The Political Economy of Mercantilism

Since the days of Adam Smith, Mercantilism has been a hotly debated issue. Condemned at the end of the eighteenth century as a 'false' system of economic thinking and political practice, it has returned paradoxically to the forefront with regard to issues such as the creation of economic growth in developing countries. This concept is often used in order to depict economic thinking and economic policy in Early Modern Europe; its meaning and content have been highly debated for over two hundred years.

Following on from his 1994 volume *Mercantilism: The Shaping of an Economic Language*, this new book from Lars Magnusson presents a more synthetic interpretation of Mercantilism as not only a theoretical system, but also a system of political economy. This book incorporates samples of material from the 1994 publication alongside new material, ordered in a new set of chapters and up-to-date discussions on Mercantilism up to the present day.

Tracing the development of a particular political economy of Mercantilism in a period of nascent state making in western and continental Europe from the sixteenth to the eighteenth century, the book describes how European rulers regarded foreign trade and industrialisation as a means to achieve power and influence amidst international competition over trades and markets. Returning to debates concerning whether Mercantilism was a system of power or of wealth, Magnusson argues that it in fact was both, and that contemporaries almost without exception saw these goals as interconnected. He also emphasises that Mercantilism was an all-European issue in a time of trade wars and the struggle for international power and recognition. In examining these issues, this book offers an unrivalled modern synthesis of mercantilist ideas and practices.

Lars Magnusson is Professor of Economic History and Dean of Social Sciences at Uppsala University, Sweden.

Routledge Explorations in Economic History

Edited by Lars Magnusson
Uppsala University, Sweden

1 **Economic Ideas and Government Policy**
Contributions to contemporary economic history
Sir Alec Cairncross

2 **The Organization of Labour Markets**
Modernity, culture and governance in Germany, Sweden, Britain and Japan
Bo Stråth

3 **Currency Convertibility**
The gold standard and beyond
Edited by Jorge Braga de Macedo, Barry Eichengreen and Jaime Reis

4 **Britain's Place in the World**
A historical enquiry into import controls 1945–1960
Alan S. Milward and George Brennan

5 **France and the International Economy**
From Vichy to the Treaty of Rome
Frances M. B. Lynch

6 **Monetary Standards and Exchange Rates**
M.C. Marcuzzo, L. Officer, A. Rosselli

7 **Production Efficiency in Domesday England, 1086**
John McDonald

8 **Free Trade and its Reception 1815–1960**
Freedom and trade: Volume I
Edited by Andrew Marrison

9 **Conceiving Companies**
Joint-stock politics in Victorian England
Timothy L. Alborn

10 **The British Industrial Decline Reconsidered**
Edited by Jean-Pierre Dormois and Michael Dintenfass

11 **The Conservatives and Industrial Efficiency, 1951–1964**
Thirteen wasted years?
Nick Tiratsoo and Jim Tomlinson

12 **Pacific Centuries**
Pacific and Pacific Rim economic history since the 16th Century
Edited by Dennis O. Flynn, Lionel Frost and A. J. H. Latham

13 **The Premodern Chinese Economy**
Structural equilibrium and capitalist sterility
Gang Deng

14 **The Role of Banks in Monitoring Firms**
The case of the Crédit Mobilier
Elisabeth Paulet

15 **Management of the National Debt in the United Kingdom, 1900–1932**
Jeremy Wormell

16 **An Economic History of Sweden**
Lars Magnusson

17 **Freedom and Growth**
The rise of states and markets in Europe, 1300–1750
S. R. Epstein

18 **The Mediterranean Response to Globalization Before 1950**
Sevket Pamuk and Jeffrey G. Williamson

19 **Production and Consumption in English Households 1600–1750**
Mark Overton, Jane Whittle, Darron Dean and Andrew Hann

20 **Governance, The State, Regulation and Industrial Relations**
Ian Clark

21 **Early Modern Capitalism**
Economic and social change in Europe 1400–1800
Edited by Maarten Prak

22 **An Economic History of London, 1800–1914**
Michael Ball and David Sunderland

23 **The Origins of National Financial Systems**
Alexander Gerschenkron reconsidered
Edited by Douglas J. Forsyth and Daniel Verdier

24 **The Russian Revolutionary Economy, 1890–1940**
Ideas, debates and alternatives
Vincent Barnett

25 **Land Rights, Ethno Nationality and Sovereignty in History**
Edited by Stanley L. Engerman and Jacob Metzer

26 **An Economic History of Film**
Edited by John Sedgwick and Mike Pokorny

27 **The Foreign Exchange Market of London**
Development since 1900
John Atkin

28 **Rethinking Economic Change in India**
Labour and livelihood
Tirthankar Roy

29 **The Mechanics of Modernity in Europe and East Asia**
The institutional origins of social change and stagnation
Erik Ringmar

30 **International Economic Integration in Historical Perspective**
Dennis M. P. McCarthy

31 **Theories of International Trade**
Adam Klug
Edited by Warren Young and
Michael Bordo

32 **Classical Trade Protectionism**
1815–1914
Edited by Jean Pierre Dormois
and Pedro Lains

33 **Economy and Economics of**
Ancient Greece
Takeshi Amemiya

34 **Social Capital, Trust and the**
Industrial Revolution,
1780–1880
David Sunderland

35 **Pricing Theory, Financing of**
International Organisations
and Monetary History
Lawrence H. Officer

36 **Political Competition and**
Economic Regulation
Edited by Peter Bernholz and
Roland Vaubel

37 **Industrial Development in**
Postwar Japan
Hirohisa Kohama

38 **Reflections on the Cliometrics**
Revolution
Conversations with economic
historians
Edited by John S. Lyons,
Louis P. Cain and
Samuel H. Williamson

39 **Agriculture and Economic**
Development in Europe Since
1870
Edited by Pedro Lains and
Vicente Pinilla

40 **Quantitative Economic History**
The good of counting
Edited by Joshua Rosenbloom

41 **A History of Macroeconomic**
Policy in the United States
John H. Wood

42 **An Economic History of the**
American Steel Industry
Robert P. Rogers

43 **Ireland and the Industrial**
Revolution
The impact of the Industrial
Revolution on Irish industry and
society, 1801–1922
Andy Bielenberg

44 **Intra-Asian Trade and**
Industrialization
Essays in memory of Yasukichi
Yasuba
Edited by A. J. H. Latham and
Heita Kawakatsu

45 **Nation, State and the**
Industrial Revolution
The visible hand
Lars Magnusson

46 **A Cultural History of Finance**
Irene Finel-Honigman

47 **Managing Crises and**
De-Globalisation
Nordic foreign trade and
exchange 1919–1939
Edited by Sven-Olof Olsson

48 **The International Tin Cartel**
John Hillman

49 **The South Sea Bubble**
Helen J. Paul

50 **Ideas and Economic Crises in Britain from Attlee to Blair (1945–2005)**
Matthias Matthijs

51 **Bengal Industries and the British Industrial Revolution (1757–1857)**
Indrajit Ray

52 **The Evolving Structure of the East Asian Economic System since 1700**
Edited by A. J. H. Latham and Heita Kawakatsu

53 **German Immigration and Servitude in America, 1709–1920**
Farley Grubb

54 **The Rise of Planning in Industrial America, 1865–1914**
Richard Adelstein

55 **An Economic History of Modern Sweden**
Lennart Schön

56 **The Standard of Living and Revolutions in Russia, 1700–1917**
Boris Mironov; edited by Gregory L. Freeze

57 **Europe's Green Revolution and Others Since**
The rise and fall of peasant-friendly plant breeding
Jonathan Harwood

58 **Economic Analysis of Institutional Change in Ancient Greece**
Carl Hampus-Lyttkens

59 **Labour-Intensive Industrialization in Global History**
Edited by Gareth Austin and Kaoru Sugihara

60 **The History of Bankruptcy**
Economic, Social and Cultural Implications in Early Modern Europe
Edited by Thomas Max Safley

61 **The Political Economy of Disaster**
Destitution, plunder and earthquake in Haiti
Mats Lundahl

62 **Nationalism and Economic Development in Modern Eurasia**
Carl Mosk

63 **Agricultural Transformation in a Global History Perspective**
Edited by Ellen Hillbom and Patrick Svensson

64 **Colonial Exploitation and Economic Development**
The Belgian Congo and the Netherlands Indies compared
Edited by Ewout Frankema and Frans Buelens

65 **The State and Business in the Major Powers**
An economic history, 1815–1939
Robert Millward

66 **Privatization and Transition in Russia in the Early 1990s**
Carol Scott Leonard and David Pitt-Watson

67 **Large Databases in Economic History**
Research methods and case studies
Edited by Mark Casson and Nigar Hashimzade

68 **A History of Market Performance**
From ancient Babylonia to the modern world
Edited by R. J. van der Spek, Jan Luiten van Zanden and Bas van Leeuwen

69 **Central Banking in a Democracy**
The Federal Reserve and its alternatives
John H. Wood

70 **The History of Migration in Europe**
Perspectives from economics, politics and sociology
Edited by Francesca Fauri

71 **Famines in European Economic History**
The last great European famines reconsidered
Edited by Declan Curran, Lubomyr Luciuk and Andrew Newby

72 **Natural Resources and Economic Growth**
Learning from history
Edited by Marc Badia-Miró, Vicente Pinilla and Henry Willebald

73 **The Political Economy of Mercantilism**
Lars Magnusson

The Political Economy of Mercantilism

Lars Magnusson

LONDON AND NEW YORK

First published 2015
by Routledge
2 Park Square, Milton Park, Abingdon, Oxon OX14 4RN

and by Routledge
711 Third Avenue, New York, NY 10017

Routledge is an imprint of the Taylor & Francis Group, an informa business

British Library Cataloguing in Publication Data
A catalogue record for this book is available from the British Library

Library of Congress Cataloging-in-Publication Data
Magnusson, Lars, 1952–
The political economy of mercantilism / Lars Magnusson.
  pages cm. – (Routledge explorations in economic history)
  1. Mercantile system. I. Title.
  HB91.M28 2015
  330.15'13–dc23   2014049457

ISBN: 978-0-415-82879-6 (hbk)
ISBN: 978-1-315-69451-1 (ebk)

Typeset in Times New Roman
by Wearset Ltd, Boldon, Tyne and Wear

Printed and bound in the United States of America by Publishers Graphics, LLC on sustainably sourced paper.

Contents

Preface   x

1   Introduction   1

2   Debates on Mercantilism   15

3   Plenty and power   54

4   The favourable balance of trade   100

5   The 1620s debates   133

6   A new science of trade   173

7   Then what was Mercantilism?   217

    Index   225

Preface

What I mentioned as a reason for writing *Mercantilism: The Shaping of an Economic Language*, published in 1994, still seems pertinent. First, that although many attempts to once and for all outroot the concept of Mercantilism had been made, the term remains to be used in depicting the intellectual, economic and political environment of Early Modern Europe. Hence, there is a continuing need to discuss its meanings and implications. Second, the concept of Mercantilism has remained open for misuse. Despite many attempts by modern researchers to replace the old interpretation built on Adam Smith's classical definition, it remains painfully powerful. Perhaps this is because it became so very useful in the nineteenth century in order to contrast industrial protectionism based upon – as it was characterised by its opponents – the erroneous mercantilist theory with liberal economics of free trade. Hence Mercantilism became a doctrine and a theory based on the notion that wealth was money, and therefore the main economy policy goal was to achieve a favourable balance of trade. Many still believe in this too-simplistic theory.

Instead of depicting it as a coherent doctrine, I rather seek to define Mercantilism as a set of discourses appearing in the Early Modern period, roughly between the sixteenth and eighteenth centuries, that discussed how national power could be achieved by economic plenty, but also how plenty was dependent upon power. On this basis, a series of discussions opened up in several countries in Europe which touched upon economic subjects, including foreign trade, money, manufactures, interest rates and so on. Hence, Mercantilism was a form of 'bellicose political economy' in an era of fierce commercial and national competition; however, Mercantilism was more than that. Over time the economic discussions led to new insights and conceptualisations: for instance, that foreign trade was not merely a zero-sum game, but that competitive edge as well as national wealth could be achieved through the introduction of manufactures and higher added-value production; moreover, that a commercial economy had laws of its own and that demand and supply was its main regulating mechanism.

This book has a different title to my previous one. But the difference between the two books goes deeper than that. While using parts of the material that appeared in the earlier version – while at the same time adding much that is new – an attempt here has been to widen the perspective. While the 1994 version to a large extent focussed on the shaping of an economic language, this book is additionally more deeply concerned with the political economy of Mercantilism and how the entanglements of a competitive commercial economy shaped ideas and discourses. This does not imply an epistemological turnover from my part. As I will hopefully show, I remain critical to attempts to reduce discourse to a mere mirror of 'real' events. Without doubt, discourse and language have their own roles to play. However, it is the interplay between discourse and reality that is my main interest here.

The book is dedicated to all those who have given opinions on the earlier version of the book, as well as those who over the years have been willing to discuss its various themes with me in seminar rooms or lecture halls in Europe, the United States and Japan.

Lars Magnusson
Uppsala, December 2014

1 Introduction

It was certainly a cry too far when, in 1980, the British economic historian D C Coleman argued that Mercantilism was not only a 'red-herring', but also a 'non-existent entity' lacking coherence both regarding theory or practice and policy. On the contrary, it seems more conducive to argue that it contained at least as much coherence and that it is useful to use the concept still.[1] Moreover, it is not off the mark to claim that it proposed at least *some* propositions regarding the *modus operandi* of an Early Modern economy in Europe. Also, it makes sense to use the word Mercantilism, or the 'mercantile system', in order to depict *some* parts of political practice, a political economy during the same period. As we will see, 'mercantilist' writers were often unsystematic in their thinking, and in policy matters the mercantilist politicians were not always very consequent. But that does not mean that they were merely pragmatists who invented ideas and policies off the back. Historical actors in fact seldom do. They are seldom without ambition or lacking an ability to reflect upon their whereabouts. Nor are their policies completely unsystematic or mere *ad hoc* responses to a confusing outside world.

To the extent that the concept of Mercantilism is accepted at all, another peculiar feature in the dwindling discussions on 'what it actually was' – which we will discuss in more depth – has been to treat it as either a theory *or* a practical policy and regulation. This undoubtedly has a historical pedigree. In the early 1930s the Swedish economic historian Eli F Heckscher published a two-volume treatise on Mercantilism in which he treated it as both practice (economic policy) and theory (the favourable balance of trade, etc.), but also as a worldview (secularism, materialism).[2] Ever since, many have been sceptical towards Heckscher's synthetical ambitions. However, in my view, it is fruitful to understand Mercantilism as both theory (or rather language as we will argue later on) and practice. Without doubt there are also connections between the practical and theoretical aspects of Mercantilism. But the relationship is of course complex. Theory cannot be seen as automatically reflecting the level of practice, nor does policy mirror theory in any immediate sense. Thus, language and theory as well as policy have a certain autonomy. At the same time they are deeply entangled.

In the following I will argue that Mercantilism might be an as useful concept as any other in order to try to make generalisations of language and ideas, but also of political practices in Europe roughly during the sixteenth to eighteenth centuries. First, I will discuss how a series of European policies developed during this time in order to handle and understand what, in the mid-eighteenth century, David Hume called 'jealousy of trade', or reason of state by economic means, in a world of trade competition where such means and power politics were deeply intertwined. This is also the time and birthplace of the modern state – as formulated by Gustav Schmoller in his foreword to his *Studien über die wirtschaftliche Politik Friedrich der Großen* (1884)[3] – which also is reflected in the policies pursued. Second, I will discuss how a language of the modern market economy was developed during approximately the same time period in order to make such a world of new challenges and possibilities intelligible and possible to handle. This language reflected how the market economy operated and how it was constructed. Hence, while they sought to understand how the price system worked or what factors triggered the interest rates or trade balances to rise or fall, the economic writers of different nationalities were also constructing a basis for our own present theories of the market economy.

Mercantilism

In his seminal *Predecessors to Adam Smith*, E A J Johnson labelled 'mercantilism' an 'unhappy word'.[4] Hence, the word 'mercantilism' has been used in a number of confusing ways and for many different designs. As reaching a common agreement with regard to the interpretation of Mercantilism has been difficult, discussions dealing with this phenomenon have often been blurred. For Adam Smith, as well as for nineteenth-century opponents of the 'mercantile system', such as the classical political economists J R McCulloch and Richard Jones, it was the confusion of wealth and money made manifest in the favourable balance of trade theory that gave the system its coherence. Moreover, it was this idea that once again reappeared in the 1930s with Jacob Viner.[5] In the late nineteenth century such historical economists as Wilhelm Roscher and Schmoller instead turned Mercantilism into a doctrine of state building, which originated during the Early Modern period in order to bolster a weak state: the transformation from a 'territorial' to a 'national' state.[6] As in Heckscher's studies, the meaning of Mercantilism was expanded even further – as noted above.

More precisely, it was after Smith that Mercantilism was constructed into a more or less coherent 'system'. Gradually, and on the basis of Smith's interpretation in the *Wealth of Nations*, it was constructed as an opposite to the 'Smithian' or 'free trade' system.[7] By 1840 its most distinct policy feature was depicted as protectionism and state regulation of the economy. Such a view was even more enforced in the debates concerning the British Corn Laws and their eventual demise in 1846.[8] However, as we will return to this, it is certainly wrong to describe all mercantilists as protectionists in a modern or even a nineteenth-century sense. Moreover, it is also wrong to characterise Smith as a doctrinaire free trader – as was done after 1846 by the followers of Richard Cobden and the Manchester men.[9] There were certainly important differences between Smith and the mercantilists, but these were overemphasised during the nineteenth century.

It is commonly known that the term *système mercantile* first appeared in print in de Mirabeau's *Philosophie Rurale* in 1763.[10] It was referred to in a passage in which de Mirabeau overtly attacked the idea that a nation may profit from importation of money. As Smith had apparently read *Philosophie Rurale*, it is not at all unlikely that he picked up this term from this book.[11] However, de Mirabeau was not the first to use the term. It was in use in the discussion on political economy within the so-called Gournay circle some years earlier. In the French discussion it referred back to the eighteenth-century French finance minister Colbert and his 'system' of trade and manufacture protection.[12] Regardless, it is with Smith that the 'mercantile system' gained its worldwide reputation. In his famous the *Wealth of Nations*, Smith devoted a very long chapter to delineate the characteristic features of this 'system'.[13] According to Smith its kernel was the 'popular' fallacy to confuse wealth with money. Smith does not directly accuse Thomas Mun and other mercantilists for this fallacy. On the contrary, he explicitly pictures Mun as an opponent of the old medieval policy in England of forbidding the export of money. Instead, Mun's main error lies (according to Smith) in that he continued to use this popular bullionist image although he ought to have known better. Whether this error originated for opportunistic reasons (i.e. a conspiracy against the public interest in order to pursue a special interest) we will never know. However, the main point is that those who have read Smith have rarely noticed this error. At least according to Joseph Schumpeter, Mun intentionally used the bullionist image; Smith insinuated this connection, according to him, 'in such a way that his readers cannot help getting the impression, which has in fact become very general'.[14]

Thus, most of Smith's readers would be tempted to draw a direct line between protectionism and the doctrines of Mun. Smith of course emphasised the devastating consequences of a system of regulation and protection. In several instances he pointed out that such a system was self-defeating as well as erroneous. Thus, instead of extending trade and manufactures, the system most often led to the opposite. Furthermore, those who gained through the system were not the general public but the monopolistic merchants and manufacturers who could increase their capital. In fact, Smith implied that the whole 'commercial system' at its core was a giant conspiracy led by powerful interest groups pursuing their own selfish interests. However, Smith's feelings towards the merchants and manufacturers were rather mixed; it was also well known that he vigorously supported them against the physiocratic accusation that their activities were 'sterile'. Furthermore, the increase of such activities was an inherent part of Smith's historical stage theory of economic development.[15] Moreover, Smith was sometimes prone to defend such typical 'mercantilist' institutions as the Navigation Acts, and he believed that free trade as a general principle was a utopia that would not be fulfilled in his lifetime, perhaps never.[16] That Smith found it difficult to make up his mind is obvious when he, in the final paragraph of the chapter, concludes:

> It cannot be very difficult to determine who have been the contrivers of this whole mercantile system; not the consumers, we may believe, whose interest has been so entirely neglected; but the producers, whose interest has been so carefully attended to; and among this latter class our merchants and manufacturers have been by far the principal architects.[17]

According to Smith, the view of the mercantile system 'as an agglomeration of commercial interferences fortified by a monetary folly' was carried further in Britain by classical political economy.[18] It became commonplace for economists such as Nassau W Senior and John Stuart Mill to ascertain that protectionism stemmed from the defunct 'surviving relic of the Mercantile Theory' (Mill) that money was the only form of wealth.[19] Auguste Blanqui, in France, and McCulloch, in Britain in particular, helped to reinforce the notion of a 'mercantile system' along the lines of Smith.[20] In his preface of the 1828 edition of Smith's *magnum opus*, McCulloch especially pointed out that this system implied that

> the wealth of individuals and of states was measured, not by the abundance of their disposable products – but by the quality and value of the commodities with which they could afford to purchase the precious metals – but by the quality of these metals actually in their possession – And here the policy, as obvious as it was universal, of attempting to increase the amount of national wealth by

forbidding the exportation of gold and silver, and encouraging their importation.[21]

And in another paragraph:

> Mr Mun lays no stress whatever on the circumstances of foreign commerce enabling us to obtain an infinite variety of useful and agreeable products, which it would either have been impossible for us to produce at all, or to produce so cheaply at home. We are desired to consider all this accession, wealth ... as nothing – and to fix our attention exclusively on the balance of £200000 of gold and silver.... And yet Mr Mun's rule for estimating the advantage of foreign commerce, was for a long time regarded, by the generality of merchants and practical statesmen, as infallible.[22]

Hence, already with McCulloch, we find everything traditionally attached to a full-fledged mercantile system: the bullionist fallacy as well as protectionism. In line with Smith, McCulloch was ready to admit that Mun's *England's Treasure by Forraign Trade* was 'a considerable step in the progress to sounder opinions'.[23] However, Mun could not help but fall victim to popular delusions which – as he said elsewhere – 'have been so widely spread ... and of few have the consequences been so disastrous'.[24]

Among other writers who helped to establish the view of a 'mercantile system', particularly Jones stands out.[25] It is ironic that he, as a historical economist, helped to establish a definition of Mercantilism, which later historical economists sought to dismantle. Certainly, in his lectures on political economy at King's College London after arriving there in 1833, he aimed to develop a more scientific approach to the subject including – as he said in his inaugural lecture when entering the chair at King's in 1833 – tracing 'the deep-seated causes of long chains of events in the history of nations'.[26] Here he also spoke on 'the errors and wanderings of our forefathers', which consisted in the belief that bullion was 'the only species of wealth which really served the name'. Hence,

> Countries which could not produce gold and silver profitably from their mines, could only procure them by foreign trade: to manage foreign trade, so as to keep gold and silver constantly flowing, and then to keep them fast, were therefore supposed to be the only arts by which a nation could be enriched.[27]

However, it was in his famous contribution for the *Edinburgh Review* in 1847 on 'Primitive Political Economy of England' that Jones began to talk about specific 'systems' of political economy and thought. Up until the seventeenth century, a specific bullionist 'balance of bargaining system' prevailed. The aim of this system was to bring silver and gold into the country and to prevent it from leaving again. This was foremost achieved through the two famous 'statutes of staples and employment' already from the Late Middle Ages in England, which explicitly forbade foreign salesmen to take money or bullion out of the country. However, due to pressures achieved by increased trade and from an increase of the social and political power of merchants – but not from 'the prevalence of scientific notions', Jones informs us – this system gradually changed during the sixteenth century. Thus, in the next century a new 'system' emerged: balance of trade. The object remained the same – to hinder an outflow of money – but new means were applied. And according to Jones, the chief promoter of this new system was the 'eminent merchant of London', Mun.[28]

Hence, also Jones saw the confusion between wealth and money as the main driving force behind mercantilist policies. He, for example, made the following forceful assertion, which for a long time influenced popular notions of Mercantilism:

> Whoever has heard of Adam Smith, has heard of the almost romantic value which our ancestors set upon the possession of the precious metals; yet few persons are acquainted with the singular processes by which they sought to bring home the golden fleece, or with much more than the names of the early writers who had the honour of first enlightening their countrymen on the true nature of this Midas folly.[29]

The hero of this tale was of course Smith, who together with 'Galiany [*sic*], Quesnay, Harris and Hume had been able to unveil … the fallacy which so long received the blind homage of mankind'.[30] He stated that most past economic writers had been blinded by the Midas fallacy. Even Charles Davenant – it is certainly a misnomer when he here adds 'not surprisingly' – is made the victim of 'the faith that bullion alone constituted wealth'.[31]

Needless to say, this conceptualisation of Mercantilism has been thoroughly criticised, especially during the twentieth century. However, the Smithian idea of a 'commercial system' gradually emerged and turned into a dogma during the early nineteenth century. For the kind of *laissez-faire* economics that developed during this period, the notion of a system of protection relying on the child-like Midas fallacy obviously served its purpose. That this dogma was strongly cemented is evidenced by, for example, its repetition in 1888 by John K Ingram, who took a rather sympathetic view of the mercantilists:

'The mercantile doctrine, stated in its most extreme form, makes wealth and money identical'.[32]

Language

During recent decades, the writing of the history of economics has taken a different turn. Writers have attempted to move away from a history of economic ideas and analysis to the history of economic language or discourse. In several cases this has implied a rigorous critique of a methodology which still – it is fair to say – dominates much mainstream history of economic thought.[33] Within this tradition, a majority of writers – often economists by training – have treated their subject as a history of economic 'analysis' rather than of 'vision' – to use Schumpeter's famous distinction.[34] This implies that they have emphasised the development of economics as *primarily* an 'internal' affair: the successive development of knowledge and the gradual perfection of theories and analytical instruments. The late Mark Blaug was an outstanding example of such an approach. In 1968 he wrote,

> it must be insisted [that] great chunks of history of economic thought are about mistakes in logic and gaps in analysis, having no connection with contemporary events. And so… I have tried to write a history of economic analysis which pictures it as evolving out of previous analysis, propelled forward by the desire to refine, to improve, to perfect, a desire which economists share with all other scientists.[35]

Such an 'internal' approach – a history of economic doctrines in the form of 'tooled knowledge', as Schumpeter called it[36] – of course has certain advantages. It is clear that a history of economic texts, to some extent, must deal with how new ideas appear and how discussions among experts lead to the perfection of concepts and analytical tools. However, this methodology poses a more problematic side. It often implies a neglect of the historical dimension of ideas and doctrines and is often anachronistic. More seriously, this methodology suggests that old economics is treated and made intelligible from the standpoint of modern economics. Following from this, the construction of doctrinal development serves the implicit or explicit task to defend modern theories. And it was this history of economic ideas that the historical economist William J Ashley scornfully attacked as 'a museum of intellectual odds and ends, where every opinion is labelled as either a surprising anticipation of the correct modern theory or an instance of the extraordinary folly of the dark ages'.[37] As a consequence of such a methodology, economic writers who were largely unkown and hidden in their own time are put at the forefront. As ideas are interpreted in the light of modern theorising, this methodology further leads to these ideas holding quite different meanings than originally articulated. Certainly, if one is interested in the historical significance of specific ideas or doctrines, they can only be understood within their proper historical context. Thus, reading history backwards leads to historical dimensions becoming lost.

In literature on the history of economic doctrine, such unhistorical procedures are customary. This is perhaps not strange as the method to read intellectual history backwards has a great past with famous exponents. An early example was when David Ricardo, Mill and McCulloch appropriated Smith for their own creation, 'classical political economy', while neglecting to mention that Smith's style and methodology were quite different from theirs.[38] Another undoubtedly anachronistic writer was Lord Keynes, who in Chapter 23 of his *General Theory of Employment, Interest and Money* (1936) reinterpreted seventeenth-century Mercantilism in order to fit it into his own approach. K Marx is another example, as he constructed a line of intellectual development that connected W Petty, Smith and Ricardo with himself – in order to point out the revolutionary impact in economic theory of the labour theory of value.[39]

To move from such a position to a history of economic discourse implies a radical shift towards a more historical reading of economic texts. In the general history of intellectual ideas, such a turn has been especially emphasised by the so-called Cambridge School of Intellectual History. Hence, scholars such as Quentin Skinner, James Tully and John Pocock have stimulated an increased interest in historical reading of texts. The idea is to pay attention to the historical context in which texts are formulated. Even more pertinently, the members of this school have suggested that we take a closer look at the performance level – inspired by linguists such as John L Austin and ultimately the philosopher Ludvig Wittgenstein – instead of putting all emphasis on the intentions of writers and/or their social environment.[40] Hence, according to Skinner, we need 'to find the means to recover what the agent may have been *doing* in saying what was said, and hence of understanding what the agent may have meant by issuing an utterance with just that sense and reference'.[41] In the same manner Pocock has stressed that in order to understand what a certain author 'is getting at' we must not only recognise what an author is doing, but also try to recognise the specific discursive tradition he is involved in. This means recovering a specific language and treating our author 'as inhabiting a universe of *langues* that gives meaning to the *paroles* he performs in them'.[42] Thus, according to Pocock, it is the historian's task to learn to read and recognise the diverse idioms of (as in this case, economic) discourse 'as they were available in the culture and at the time he is studying'. As any discourse, or language, betokens a specific political, social or historical context within which it is itself a situated language, it also 'selects and prescribes the context within which it is to be recognized'. Language is self-reflective; it supplies the categories, grammar and conceptual framework through which experience is articulated.[43]

This does not necessarily imply that we prescribe an elevated ontological status to 'language'. We do not have to reduce an author to be 'a mere mouthpiece of his own language'.[44] Instead, the relation between language and experience is processual and interactive. Furthermore, due to pressures from outside, languages change. When language is used in communication, the *paroles* will necessarily eventuate modifications and change of language itself.[45] Such an interactive and processual relationship between language and practice is also emphasised by modern social science scholars' (such as Anthony Giddens 'structuration theory' and Marshall Sahlins) discussion on European encounters with the 'other' in the Early Modern period.[46]

To discuss Mercantilism as a language, as discursive practice, has some important consequences. First, it questions the statement that has been made – as we will see – that Mercantilism was never a 'living doctrine' or a 'coherent set of principles'. Certainly, if such a 'doctrine' is an agreed on set of principles and solutions building on a common methodology – a box of theoretical and methodological tools – it is perhaps right to say that the mercantilists never shared such a doctrine. However, nobody with at least some first-hand knowledge of the immense economic literature from the early seventeenth century onwards can avoid grasping their common ground. After all, authors such as Mun, Edward Misselden, Josiah Child, Nicholas Barbon, Dudley North and Davenant all struggled with the question how the nation could grow rich, what constitute the riches of a country, the importance of money and so on. Moreover, not necessarily in agreement, they used a common vocabulary of concepts and discussed a specific set of questions and issues. Thus, it is clearly a mistake to argue (as by A V Judges, Coleman and others, as we will see) that the mercantilist 'school' had no 'priest to defend it'. This is true only if we define 'school' in a very restricted way. If we instead regard Mercantilism as language and discourse, we can certainly identify a common terminology and traces of answers to a certain set of questions.

* * *

As we will discuss more thoroughly in the next chapter, the debates on Mercantilism and its interpretation have to a great extent circled the question of how to relate mercantilist texts to economic 'reality'. Thus,

Heckscher took the extreme position that mercantilist ideas – and policies – did not rely on any 'true' empirical knowledge of economic reality whatsoever.[47] As a reaction to this, a number of economic historians – as we will see – instead tried to explain the peculiarity of mercantilist thinkers by referring back to specific conditions that prevailed during the Early Modern period. However, to percieve 'mercantilist' texts as pure reflections of economic reality is without doubt to fall into the reductionist trap. It is certainly difficult from this point of view to make intelligible why the same kind of ideas seems to have sprung out of widely different economic, political and social environments.[48] Quite clearly, 'mercantilist' ideas were applied to a number of different practical problems in different socio-political frameworks. Therefore, it is difficult to make sense of such suppositions – as for example made by Schumpeter[49] – which underline that the mercantilist literature should be regarded primarily as a commonsense response to practical problems. After all, also 'commonsense' responses have their own discursive rules of the game, which any author must adhere to in order to be rightly understood. We can conclusively not understand writers such as Mun if we do not see that they put forward simplified models or visions of how they believed that what we today would call the 'economic' or 'market' system operated in a general sense (this does not mean that they perceived it as a 'system' in our sense of the word). Certainly they did not simply 'describe' economic reality in any mechanical sense. Simultaneously they also invented and constructed the very same categories by which they can make their complex reality intelligible.

Moreover, it is clear that the seventeenth century saw the emergence of what the cultural historian Peter Burke has called 'literal mindness'.[50] It included an increasing awareness of the difference between literal and symbolic meanings, but also the replacement of a more concrete form for a more abstract one. Thus paradoxically, the seventeenth century saw the emergence of empiricism at the same time as abstract and general categories were increasingly introduced. Certainly, the economic literature during this period heeds to this increasing tendency to use more complicated categories and base arguments upon stylised facts. Especially the use of stylised facts and abstract categories stands out in this context. Hence, to talk of 'commonsense' in this context is to conceal a very important historical process of cultural and discursive change that took place during this period.

Consequently, the relationship between economic texts and the contemporary economic 'reality' is very difficult to disentangle. As part of a specific discourse, they inhabited their own territory and followed their own set of rules. The *paroles* of their discourse were uttered through a specific *langue*, which provided special significance and meaning. As the 'economy' is an intellectual construction and cannot be detected in 'reality', it also designated its own privileged territory. As we argued previously, this does not mean that mercantilist language was unaffected by the tensions and developments of an outside reality. Rather, we once again stress the interrelationship between language and such 'realities'. However, this most certainly implies that it is impossible to reduce the 'mercantilists'' visions and ideas to be a mere mouthpiece of a reflective 'reality'. This relation is certainly much more complicated to trace.

Languages, no doubt, are put together by inherited concepts, words, intellectual tools and artefacts. To the same extent they make up their own rules. But, simultaneously, they are used for communication purposes. This implies that, to the extent that the 'realities' confronted by language change, language must change too. But this may take some time. Therefore, old interpretations of concepts are used alongside new interpretations – until the dissonance becomes too obvious.

A last point to mention in this brief introductory is that the debates concerning Mercantilism since Smith have been seriously dogged by attempts to define it as a very specific piece of economic policy. Smith thus blamed the 'mercantilist' writers for protectionism, monopolistic devices and corruptive economic policies. Such a 'selfish national commercial policy of a harsh and rude kind', in Schmoller's words, could all be traced back to the same source.[51] Its cause was the popular Midas fallacy of believing that money was the same as wealth, which Mun and his followers had not been able to see through. Heckscher blamed the prejudice upon a 'fear of goods'. Basically, however, also Heckscher was ready to define Mercantilism as a system of policy: as protectionism in a very general sense. According to him, Mercantilism turned out to be a commonsense answer to a timeless set of economic problems which emphasised economic nationalism and protective measures. This is primarily the reason why he so strongly pressed the viewpoint that Mercantilism had nothing to do with economic reality whatsoever.

However, economic ideas constitute only one of many factors behind the formulation of concrete policies. It is certainly a mistake to ascribe a total primacy of doctrines or ideas over policies. Not least the more recent discussion with regard to British economic history has accomplished much in clearing up missapprehensions of this kind. Thus, it has been emphasised that it is wrong to see Mercantilism as *mere* economic policy. Most of this literature cannot be regarded as mere defence of protectionism or of the traditional regulative policies which princes and rulers pursued during the seventeenth and early eighteenth centuries. Quite on the contrary, many of the mercantilist writers were highly critical of such policies. We can here refer to Barbon, Child, Davenant or William Petyt

– the presumed author of *Britannia Languens*, a text appraised highly by McCulloch for its 'free trade' tendencies.[52] One should not forget that one of Mun's objectives was to attack the old policy of prohibition against the export of gold and silver – a serious assault against the interests of the East India Company. However, it would also be wrong to attribute this critical attitude of governmental policy only to partisans of this company's interest.[53] Such a critical attitude was also shared by many others who were not partisans of this special group interest.

The content of the book

The aim of this book is twofold: first, to provide the historical context concerning a set of economic discussions that opened up already in the sixteenth century, and which explicitly dealt with how the wealth of the nation was best to be achieved and how this goal was connected to international trade in particular. As we will see, such a debate was carried out in England but also in many other places in Europe. Second, and simultaneously, we will try to show how a set of concepts and analytical tools were developed. They aimed to tackle the world of international trade competition and understand how markets worked and operated. In the history of economic thought this process is commonly described as the emergence of mercantilist economic thought. But it was more than that. Much of what we today know as economics was born as a consequence of these debates and discussions.

In the next chapter I will deal with the controversies around the concept of Mercantilism, which have raged for more than a century. Chapter 3 is set out to demonstrate the context of the discussions particularly concerning international trade that was carried out in Europe during the seventeenth and eighteenth centuries. Then in Chapter 4 the focus will be on interpreting the doctrine of the favourable balance of trade, as well as the mercantilists' conceptualisation of wealth. In chapters 5 and 6 we will deal exclusively with the English discussion during the century following the breakthrough of the 1620s. Here we trace the development of a new 'economic' language that was more or less an unintended consequence of the discussion concerning how the economy and marketplace worked during this stretch of the Early Modern period. Chapter 7, last, will provide some conclusions in a discussion of the wider implications of our main arguments.

Notes

1 L Magnusson, 'Is mercantilism a useful concept still?' In: M Iserman (hg), *Merkanilismus. Wiederaufnahme einer Debatte.* Stuttgart, Germany: Franz Steiner Verlag 2014.

2 E F Heckscher, 'Mercantilism as a conception of society'. In: *Mercantilism*, vol. II: 5, London: Routledge 1994, pp. 285f.

3 Trans. G Schmoller, *The Mercantile System and its Historical Significance.* New York: The Macmillan Company 1897, p. 77.

4 E A J Johnson, *Predecessors of Adam Smith.* New York: Prentice-Hall 1937, p. 3.

5 I will discuss these authors in Chapter 2 of this book.

6 Schmoller, p. 76.

7 On this see L Magnusson, *The Tradition of Free Trade.* London: Routledge 2004.

8 Magnusson, *The Tradition of Free Trade*, ch. 4.

9 Magnusson, *The Tradition of Free Trade*, pp. 57f.

10 M de Mirabeau, *Philosophie Rurale ou Economie Génerale et Politique de L'agriculture.* Amsterdam, The Netherlands: Libraires associés, 1763, p. 329.

11 A V Judges, 'The idea of a mercantile state'. In: D C Coleman (ed.), *Revisions in Mercantilism.* London: Methuen 1969, p. 38. Judges here refers to a passage in A Smith, *An Inquiry into the Nature and Causes of the Wealth of Nations.* Oxford: Oxford University Press 1976, Book IV, ch. 9, p. 679.

12 See S Reinert, *Translating Empire: Emulation and the Origins of Political Economy.* Cambridge, MA: Harvard University Press 2011, pp. 146f., 281. For a recent presentation of Gournay and his circle, see C Loïc, F Lefebvre, C Théré (eds.), *Le cercle de Vincent de Gournay. Savoirs économiques et pratiques administratives en France au milieu du XVIIIᵉ siècle.* Paris, France: Ined 2011.

13 A Smith, *An Inquiry into the Nature and Causes of the Wealth of Nations.* Oxford: Oxford University Press 1976, Book IV, ch. 1.

14 J A Schumpeter, *History of Economic Analysis.* London: Allen & Unwin 1972, p. 361.

15 On the stage theory of A R J Turgot and Smith, see R L Meek, 'Smith, Turgot and the Four Stages Theory'. In: *Smith, Marx and After.* London: Chapman & Hall 1977, pp. 18f.

16 Smith, Book IV, ch. 2, p. 471.

17 Smith, Book I, ch. 8, pp. 661f.

18 Magnusson, *The Tradition of Free Trade*, pp. 36f.

19 J S Mill, *Principles of Political Economy (1909).* Fairfield, NL: Augustus M Kelley 1987, p. 579.

20 Magnusson, pp. 36f.

21 J R McCulloch, 'Introductory discourse'. In: A Smith, *An Inquiry into the Nature and Causes of the Wealth of Nations*, vol. I, Edinburgh: Adam Black and William Tait 1828, p. xii.

22 McCulloch, p. xviii.

23 McCulloch, p. xv.

24 McCulloch, pp. vii f.

25 For more on this, see Magnusson, pp. 81f.

26 R Jones, 'An introductory lecture on political economy'. Delivered at King's College London, 27 February 1833. In: R. Jones, *Literary Remains Consisting of Lectures and Tracts on Political Economy* (1859). New York: Augustus M Kelley 1964, p. 543.

27 Jones, p. 545.

28 Jones, p. 312.

29 Jones, p. 293

30 Jones, p. 333.

31 Jones, p. 333.

32 J K Ingram, *A History of Political Economy.* Edinburgh, Scotland: A & C Black 1893, p. 37.

33 For such a critique, see for example Magnusson, ch. 1. For a defence, see R E Ekelund

and R Tollison, 'On neoinstitutional theory and preclassical economics: mercantilism revisited'. *European Journal of the History of Economic Thought*, vol. IV: 3 (1997), pp. 375f.

34 Schumpeter, chs 1, 4.

35 M Blaug, *Economic Theory in Retrospect.* Homewood, IL: Richard D Irwin Inc 1968, pp. xi, 1ff., 681ff.

36 Schumpeter, p. 7.

37 W J Ashley, *An Introduction to English Economic History and Theory*, vol. II, New York: G P Putnam's Sons 1893, p. 381.

38 See T W Hutchison, *On Revolutions and Progress in Economic Knowledge.* Cambridge, UK: Cambridge University Press 1978, chs 1, 2.

39 K Marx, *Theories of Surplus Value*, vol. I, Moscow: Progress Publishers 1969, pp. 354f.

40 See Q Skinner, 'Social meanings and the explanation of social action'. In: P Laslett, W G Runciman and Q Skinner (eds.), *Philosophy, Politicis and Society.* Oxford: Oxford University Press 1972; Q Skinner, *The Foundation of Modern Political Thought*, vol. I, Cambridge, UK: Cambridge University Press 1978; Q Skinner, 'Interpretation and the understanding of speech acts'. In: Q Skinner (ed.), *Visions of Politics, Volume I: Regarding Method.* Cambridge, UK: Cambridge University Press 2002; J G A Pocock, 'The machiavellian moment revisited: A study in history and ideology'. *Journal of Modern History*, vol. LIII: 1 (1981); J Pocock, *Virtue, Commerce and History.* Cambridge, UK: Cambridge University Press 1985.

41 Skinner, *Visions of Politics*, p. 104.

42 Pocock, *Virtue, Commerce and History*, p. 5.

43 Pocock, *Virtue, Commerce and History*, pp. 9, 12.

44 Pocock, *Virtue, Commerce and History*, p. 5.

45 See for example S Fish, *Is There a Text in This Class? The Authority of Interpretative Communities.* Cambridge, MA: Cambridge University Press 1980; Pocock, *Virtue, Commerce and History*, ch. 1, p. 5.

46 A Giddens, *The Constitution of Society.* Cambridge, UK: Polity Press 1984; M G Sahlins, *Islands of History.* Chicago, IL: University of Chicago Press 1985.

47 Heckscher, *Mercantilism*, Part 2 (ed. Söderlund). London: Allen & Unwin 1955, p. 347 (the chapter here on Keynes was added to Söderlund's edition).

48 See for example A W Coats, 'Mercantilism, yet again!' In: P Roggi (ed.), *Gli economisti e la politica economica.* Naples, Italy: Edizione Scientifische Italaiane 1985, p. 33.

49 Schumpeter, pp. 335ff.

50 P Burke, *Historical Anthropology of Early Modern Italy.* Cambridge, UK: Cambridge University Press 1987, ch. 16; P Burke, *The Fabrication of Louis XIV.* New Haven, CT, and London: Yale University Press 1992, pp. 128ff.

51 Schmoller, p. 77. Of course Schmoller himself did not agree with this harsh condemnation of Mercantilism, which instead meant practically 'nothing but the creation of a sound state and a sound national economy' (p. 76).

52 For a longer list see W D Grampp, 'The liberal elements in english mercantilism'. *Quarterly Journal of Economics*, vol. IV (1952).

53 See below p. 179f.

2   Debates on Mercantilism

To some extent, the enduring interest that economists, economic historians and historians of economic thought have taken in the topic of Mercantilism is baffling. Hence a lively debate concerning its interpretation opened up more than a hundred years ago – and has been going on ever since. Using a term invented by the Physiocrats in the eighteenth century, the discussants have focussed on both the ideas and the events of Mercantilism; on the intellectual core ideas as well as on economic policies. And the subject still arouses interest. As we will see, there is a current discussion concerning the use of the concept in order to understand the relationship between wealth and power during the Early Modern period at large. Obviously, how to interpret Mercantilism, or to understand concepts like 'the favourable balance of trade', can still serve as targets for professional careers and to arouse recognition within the scholarly world.

Yet, perhaps this enduring interest in Mercantilism might not be so difficult to understand after all. Most certainly, if the discussion mainly had focussed on 'pure' historical issues regarding what mercantilist writers or politicians really did say, it would probably only have gained the interest of a small number of antiquarian historians. However, this has certainly not been the case. Instead, the topic of 'mercantilism' has served as an excuse for broad discussions on methodological, theoretical and – indeed – political issues. Here economists and historians have toyed with their favourite ideas. Within such a discussion combatants of different theoretical as well as political schools have clashed over general issues of methodology as well as over interpretative frameworks – sometimes very bitterly so.

First, it is clear that the *Methodenstreit* within economics during the nineteenth century triggered an increased interest in the otherwise rather obscure undertaking to make sense of seventeenth- and early eighteenth-century economic thinking. This discussion, of course, had many political overtones. For German protectionists such as List, as well as historical economists like Roscher and Schmoller, it was important *not* to treat seventeenth-century economics as pre-scientific nonsense only worth the attention of the antiquarian. Instead, it was crucial for them to emphasise the historical rationality of Smith's mercantile system instead of its mistakes and analytical errors. To this effect they made use of the classical historicist argument: that Mercantilism must be studied from the contemporary viewpoint and not from what economics might have achieved later on. They strongly defended the notion that mercantilist ideas were rational for their own time. This approach obviously fitted into their general critical attitude towards classical political economy, especially Ricardo and Mill. It was also known that they argued that there were no general laws attached to the economic world ready and ripe to be detected by the economic scientists. Rather, the rationality of economic behaviour was institutionally bound to time, place – and nationality. Hence the message was clear: *laissez-faire* was *not* the universal language of economic commonsense. And as mercantilist ideas had been a rational response to seventeenth- and eighteenth-century conditions, so too were their economics of protectionism appropriate for the German *Sonderweg* to modern industrial society.

This was largely the intellectual and political *milieu* in which the mercantilist debates emerged in the late nineteenth century. From this stemmed the historical economists' – Roscher, Schmoller, Werner Sombart, William Cunningham, Ashley and others – attempt to present Mercantilism as a broad school of thought and an economic policy with an aim to promote economic growth and modernisation through means of protection and economic nationalism. Their definition slipped into the first edition of *Palgrave's Dictionary of Political Economy* published in 1894, which became the standard for many years to come: 'By the mercantile system we mean the economic policy of Europe from the break-up of the medieval organisation of industry and commerce to the dominance of Laissez-faire'.[1]

Hence, the question what Mercantilism was and ought to be became a battleground for or against *laissez-faire* and classical political economy. Moreover, this was probably the main reason why it became so important to stress the difference between Smith's new 'system' and the 'mercantile system'. Well into the twentieth century such a proposed great divide was used both by Heckscher and Keynes to amplify economic-political statements – of different sorts, of course. Furthermore, Viner and others saw the potential in using the seventeenth and eighteenth century for their ideological purposes. The price of these procedures was high, however. By dichotomising the 'systems', their differences became too wide, while their similarities were largely disregarded.

Second, not only has the prolonged discussion on Mercantilism drawn on the general issue for or against *laissez-faire* or classical political economy: as already stated, it has also served as an excuse for raising general methodological and theoretical issues. For example, the relationship between economic *ideas* and *policies* has been a widely discussed topic. As we will see, this stirred up controversy especially in the aftermath of Heckscher's work, which particularly highlighted this problematic issue. Moreover, most post-Heckscher debaters have tended to take a rather sceptical turn against a too-close identification of economic thought with the policies pursued during this period.

Against this background it is paradoxical to note that especially economic historians have been rather disinterested with regard to the problematisation of the interrelationship between *ideas* and *events*. Hence Barry Supple, Charles Wilson, Joyce Oldham Appleby and others seem ready to accept that mercantilist thinking was a 'true' reflection of what really occurred within polity and economy. For example, the favourable balance of trade doctrine could thus be explained by the fact that, due to the underdeveloped nature of international trade and exchange during the seventeenth century, a concern over specific balances was a crucial *de facto* issue.[2] Or it could be argued that the discussion between Gerrard Malynes, Mun and Misselden 'in reality' reflected the trade depression of the early 1620s. It is typical indeed when Coleman makes the following comment regarding the challenge from economic history to Heckscher and the historicists: 'recent research has shown that in fact much of Mun's formulation of the balance-of-trade doctrine sprang directly from his inquiries into the depression of 1622–3'.[3] But must we not rather admit that major historical events can only be grasped by observers through a process of interpretation and conceptualisation? The problem involved here is not only that an epistemology which regards ideas as mere reflections of events are unsophisticated by modern standards, but also that, from this basis, it is impossible to understand why concepts such as the favourable balance of trade was used in so many different frameworks and over such a long time. The general conditions of trade and industry without doubt changed dramatically in Britain during the century following the 1620s – but still the concept or 'theory' was used. We will discuss this paradox further later on. Here, it suffices to make the point that different epistemological standpoints have been viewed in the debate. Without doubt this has made the discussion more heated and long lived than otherwise would have been the case.

The issue of Mercantilism has also provided an opportunity to discuss the general relationship between *ideas, policies* and *special interest*. It is also known that already Smith made the point of a clear link between different group interests and Mercantilism. This line of thinking has later been followed up by for example Viner and, in a more recent intervention, Robert E Ekelund and Robert Tollison (see further below). But also Schumpeter used this argument for giving at least some credibility to the historicist 'pro-mercantilist' position. Such an interpretation was valid, he believed, if it was admitted that mercantilist doctrines largely ought to be regarded as partisan stand-points developed in the interest of the merchant interest groups:

> Many policies of the mercantilist age may in fact be traced to the interests of, or to the pressure exerted by, groups that can be defi-nitely identified and from whose standpoints they may acquire a character of rationally that otherwise would be lacking.[4]

Also to this issue we will return in a short while.

Lastly, methodological issues on how to write the history of eco-nomics have also been highlighted in the discussion around Mercantil-ism. Thus the 'entelechies' of Mercantilism – to use the phrase invented by Robert Schaeffer – most certainly depend upon from which point of view this is done.[5] In the preceding chapter we dis-cussed the method of writing the history of economics backwards from a modern standpoint. In such a case the task of an intellectual history of economic ideas becomes to trace the origin of discrete 'unit ideas' (as phrased by Arthur Lovejoy).[6] The problem with such an under-taking was at least admitted by Schumpeter. Thus he pointed out: 'To read our meaning uncritically into old texts amounts to betrayal of the historian's duty as much as does overemphasis on every mistake in formulation'.[7] Others, however, have been less cautious. Thus Viner for example was a partisan of a quite different viewpoint. He formu-lated his methodology in the following fashion:

> [T]he economic historians and the economists of the German historical school have been almost alone in studying the mercantil-ists, and they have generally been more interested in the facts than in the ideas of the mercantilist period, have often based sweeping generalizations as to the character of mercantilist doctrine on what they found in a handful of the mercantilist writings, have displayed neither interest in, nor acquaintance with, modern economic theo-rizing with respect to monetary and trade process, and have almost without exception shown a tendency to defend the mercantilist doctrines by reasoning itself of decidedly mercantilist flavor.... The present study, is therefore, primarily an inventory of the English ideas, good and bad, with respect to trade prevalent before Adam Smith, classified and examined in the light of modern monetary and trade theory.[8]

This methodology has also found other previous followers, for example Robert Eagley,[9] Blaug and William Letwin. Especially with

Letwin one cannot avoid the feeling of partaking in an economics seminar in which Professor Letwin snubs his students of mercantilist inclination for not having read Paul Samuelson thoroughly enough.[10] However, their kind of methodology has often been challenged, mainly by historians.

In the following we will deal with some of these discussions related to the issue of Mercantilism. An attempt will be made to summarise the main arguments put forward in this long discussion. To what extent it really makes sense in relation to what Mercantilism was is open to discussion. Schumpeter's general advice to the reader – to forget everything read about the mercantilists and start afresh – was perhaps not such a bad piece of advice after all!

The historical reaction

In the previous chapter we highlighted the invention of the concept of Mercantilism – or rather 'the mercantile system' – by the Physiocrats in the 1760s. We also saw how it was made even more system-like in the hands of Smith, who used it as a straw man handy in order to contrast his own ideas on commerce, the definition (as well as creation) of wealth and other issues. Moreover, we suggested that this definition of Mercantilism was forcefully defended by classical political economists such as McCulloch and Jones in the early nineteenth century.

However, both in Germany and Britain a reaction emerged some decades later concerning this orthodox interpretation of Mercantilism originating from Smith. Basically, the revisionists questioned the Midas-folly argument and argued that the much-scorned favourable balance of trade theory might have had a rational basis. This was especially the case if Mercantilism was more realistically looked upon as a process of state making in a broad sense, such 'revisionists' argued. Moreover, according to their interpretation, it not only became a broad concept focussing on certain forms of policy making and the economic management of the state during the Early Modern era; it also seriously questioned Smith's insistence that Mercantilism must be regarded as a doctrine pursued in order to gain a particular interest. Thus, instead, the revisionists argued that at its core Mercantilism represented the nation–state interest.

A full account of this new and wide definition of Mercantilism as a process of state making first appeared in the form of 12 long articles in the *Jahrbuch für Gesetzgebung, Verwaltung und Volkwirtschaft*, published between 1884 and 1887. Their author was the German historical economist Schmoller. Schmoller dealt with how the electors and kings in Prussia from 1680 to 1786 – most especially Frederick the Great – laid the groundwork for later German unification. Mercantilism was the term he used to designate the policy of unity and centralisation pursued by Prussia administrative powers during this period: 'The whole internal history of the seventeenth and eighteenth centuries ... is summed up in the opposition of the economic policy of the state to that of the town, the district, and the several Estates'.[11] Faithful to his historicist methodology, Schmoller regarded the emergence of the strong territorial state part of a great evolutionary chain of historical development. Thus he believed that in every phase of historical development 'controlling organs of social and political life' essential for the 'life of the race or nation' was developed. As such, he regarded the village, the town, the territory, and, lastly, the national state as successive phases or 'bodies'.[12]

Mercantilism thus became something quite different in Schmoller's hands than it had been with Smith. First and foremost, it expressed the 'economic interests of whole states ... [which] found a rallying-point in certain generally accepted postulates'.[13] Viewed as a 'national policy', the particular views and ideas of mercantilist thinkers and writers were only of minor interest. Thus, for example, 'the whole idea and doctrine of the Balance of Trade ... was only the secondary consequence of economic processes which grouped them according to states'.[14] Accordingly, Schmoller defined Mercantilism in the following fashion:

> What was at stake was the creation of real **political** economies as unified organisms, the centre of which should be, not merely a state policy reaching out in all directions, but rather the living heartbeat of a united sentiment. Only he who thus conceives of mercantilism will understand it; in its innermost kernel it is nothing but state making – not state making in a narrow sense, but state making and national-economy making at the same time; state making in the modern sense, which creates out of the political community an economic community, and so gives it a heightened meaning. The essence of the system lies not in some doctrine of money, or of the balance of trade; not in tariff barriers, protective duties, or navigation laws; but in something far greater: – namely in the total transformation of society and its organisations, as well as of the state and its institutions, in the replacing of a local and territorial economic policy by that of the national state.[15]

Most certainly, Schmoller's broad definition of Mercantilism, which portrayed it rather like the *Zeitgeist* of a specific historical epoch, had of course older roots. Both's monumental *Geschichte der National-Oekonomik in Deutschland* (1874) and Edmund von Heyking's treatement of Mercantilism in *Zur Geschichte der Handelsbilanztheorie* (1880) served as an inspiration for Schmoller.[16] Thus Schmoller agreed with Roscher that the rationale of 'mercantilist' policies in Prussia during the eighteenth century must be sought in the specific conditions prevailing in the German states. More particularly, it was the consequence of a conscious policy pursued especially by the great Elector. Schmoller must have found strong support for his interpretation by reading von Heyking, who depicted the balance theory as a more or less accurate illustration of the bitter power struggle among the European states during the Early Modern epoch. Hence in his treatise, von Heyking outright defined Mercantilism as a system of economics in order to achieve national power.[17] However, he in turn relied on an older school of historical economists like Karl Bücher and Bruno Hildebrand. Ultimately, it was of course List, 'the National Economist' *par exellence*, who first treated Mercantilism as a national economic programme for modernisation and power. Thus the 'idea of a mercantile state' was deeply embedded in the thinking of historical economics in Germany.

In the German-speaking countries, the discussion between the younger school of historical economists and the neo-classicist Carl Menger exploded in the so-called *Methodenstreit* during the 1880s. However, also in Britain such a fight occurred. As argued by Gerrard M Koot, this conflict must not only be seen as a mere duplication of the German discussion.[18] First, instead, it must be related to the specific British discussion during this period and the rise of so-called neo-Mercantilism in this country. From the 1880s onwards the 'neo-mercantilists' opted for higher tariffs, social reforms and 'constructive' social imperialism – the most spectacular result of their lobbying efforts was Joseph Chamberlain's tariff reform in 1903. In their campaigning they mainly found intellectual support among historically minded economists. The most important of these included Cunningham, Ashley and W A S Hewins.[19]

Second, the origin of the *Methodenstreit* in Britain, for example the heated debates between Cunningham and Alfred Marshall during the 1890s, must be sought in the existence of a special variant of historical economics in Britain.[20] Jones is often regarded as a forerunner of such a 'school' of historical economics in Britain. This is perhaps true, but it is essential to remember that Jones regarded himself as a follower of Smith. He saw himself as Smith's brother in arms against the deductive and unhistorical economics of the Ricardian school. However, a historical approach, which included a critical attitude towards the Ricardian school, also united economists such as Thorold Rogers, Arnold Toynbee and Thomas E C Leslie. Especially Leslie attacked orthodox political economy throughout the 1870s for its alleged deductive method and its free trade illusions. In a tone undoubtedly reminiscent of the Germans, he campaigned against the hedonism contained within the orthodox gospel. Man was motivated by not only selfishly seeking wealth, but also moral and religious sentiments, family obligations and so on, he argued – instead of *laissez-faire*, he claimed, for government regulations, protection and a balanced home market.[21]

However, it awaited the threesome Cunningham, Ashley and Hewins to launch a full-blown British version of historical economics in the 1880s. The most spectacular side of the clash between historical economics and the emerging neo-classical school was the bitter conflict between Cunningham and Marshall. This conflict, which over the years turned increasingly bitter, ultimately led to Cunningham resigning from his lecturing post at Cambridge University, while Marshall was able to established an almost hegemonic position within British academic economics.[22]

Cunningham, Ashley and Hewins were all three deeply sceptical towards the deductive ambitions of the neo-classical school. Instead of a hedonist motivated 'economic man', Cunningham, Ashley and Hewins perceived man as a historical creature formed by evolving institutions and social conditions. They strongly resisted *laissez-faire* and defended neo-mercantilist policies. In their political attitudes they differed much, of course: Cunningham was a religious conservative, almost reactionary in style and temperament; Ashley was a kind of social democrat and a warm supporter of both trade unions and social imperialism; while Hewins, lastly, was a social liberal who worked closely with J Chamberlain as his academic advisor.[23] According to Judges, Hewins had been almost shocked by Cunningham's outright praise of almost all kinds of regulative measures and mercantilist policies.[24] However, in his dislike of orthodox political economy, and in order to establish a historical programme for economics, he was willing to join forces with Cunningham and Ashley.

Hence, in his textbook *The Growth of English Industry and Commerce* (1882), Cunningham defended the national regulatory policies pursued by the Tudor monarchy. From a general point of view, its historical role had been to break away from the medieval particularism and establish a national spirit that would provide a basis for later national power and a glorious colonial system, he argued. Cunningham saw the advantage in the breaking up of some regulative orders during the seventeenth century. However, at the same time, he warned against too much *laissez-faire* and freedom of enterprise. By and large he shared Toynbee's pessimistic view that unhampered industrial freedom during the nineteenth century had led to a declining living standard among the poorer classes.[25] The rapid transformation of English economy and society – from an order built on organic *Gemeinschaft* to an industrial order based on *Gesellschaft* – had lead to increased alienation and a loss of national spirit. Cunningham's general attitude was thus clear and resembled the position taken by Schmoller:

The State is after all the embodiment of the national spirit, it reflects the general tone of feeling and thought among the people; such as they are.... The State is the embodiment of what is common to the different persons in the nation, it expresses the spirit in which each shares.[26]

In his *The Growth of English Industry and Commerce*, Cunningham depicted Mercantilism as a system that sought power instead of plenty. The power of the state was the ultimate end to which the regulative policies of successive monarchies and statesmen were geared. It was this system of national power he defined as 'the Mercantile system'.[27] This was of course something quite different than what Smith had in mind a century earlier. In a contribution to a scholarly German *Zeitschrift*, Schmoller explicitly dealt with Smith's interpretation. He was especially critical towards Smith's opinion that Mercantilism mainly represented a particular group interest. On the contrary, he argued, mercantilist policies manifested the national interest and the quest for national unity against particularism.

Like Schmoller, Cunningham was not particularly interested in the specific ideas held by mercantilist writers. They were at best of secondary interest to him. He in fact tended to agree with Smith that the mercantilists produced poor theory. But that was of small matter. When looked upon from a more elevated perspective they were historically justified, he argued. Thus in a longer view they were perfectly rational. The ends the mercantilists had pursued were historically correct. Also most of their means made sense. Together these means and ends served to build a strong national state.[28]

Heckscher

The first Swedish edition of Heckscher's massive interpretative work *Merkantilismen* appeared in 1931.[29] It was translated into German the year thereafter, and the first English edition appeared in 1935 under the title *Mercantilism*. Almost instantaneously it made this liberal Swedish economist and economic historian famous for a wide international audience. His work, however, was by and large critically received both by economists and economic historians. His reviewers would acknowledge the great labour that had gone into the work, as well as Hecksher's great learning and skill. However, they emphasised the following shortcomings of the work:

- The fact that Heckscher tended to treat mercantilist politics in *vacuo* from economic practice as well as economic ideas (Thomas H Marshall);[30]

- His inability to establish a synthesis between 'the situation, the ideas and the actions' of Mercantilism (Herbert Heaton);[31]
- That his system of 'mercantilism' had something unhistorical about it (Marc Bloch);[32]
- That it was highly doubtful whether all regulative policies of the state from the Middle Ages onwards could be seen as bolstered by common and systematic intentions and goals (Bloch, Heaton);[33]
- The fact that he interpreted power in itself as a main end of Mercantilism (Viner);[34]
- His notion of a 'fear of goods' and its explanation in the transition to monetary economies in western Europe after the Middle Ages was too general and unrealistic (Heaton).[35]

Yet, some of this critique must have sounded strange to Heckscher's ears. Especially Viner's insistence that Heckscher had defined power as the main end of Mercantilism seemed to place him in line with historical economists such as Cunningham. This must certainly have been a shock. Paradoxically, really, Viner appeared as one of his strongest opponents, not only because Heckscher in his work had referred so approvingly of Viner: 'When I had the opportunity to study his treatment of the subject, I was happy to find a high degree of agreement between our presentations'.[36] More curious perhaps was that Heckscher regarded himself as a stern opponent of the historical school. In articles dealing with theoretical and methodological issues he always directed severe criticism towards historical economics.[37] Moreover, in the first chapter of his work he critically points out that the 'economic aspects' of Mercantilism – in the form of a protectionist and monetary system – was neglected by Schmoller and Cunningham. Instead he spoke approvingly of Smith's position.[38] Certainly, Heckscher had started out as a conservative historian under the aegis of the enigmatic professor Harald Hjärne in Uppsala. However, later on, as a professor at *Handelshögskolan* (Stockholm School of Economics) in Stockholm, he defended *laissez-faire* and an international system of free trade (see also his contribution to international trade theory known as the Heckscher-Ohlin theorem).[39] Moreover, from the 1920s, he became more liberal in his political aptitudes.

Also, he would see himself in agreement with Viner on a second point. As his American colleague, Heckscher was highly critical of the historicist position that Mercantilism was at heart a rational response to what occurred in the real economic world. As we have seen, he went so far that he denied that the economic ideas of Mercantilism had anything to do with economic realities whatsoever. By and large, then, he must have looked approvingly to the onslaught on what he called the 'economic historians' (mainly of the German historical school) that was carried out by Viner in 1930.[40]

However, that Heckscher's *magnum opus* might be read as a defence of historicism is mainly his own fault. Hence, exactly as Schmoller did, he took a very wide view of Mercantilism. In fact, he extended it even further than Schmoller and Cunningham. Thus, in his book, Heckscher treated it as a system of economic, regulative, administrative and political thinking with roots back to the town policies of the medieval period. Thus, Mercantilism was at its base 'a phase in the history of economic policy'.[41] However, it is at the same time a system of economic doctrine: a 'system of protection and money'. With Heckscher, the economic aspect of Mercantilism achieved a much more coherent character than with Schmoller. He treated it as some kind of commonsensical and popular economic thinking that appeared throughout history. It was not limited to a specific historical period, he maintained. But even this was not all. Henceforth, according to Heckscher, it was third also a specific conception, egotist and materialist, of man and society; almost a worldview.

Therefore, although Heckscher's definition goes even further, it seems closely related to Schmoller's. Furthermore, it seems to fit very neatly into a kind of stages theory of history promoted by the historical school – an approach of which Heckscher was programmematically critical.[42] That Heckscher might be seen as a historicist was further enforced by his suggestive, almost Marxian or Hegelian, conception of a 'fear of goods'. As a form of 'fetishism of money', the want of money and the 'fear of goods' reflected the transition from a barter to a money economy.

Surely, the main reason why Heckscher's book was critically received and partly also misunderstood was due to its complicated structure. For example, it is often hard to grasp how its parts relate to one another. To a large extent, this was caused by his failure to make up his mind regarding what his object really was. Clearly, also, this is the reason why his definition becomes so encompassing and yet so elusive. Further, this is the main explanation behind why he could treat Mercantilism in such an eclectic fashion without really turning out a true synthesis – as Alfred Marshall complained. Hence he treated the system-like features of regulative policies, economic doctrines and general conceptions of society without making clear the relationship between these entities.

We may, however, reconstruct Heckscher's general argument in the following fashion. He started out by emphasising the system-like character of Mercantilism perceived as a specific economic policy. 'It has often been discussed whether mercantilism compromised a theoretical system or not, but this question is badly stated', he said. And he continued,

> For everybody has certain ideas, whether he is conscious of them
> or not, as a basis for his actions, and mercantilists were plentifully
> provided with economic theories on how the economic system was
> created and how it could be influenced in the manner desired.[43]

Furthermore, in order to understand Mercantilism, we must differen-
tiate between its ends and means, he explicated. The ultimate *end* of
mercantilist policies was to strengthen the external power of the
state.[44] This was explicitly contradictory to Smith and liberal economics that preferred the wealth of the individual before the wealth
of the nation state. Still, however, this was not Mercantilism's most
pertinent distinctive character. What gave this system its characteristic stroke was the *means* attached to this general end, he stressed.
Such economic means to bolster the political strength of the state
was part and parcel of Mercantilism regarded as a protectionist and
monetary system. The ambiguity whether this 'system' ought to be
regarded as economic policy or economic thinking – or both – is not
made clear at the outset and follows the reader throughout the full
two volumes. Regardless whether it was policy or doctrine, Heckscher was most anxious to point out that Mercantilism must *not* be
seen as a rational reflection of how the economic system may have
worked during the early modern period. In the introductory chapter
he was more cautious than later on in the text. Here he pointed out
that: 'The description of the economic policy pursued in a particular
period should never be regarded as a sufficient explanation of the
economic circumstances of the time'.[45] But later on he was more cat-
egorical: 'But if economic realities sometimes made themselves felt,
this did not divert the general tendency of economic policy'.[46] In a
chapter which was added to the second edition he was even more
explicit. Now, however, he had turned the argument around and
referred to the economic thinking of the period: 'There are no
grounds whatsoever for supposing that the mercantilist writers constructed their – with its frequent and marked theoretical orientation –
out of any knowledge of reality however derived'.[47]

On the basis of this, no doubt from an overtly exaggerated position,
Heckscher informs us that there are five aspects of Mercantilism that
he will deal with. The first aspect is as a system of unification –
Schmoller's main point, of course. Second, he deals with it as a system
of power, expounded earlier by, for example, Cunningham. Third and
fourth, he discusses Mercantilism as a protectionist and monetary
system taking his point of departure from Smith. Fifth, and lastly, he
emphasised that Mercantilism must be regarded as a conception of
society. This is an often forgotten aspect, he points out. Against this
background, Heckscher's main aim is to provide a synthesis of all

these aspects, and establish a general interpretation of his phenomenon viewed in systematic terms.

Hence, in the first part of his work he treated Mercantilism as a system of unification. This was an ambitious and brilliant piece of economic and legislative history that runs over four hundred pages, but it does not in principle go beyond Schmoller. 'Mercantilism as a system of power' was briefly treated as part 2 of the work (40 pages). Here he mainly reiterated Cunningham's position that the aims and ends of mercantilist policy were to strengthen the power of the state in itself. Part 3, thereafter, was devoted to a discussion of Mercantilism as a system of protection. Here Heckscher presented his famous distinction between a 'policy of provision', so characteristic for the economic administration of medieval towns, and the 'system of protection', which belonged to the mercantilist period. The system of protectionism is, by and large, explained by a psychological inclination and attitude: 'a fear of goods'. According to Heckscher this peculiar mercantilist mentality was characterised by the fact that 'selling was an end in itself'.[48] The object was, he said, to dispose of goods by any possible means. Hence, this also served as an argument for the balance of trade doctrine that became so widespread during this period. Furthermore, this psychological aptitude to fear goods had its historical roots in the autarchic conditions of the medieval age, Heckscher suggested. However, another factor was of even greater importance. By and large it was the extension of the money economy which propelled that 'the money yield appears as the only aim of economic activity'.[49]

Heckscher came back to the Midas fallacy in his next section on Mercantilism as a monetary system. From his interpretation of Mercantilism as a system of protection, it would be logical to expect that Heckscher agreed with Smith that the mercantilist writers had confused money with wealth. However, here he was careful to take notice of the fact that such bullionist attitudes may have been common among early mercantilist writers, but they became much less so during the seventeenth century. In fact, he wrote:

> Mercantilism as a monetary system is thus not to be explained as a conscious idolatry of money. This vital point in it in the field of the rational was the conception of the function of money and the precious metals in society and for the development of economic life.[50]

In this section Heckscher set out to show how mercantilist thinking was obsessed with an elevated attitude of the role of money. Hence economic development, according to the mercantilists, depended upon a vast circulation of money. It was this argument rather than some mystical belief in the wealth-creating capacity of money that helped to explain the mercantilist's high propensity of money, he argued.

In the last section Heckscher discussed Mercantilism as a conception of society. Initially, he stressed the similarities between 'liberalism' and 'mercantilism'. Thus both systems were based on the notion that man was a social animal inspired by contemporary doctrines of natural rights. But, he asked, how could the same kind of social philosophy give rise to such different economic systems as *laissez-faire* and Mercantilism? One answer he presented pointed out that natural rights philosophy in the hands of the mercantilist had a certain a-moralistic flavour. Thus mercantilists were recognised for their 'widespread indifference towards mankind'.[51] An earlier ethic to protect the poor through laws that prohibited usury, and so on, had been replaced by materialist and secular images. Further, as a general principle, the welfare of the individual was always sacrificed for the might of the state. Hence, the Early Modern period saw the rise of 'pure Machiavellianism'. Typical indeed was the attitude towards the poor. The poor classes were by and large looked upon as a 'free good' at the disposal of the propertied classes, he believed.

However, this was not all. The most important divide between Mercantilism and *laissez-faire* lay certainly in the more humane attitude of the latter doctrine. However, the main peculiarity of the mercantilist viewpoint was the strong belief in the regulating power of the state. While *laissez-faire* proponents often could be as unethical and ruthless as the materialist mercantilist, they nevertheless believed in the existence of a pre-established harmony, which the mercantilists did not. In a rejoinder to his critics, Heckscher wrote: 'In the eyes of mercantilists the desired results were to be effected by the dextrous management of a skilful politician; they were not expected to follow from the untrammelled forces of economic life'.[52] Thus doubts in the existence of an invisible hand was really, according to Heckscher, the main dividing line between the world of Smith and the world of Mun. By and large, then, Mercantilism in the hands of Heckscher had turned into a worldview of great dimensions.

Plenty or power?

In line with Schmoller and the historical school, Heckscher expanded the term Mercantilism to become a system of economic thought and a conception of society, as well as a system of economic policy with roots back to the Middle Ages. He had made the state its main agent and propelling force. And although he admitted to his reviewers that both power and opulence were the goal of mercantilist policies, Heaton's dictum certainly had some truth in it, namely, that Heckscher 'insists that mercantilism put power above opulence, in contrast with *laissez-faire*, which made the creation of wealth its lodestar, with small regard to the effect on power of the state'.[53]

In a long article published in two parts in 1930, Viner paid homage to Smith by challenging the historicist's position. As we already have noted, he was very explicit in his critique of historical economics and economic history. Not only had the historical school 'displayed neither interest in, nor acquaintance with, modern economic theorizing with respect to monetary and trade process'. By introducing historicist argument regarding the rationality of this school, the historical school had furthermore 'almost without exception shown a tendency to defend the mercantilist doctrines by reasoning itself decidedly mercantilist flavour'.[54] Instead of trying to understand the mercantilists from their own point of view Viner propounded the strategy to start out from 'modern monetary and trade theory' and on this basis provide 'an inventory of English ideas with respect to trade prevalent before Adam Smith, classified and examined in the light of modern ... theory'.[55] Thus he thought that by such a critical examination the evolution of the doctrines would be better understood than by the historicists' way of arguing that such ideas in some sense reflected the reality of the economic world during the pre-Modern Era.

According to Viner, the mercantilists erred exactly where Smith had said they did: they mixed up real wealth with money. If this was not recognised, he stressed, it is impossible to understand the favourable balance of trade doctrine as well as the view that foreign trade was the only path to national gain. Thus, the mercantilists 'believed, momentarily at least, that all goods other than money were worthless'.[56] Hence, much stronger than Smith, even, Viner emphasised that the mercantilists – by picking citations out of their proper context – were straightforwardly of bullionist stance. Moreover, he refused to see something new come out of the discussion concerning a favourable trade balance during the 1620s. The often drawn distinction between a balance of individual bargain to a balance of trade in general stage was denied by Viner. As we saw, this distinction was implicit already in Smith's *Wealth of Nations*, and with Jones in the 1820s it became an orthodox standpoint. However, such a distinction is only a product of a vivid imagination, Viner stated.[57] Instead, the real division came in the late seventeenth century with the emergence of the employment argument: the labour balance of trade (see further Chapter 4). This successively helped to root out the old dogma of a favourable balance of trade.

However, Viner was ready to admit that a total identification between money and wealth only occurred among some extreme mercantilists. Among the more moderate, an emphasis on gold and silver as wealth must be understood from a different angle. It is ironic that he in his argumentation regarding why money was seen as so pivotal during the sixteenth and seventeenth centuries conceded to an explanation which stressed the 'material' base of this fallacy. In this context he emphasised:

> Much more important in the writings of the abler mercantilist than the absolute identification of wealth with gold and silver was the attribution to the precious metals of functions of such supreme importance to the nation's welfare as to make it proper to attach to them a value superior to that of other commodities.[58]

However, by attending this road, he rather opened the way for yet a new series of historical interpretations that, as we will see, emerged after the Second World War. Thus his critique of the methodology of historicism in reality turned into a plea for better and more profound historical explanations.

Viner also challenged another kind of assumption made by the historical economists, most pertinently of course by Schmoller. In contrast with him, and in accordance with Smith, he emphasised that the mercantilist writers were not devoted to *etaisme*. This is empirically demonstrated, he thought, by that they seldom paid homage to the general good or defended state legislations and policies. Rather, most of them were critical of current politics and saw themselves as reformers in this context. But, as Viner maintained, they were certainly reformers of a particular kind. Hence in their endeavour to reform the old structure they were first and foremost bearers of 'special interests' (they were rent-seekers to use modern vocabulary). Each group constantly lobbied for legislative reform that could conform to their economic interests. Clearly inspired by Smith's rhetorical style, Viner wrote that:

> The laws and proclamations were not, as some modern admirers of the virtues of mercantilism would have us believe, the outcome of noble zeal for a strong and glorious nation, directed against the selfishness of the profit-seeking merchants, but were the product of conflicting interests of varying degrees of respectability.[59]

Viner's two articles appeared before Heckscher's work had been published and translated. However, after Viner had read Heckscher, he was reinforced in his critique against historical economics. Thus, in his review of Heckscher's book and in an article published a decade later, he severely criticised the notion that power for the mercantilists had been an end in itself.[60] As we saw, it is quite possible to argue that

Heckscher in this context stood close to Cunningham. However, a more charitable reading of Heckscher suggests that he saw the struggle for power as only *one* of the ends of mercantilist policy. After all, his ambition was clearly to put forward a general synthesis in which the struggle for power was only one among several aspects. Moreover, Heckscher was always in principle careful not to press for a single explanation. As we saw, in his answer to Viner and others, he was ready to concede that *both* power and opulence were a central theme in mercantilist economic policy during its heyday. Here he also seemed to suggest that behind these two linked aims lurked a very peculiar social philosophy: the worldview of Mercantilism.

However, Viner had made up his mind once and for all. Thus Heckscher, according to him, had supported the 'thesis that the mercantilists subordinated plenty to power'.[61] In his 1948 article, he made notice of Heckscher's acquiescence but seems to have regarded it mainly as a tactical retreat. Heckscher failed to demonstrate, he maintained, that mercantilist writers ever regarded power as 'the *sole* end of national policy, or that wealth matters *only* as it serves power'.[62] Instead, as a 'correct' interpretation, he (not so very) modestly proposed something which Heckscher might have readily agreed with:

> [P]ractically all mercantilists ... would have subscribed to all of the following propositions: (1) wealth is an absolutely essential means to power, whether for security or for aggression; (2) power is essential or valuable as a means for the acquisition or retention of wealth; (3) wealth and power are each proper ultimate ends of national policy; (4) there is long-run harmony between these ends.[63]

The economic history of mercantilism

Heckscher's two volumes on Mercantilism without doubt led to a revitalisation of the discussion. In the early 1930s, when this work first appeared, Mercantilism was of course a controversial political issue. In Europe, protectionism and economic nationalism had re-emerged on a wide scale. And the voice of contemporary totalitarianism sounded peculiarly like the *dirigisme* tone of old Mercantilism.[64] Also, as we will see, in his *General Theory*, Keynes spoke approvingly of it – to the abhorrence of 'old' liberals such as Heckscher.[65]

After the war, however, and in a very different political climate, the discussion on Mercantilism continued. But now the debate to a lesser degree caught the ears of politicians and economists. Hence it was instead the economic historians who added the subject of Mercantilism to their *curriculum vitae*. Especially the 1950s and 1960s were characterised by the fast rise of economic history as an academic undertaking, especially in the Anglo-Saxon world.[66] At least in Britain its success relied not to a small extent upon the scholarly controversy concerning Mercantilism. In Britain the discussion came to focus especially on two issues. First, the value of Heckscher's broad and encompassing definition of Mercantilism was questioned and criticised. Second, new historical research on international trade relations seemed to suggest new ways to understand and interpret the phenomena. Hence, a lively discussion emerged which sought to establish a sound economic-historical base for the superstructure of mercantilist thinking.

With regard to the first of these aspects, A W Judges had already in 1939 vigorously rejected the notion of 'a mercantile state'. Judges was a fellow of King's College London and a renowned scholar on English literature, especially the Elizabethan period. His campaign was officially directed against the *Historismus* of 'German scholarship', including fellow travellers such as Cunningham and Ashley. Although Heckscher was only briefly mentioned, much of Judges' critical remarks could as well have been directed against him. Judges put the question whether it was appropriate to regard Mercantilism as a coherent 'system'. He was certain of the answer himself. Mercantilism 'never had a creed; nor was there a priesthood dedicated to its service', he wrote. Moreover, it did not, he argued, offer a coherent doctrine or 'at least a handful of settled principles'. Thus, Mercantilism was a straw man constructed 'in the eighteenth century by men who found security for their own faith in a system of natural law'.[67]

Some two decades later this standpoint was further developed by a leading economic historian, Coleman. Coleman openly confronted Heckscher and his 'synthesising treatment' of his topic. Almost in a Hegelian fashion Mercantilism had become a real entity, which had manifested itself through the centuries in different guises.[68] Coleman's conclusion is often cited:

> [W]hat was this mercantilism. Did it exist? As a description of a trend of economic thought the term may well be useful.... As a label for economic policy, it is not simply misleading but actively confusing, a red-herring of historiography. It serves to give a false unity to disparate events, to conceal the close-up reality of particular times and particular circumstances, to blot out the vital intermixture of ideas and preconceptions, of interests and influences, political and economic, and of the personalities of men which is the historian's job to examine.[69]

As already noted, in later articles Coleman extended this argument also to Mercantilism perceived as a trend of economic thought. In

1980 he conceded that the term Mercantilism may have a certain heuristic value. It was in fact an example of such 'non-existent entities that had to be invented in order to prevent the study of history of falling into the abyss of antiquarianism'.[70] However, as a description of a *real* specific stream of thought or economic policy the term was not legitimate and misleading, he maintained.

Although having a great and distinct influence on the discussion in the 1950s, it is at the same time clear that most partakers in the discussion since then have been reluctant to conform to Judges' and Coleman's rather extreme views on this matter. However, a general sceptical view towards the system-view has been widespread. As already noted, Johnson already in his influential work from 1937, *British Predecessors to Adam Smith*, believed that Mercantilism was an 'unhappy term'. Also Schumpeter's dictum in *History of Economic Analysis* that the mercantilists – his 'consultant administrators' – were practical men unable to theorise fitted quite well with such a position.[71] In line with this, Terence W Hutchison argued that the term Mercantilism ought to be avoided if possible as it had become too broad and general. It would not be wise, he thought, to use such an encompassing concept to describe economic thinking over several decades and in many socio-economic contexts.[72]

However, while often sympathetic with attempts to qualify the 'curiously unrealistic' stew that Heckscher had made of Mercantilism, many have continued to use the term and indeed argued for preserving it.[73] Surely, certain leading ideas can be found in the economic literature from the early seventeenth century up to the time of Smith. So why not use the label 'Mercantilism' to denote these ideas and formulations? And if the term has a heuristic value and might be used as an ideal type in a Weberian sense, does it not then at least to some extent reflect some underlying reality? It is also extremely difficult to make sense of Schumpeter's view that the consultant administrators did not theorise at all. It is of course true that they did not use a methodology invented by twentieth-century economics – and to some point we may even agree with Schumpeter that the mercantilists were poor theorists. But is this all there is to it? It is improbable that even Schumpeter would have believed that the mercantilist thinkers did not think – however faulty – in any systematic fashion at all.

Nor is it, as Bob Coats once remarked, in principle illegitimate to make generalisations about economic policy. Thus it is clear that 'economic policies' – the myriad of decisions on different levels made by legislative or executive organs of the state or other communal properties – must be illuminated by at least some visions and views regarding both how 'the economy' operates and the ultimate ends of legislative or regulative action. 'Historians of economics recognize that without *some* conception of the way the economic system works, and the relationship between "means" and "ends", there can be no coherent policy making whatever', Coats writes.[74] It is of course in principle possible to argue that such coherent policy making was absent from the governing structures of the eighteenth and early nineteenth centuries. But is such a view really realistic? Surely, it is more fruitful to argue that also during this age administrators and politicians were trying to find means for a set of ends that they had put forward – irrespective of their content or soundness. On this whole discussion, opened up by Judges and Coleman, probably a majority would agree with Richard C Wiles's rather sombre attitude when he put up a warning for over-generalisation:

> [T]his does not necessarily argue for the charge often made in the critical literature that the mercantilists were unsystematic, ad hoc, and merely pleaders in their economic writings who rushed to suggestions for state policy in a haphazard manner to enrich the sovereign. For there is more continuity and cohesiveness in mercantilist literature than such a view allows.... Mercantilist ideas, like most periods and schools of economic thought, did change and develop. Yet a continuity remained.[75]

A second important theme in the discussion on post-1950s' Mercantilism – also dominated by the economic historians – was to consider the relationship between economic ideas, events and policies during the mercantilist period. Although Heckscher, as we saw, was ready to establish a clear connection between thought and policy, he was totally negative towards the ideas of a positive relationship between thought and events. For this he was critically summoned in stark language by, for example, Coleman. Coleman put an emphasis on the materialist base for economic ideas:

> The continuity of ideas which Heckscher was eager to stress was paralleled by a continuity of basic conditions which he ignored. It is upon these substrata of economic life that are built the general conceptions of economic life which men hold.[76]

Hence, from the 1950s, Coleman's economic historical colleagues set out to discover the real grain that the writings of the mercantilists were based upon. Hence, for example, Wilson in a series of articles set out to prove what George N Clark earlier had argued for, namely, that 'the explanation of the mercantilist attitude seems to lie in the commercial conditions of the time, and especially in the needs of traders for capital in a solid and ponderable form'.[77] A common fault with interpreters of

Mercantilism since Smith was, as Wilson said, that 'The possibility that the obsession with bullion might have rational historical roots is scarcely examined'.[78] Hence, according to Wilson, the central theme in early British mercantilist writing (Mun, Misselden and others) was the worry over some particular trades balances – especially the Baltic trade. Much trade during this period was carried out in a bilateral form, he argued. The import of grain, timber, iron and copper from the Baltic countries was crucial to Britain. But it was a remaining problem that this trade only could be carried out through the export of real money from Britain. An important cause behind this was the dominant position of the Dutch as exporters to the Baltic area.[79] Hence this outflow of species had to be counter-balanced by a positive 'overplus' in the trade with other countries and regions. It was this peculiar situation which explained the rationale behind the mercantilists' concern for a positive balance of trade, Wilson believed. As trade turned more multilateral during the seventeenth century, this doctrine became increasingly obsolete and was in the end discarded.[80] In his answer to Wilson, Heckscher denied that bilateralism was common during the seventeenth century. The existence of exchange bills, especially, spoke against Wilson's bullionist interpretation, he argued.[81] In a rejoinder, Wilson restated his view that 'in a number of branches of international trade, precious metals played a unique role which gives an element of rationality to mercantilist thought'.[82] Further, the 'hard currency' view was 'rooted in the views of individual merchants about the requirements of their business'. Therefore, he stated, 'Trading capital *in money* was regarded as an indispensable link in the exchange of goods'.[83]

During the early 1950s also another strand of research, explicitly aimed at explaining the historical rationality behind the mercantilist discussion, caused intense discussion. Hence in two articles, in 1954 and 1955, John D Gould argued that the great commercial and industrial depression in Britain in the early 1620s was a formative factor for the rise of mercantilist doctrine. According to Gould, most contemporary observers had shared the view that the crisis was primarily caused by 'some shortcoming of the monetary system and the machinery of foreign exchange'.[84] From this followed that:

> To one who studied the trade depression of the 1620s in detail ... it is clear that a very substantial part of 'England's Treasure' [Mun's most famous book] represents simply the fruits of reflection on the events and discussion of those years.[85]

By referring to the monetary situation, Gould without doubt drew on Raymond de Roover's pathbreaking study of Thomas Gresham and international exchange relations during the sixteenth century. In this study de Roover showed how the discussions around exchange and monetary questions in Britain during this period and up until the crisis of the 1620s to a large degree was formed by a specific set of conditions, which had given exchange dealers in Antwerp a central position vis-à-vis Britain and its merchants. Thus Gresham's and perhaps also Malynes's notion that the power of the malicious foreign exchangers must be broken most probably had such a background.[86]

The position Gould took to these issues was carried further in a study by Supple, *Commercial Crisis and Change in England 1600–1642* (1959). In this important study Supple emphasised the existence of a real 'drain of silver' from England especially during the 1620s. Its main cause was the overvaluation of British silver money – in its turn largely caused by monetary chaos and debasement on the continent in the wake of the Thirty Years' War – which led to a severe drop of demand especially for British cloth. This was in fact the phenomenon, Supple emphasised, which underlay 'so many contemporary complaints concerning a scarcity of money'.[87] The heated discussion between Mun, Misselden and Malynes thus hinged upon how this deflationary process and scarcity of money should be explained. Both Gould and Supple tended to prefer Malynes's conclusion that it was the existence of international currency manipulations which were at the root of the problem. As monetary problems were the pivotal issue, his position was without doubt more realistic than Mun's and Misselden's, who rather saw the dearness of British coin as a secondary phenomena caused by a negative trade balance. But the heart of the matter was, Supple maintained, that 'the reiterated claims of these years that England had an unfavourable balance of trade were founded on uncomfortable fact'. And the conclusion he draws from this comes immediately: 'Indeed much of the economic literature which historians have interpreted as "typical" of mercantilism is, in fact, the product of a specific situation and a short-run crisis'.[88]

Against this background, Supple, along the line of Judges, Coleman and Schumpeter, manifested a negative attitude to notions of Mercantilism's system-like character. 'In calling such writers "mercantilist" there is the danger of implicitly attributing to them a continuity of doctrine, based on a set of supposedly logical principles, which was not theirs', he warned us.[89] In fact their writing as being 'consistent and pragmatic responses to consistent fluctuations in an economic environment whose basic elements were slow to change hardly merit treatment as a full-blown system'.[90]

Without doubt, the emergence of economic historical studies has contributed much to an increased understanding of mercantilist doctrines. First, they have shown how the mercantilist literature was related to current political and economical issues and debates. Second, they have convincingly showed the complex interrelationship between economic ideas, politics and interest groups during this period. For example, the British historian R W K Hinton has clearly demonstrated that governmental politics especially during the seventeenth century had a high degree of autonomy and could certainly not be seen as an instant outcome of 'mercantilist thinking'.[91] Not until well into the eighteenth century, protectionism in the sense of a policy to promote home production became established as a coherent working rule of British governments.[92]

At the same time, however, many of the interventions from the economic historians display, to a different degree, a reductionist tendency to 'explain' texts as the immediate result of economical, political and social circumstances. However, as we have argued, complex 'circumstances' of the kind we deal with here are never immediately observable. They are always interpreted against the backdrop of a certain language; in concepts and words that are historically inherited and made intelligible to the actors. It is hardly enough to argue that Mun and Malynes were involved in a discussion which concerned pragmatic issues. Instead, it is totally clear when they discussed 'practical' economic matters such as the effect of monetary speculation on the trade balance that they did so with the help of a conceptual framework deeply rooted in earlier conceptions and views for how the economy functioned and ought to be understood. They discussed with conceptions that made sense to them: 'overplus', 'underweight', 'exchange' and so on. As for example Coats has stressed, this is as much an empirical issue as an epistemological one:

> For example how can 'events' as such explain the co-existence of conflicting opinions unless some effort is made to demonstrate which events conditioned any particular ideas or set of attitudes? Among those who respond to events are cranks, eccentrics, partisan promoters of vested interests, office-seekers, statesmen, and those rare individuals motivated chiefly by the disinterested pursuit of 'truth'.[93]

Keynes and Mercantilism

Apart from Smith's *Wealth of Nations*, probably the most well-known economic text is by Keynes, *The General Theory of Employment, Interest and Money*, which appeared in 1936. Its Chapter 23 was devoted to the discussion of old economists who in the past, in Keynes's eyes, had been mistreated by members of 'the classical school'. The mercantilists were no mere cranks nor can their ideas be dismissed as nonsense based on intellectual confusion, he argued.[94] He stated what he regarded the most important element of 'scientific truth' in mercantilist doctrine:

> When a country is growing in wealth somewhat rapidly, the further progress of this happy state of affairs is liable to be interrupted, in conditions of *laissez faire*, by the insufficiency of the inducements to new investments.[95]

Furthermore, 'the opportunities for home investments will be governed, in the long run, by the domestic rate of interest; whilst the volume on foreign investment is necessarily determined by the size of the favourable balance of trade'.[96] Moreover, the rate of interest is determined by 'the quantity of the precious metals'. From this the logic of the mercantilists' insistence upon the gains from a favourable balance of trade becomes quite clear. Hence,

> measures to increase the favourable balance of trade were the only **direct** means at their disposal for increasing foreign investments; and at the same time, the effect of a favourable balance of trade on the influx of the precious metals was their only **indirect** means to reducing the domestic rate of interest and so increasing the inducement to home investment.[97]

According to Keynes, this is in principle the central argument of mercantilist thought. By choosing this approach – which needless to say fitted well into Keynes's own theoretical aspirations – he had to assume that the general aim of mercantilist thinking and policies was full employment. He does not really go into whether such an aim really can be observed in an identifiable body of mercantilist literature – he simply takes it for granted. But this supposition would most certainly have needed a more extensive discussion. As Viner pointed out early and Wilson later wrote, 'Re-reading the works of the mercantilists, one cannot avoid an uneasy feeling that employment was seen as a means to increasing bullion supplies rather than vice versa'.[98] Instead of elaborating on this point, he continued with a discussion on which specific mercantilist viewpoints made sense and could even be regarded as superior to the views of the classical *laissez-faire* position.

First, Keynes praised the mercantilists for *not* assuming a self-adjusting tendency existed by which the rate of interest would be established 'at the appropriate level'. On the contrary, he argued, they saw a high rate of interest as a main obstacle to economic growth, and they were 'even aware that the rate of interest depended on liquidity-preference and the quantity of money'.[99]

Second, he pointed out that they were aware of the danger that excessive competition may turn the terms of trade against a country. Third, he hailed them for a viewpoint 'which the classicals were to denounce two centuries later as an absurdity', namely, that a scarcity of money could be a cause for unemployment. Fourth, and last, 'The mercantilists were under no illusion as to the nationalistic character of their policies and their tendency to promote war'. It was '*national* advantage and *relative* strength at which they were admittedly aiming'.[100]

It would be easy to dismiss Keynes's interpretation of mercantilist thought as a mere invention in order to provide support for his own case. Thus, according to Wilson, as so typical for economists writing the history of economic thought, Keynes falls into the anachronistic trap.[101] Thus he took for granted that the end result which the mercantilists tried to achieve was full employment, while they perhaps rather aimed to put forward a wide programme of national growth, power and modernisation. Nor were his insights into the mercantilist literature exhaustive and very penetrating. Therefore, we may also expect some factual errors in his texts – as there certainly are.[102]

As expected, Heckscher took a rather negative attitude towards Keynes's interpretative scheme. Thus he was anxious to point out that 'there are no grounds whatsoever' to allege that the mercantilists derived their opinion from an observation of economic facts.[103] Certainly, any attempt to explain the mercantilist viewpoint from a rational and historical point of view would of course meet objection from Heckscher. But, with regard to Keynes, he seemed particularly critical of the view that unemployment during the mercantilist period might be seen as a consequence of inadequate investments. Instead, according to Heckscher, unemployment depended on bad harvests and war and had very little to do with 'modern' business cycles.[104] However, this position seems untenable from what we know of the causes for the great trade crisis in England in the 1620s. As it seems, this crisis was clearly a 'modern' one. Furthermore, we will later on see that some mercantilist writers quite explicitly connected unemployment with low investments and growth – although using other words.

After all, it is not so easy to dismiss Keynes as an interpreter of Mercantilism.[105] First, it is clear that full employment of resources *was* an important policy end put forward by mercantilist writers. However, this aim should be regarded as part of a wider design, which emphasised national power and opulence. Second, Keynes was fully aware of the fallacy of anachronism. He was in fact quite alerted *not* to put his own words in the mouth of mercantilist writers. Furthermore, he was careful to take notice of the specific institutional conditions that prevailed at the time and how they differed from his.[106] Additionally, his historical understanding was not so shallow as sometimes suggested. In the first place he was well informed of, for example, the economic history of Spain. Second, the remarks he made about the specific institutional framework which confronted the mercantilists does not seem unreasonable from a historical point of view.

However, at the same time, there are some important problems with Keynes's interpretation. Some of them we are already familiar with. First, it is clear that Keynes had an affinity of grand oversimplification. He depended overtly on his own intuition and was fond of sweeping generalisations. Second, he shared with many others an oversimplified view of the relationship between ideas, events and policies. In Keynes's version, all these levels become part of a coherent, but vague, 'system'. Third, it is highly questionable whether 'full employment' was the sole end of mercantilist thinking and policy making. It is true, as we will see, that a large population in work was a cornerstone in this thinking. However, what 'full employment' might have meant at the time cannot be apprehended easily. Fourth, Keynes's attempt to find an inner logic of mercantilist thinking had a tendency to prove too much. As noted by many scholars, many seventeenth-century writers were sometimes illogical when discussing how prices, money, interest rates and so on were connected. Quite clearly, to some degree, we must admit to the existence of such flaws and logical mistakes. How shall we otherwise, for example, perceive their belief that an inflow of money lead to lowered interest rates, while at the same time low prices was an important policy end? How indeed did interest rates interrelate with the level of prices and with demand and employment? It is wrong to believe that mercantilist writers were always clear on such matters. Especially, against this background, Keynes's insistence on the coherent structure of their thinking was really wide over the mark.

Nevertheless, during the halcyon days of Keynesianism, the view that the mercantilists had been forerunners of Keynes in pursuing a policy of full employment was quite common. Thus the American economist Douglas Vickers in a study dealing with monetary theory during the eighteenth century did not only find that a mercantilist like William Potter had discovered the multiplier effect.[107] In general terms, Vickers would also draw the conclusion that 'the important characteristic of the pre-classical literature was that it developed a theory of money which was addressed to the explanation of the problems of employment, prosperity, and economic development'. Furthermore,

> It was not merely the case that a relationship was noticed between a larger or smaller supply of money in circulation on the one hand and a larger or smaller volume of employment or effective level

trade activity on the other. The nature of the dependence which here subsisted was also examined.[108]

Was it indeed? The same thinking was also prevalent in A K Sen's study of the 'late mercantilist' James Steuart. Sen stated outrightly about Steuart:

[I]t is only in the light of the Keynesian analysis that what he was really groping for finally becomes clear. His analysis of the nature and importance of ready money demands his conclusion that their volume depends on the state of trade and industry, the mode of living and the customary expenditures of the people, etc., and his stress on the fact that an increased quantity of money tends to affect trade and industry not only by facilitating circulation but also by lowering the rate of interest, are ideas which we have become quite familiar with in recent years and which does not sound, after all, quite so preposterous to us as they did to our nineteenth-century forebears.[109]

We will return to these questions later on. Here we will only note that a Keynesian interpretation of Mercantilism became quite widespread during the 1950s and 1960s. It was, for example, prevalent in an influential article published by William D Grampp in 1952. In this article Grampp especially emphasised 'the importance of full employment in mercantilist policy'. Hence, he assumed that full employment really was the main objective of mercantilist policy and thinking.[110] The core of this, as we noted, anachronistic argument was borrowed from Keynes:

It is my opinion that their [the mercantilists'] desire to maintain a favourable balance of trade was based on the assumption that England would be able to increase employment by exporting more than it imported – an assumption which is plausible in the short run.[111]

After all, as we saw, it was Keynes who strongly stressed that foreign investments and an inflow of bullion would lower the domestic rate of interest and thus increase employment. In his article Grampp especially pointed to the role of foreign investment in this context. However, although Grampp was clearly influenced by Keynesian macro-economics, his argument was at the same time based on the actual writings of the mercantilist writers themselves. Furthermore, by referring to their texts he was able to modify the Keynesian tale in certain respects.

Mercantilism as a rent-seeking society

More than anybody, Smith emphasised egotistical self-interest from 'men whose interests never is exactly the same as that with the public' as an impelling driving force behind 'the mercantile system'. As we have seen, this idea has continued to gain support over the years. Some decades ago it was reinstated in a public choice inspired version: Mercantilism as rent-seeking. Hence two American economists, Ekelund and Tollison, in a study provide an interpretation in which 'the supply and demand for monopoly rights through the machinery of the state is seen as the essence of mercantilism'.[112] Their ambitions were highly put. In their model they set out to not only 'explain mercantile political economy', but also 'rationalize the emergence and decline of the social order of mercantilism in England and France'. Indeed, because it suggests a positive explanation of all this simultaneously, they state that their model is more 'robust' than previous ones. Furthermore, their aim is to explain 'the order of mercantilism' in terms of individual behaviour, 'in the face of varying institutional constraints rather than in terms of the irrationality of error'. By this they desire to avoid the 'conventional paradigm', which focusses mostly 'on the stupidity of the mercantile writers'.[113]

Instead they offer us public-choice 'positive economics' stemming from Chicago. We are thus informed that rational profit-seeking, methodological individualism and evolving institutional constraints are the key variables involved here. But at the same time rent-seeking is regarded as something more specific than profit-seeking: it is an expenditure 'of scarce resources to capture a pure transfer'. Hence the rise of Mercantilism implies at the same time the rise of such actors

> who perceive potential gains from procuring monopoly rights to produce particular goods and services. These individuals will attempt to subvert the forces of the market and to monopolize the production of goods by having the state limit production to themselves by fiat.[114]

Ekelund and Tollison used the cases of England and France to illustrate their thesis. For England the task is to explain the gradual decline of regulation and the 'social order of Mercantilism', while the preservation of regulation is a main characteristic feature in France. In the heyday of old absolutism, the cost of seeking monopolies was relatively low in Britain, they suggested. However, the rise of parliament costs due to 'uncertainty' as well as 'growing private returns' led to the demise of the old regulative system. 'Seeking monopoly through the shelter of the state was clearly going to be a less profitable activity under these circumstances', they state.[115] In France, old absolutism and authoritarian power of the monarch lingered on. Here, therefore, to seek monopoly positions continued to be a top priority among individuals.

However, like Ekelund and Tollison, the authors already at the outset define Mercantilism as a system in which individuals seek monopoly positions, such an argument comes close to being circular; a simple tautology. Nevertheless, they conclude that 'our theory ... presents an explanation for the decline of mercantilism in England and for its simultaneous intensification in France'.[116] However, from this basis, one cannot help wonder – as one critic stated – 'what evidence, if any would constitute falsification of their theory, or what counter-examples, if any would persuade them to abandon it?'[117]

Furthermore, with Ekelund and Tollison's interpretation it is not only that it is difficult to find a transfer mechanism between ideas, events and policies; they explicitly regard it as a non-question. 'Our interpretation of mercantilism as a rent-seeking society does not suggest that intellectual developments will have much impact on public policy', they confess.[118] In their universe it is merely self-interested merchants, monarchs and publics that counts. Their story deals with the costs and benefits that accrue to actors that participate in the process of mercantile rent-seeking.

A peculiar feature of the Ekelund and Tollison approach is that they seem totally disinterested in what the mercantilist writers actually wrote themselves. This lack of interest is furthermore documented in a longer work *Politicized Economies* published 16 years after the above-mentioned book. Although the criticism of several historians of economic thought – as we saw – they still declare themselves to be 'stubbornly neo-classical'.[119] But not only that. Here and elsewhere they reject any historical reading of the mercantilist texts as a false start, as a red herring. Instead they uncompromisingly state that, whatever occurs in them, they are – consciously or not – pure rationalisations of egotistical private interests. Reminiscent of Marx's notion of agents being unconscious concerning their 'true' interests, Ekelund and Tollison continue in the book to demonstrate how in England, France and Spain a political economy emerged which they state was an outcome of rent-seeking. In the same manner, institutional change (especially in Britain) during the eighteenth century was a mere consequence of 'economizing activity'.[120] Hence, departing from public choice theory, they work backwards to the seventeenth- and eighteenth-century European history and find exactly what they set out to find in the first place.

Development and underdevelopment

The main originator of radical economics, Karl Marx, seems on the whole to have said nothing very original about the mercantilists. Like Smith, he tended to treat them mainly as erroneous and pre-analytical. Marx certainly paid tribute to Petty, of course. But this was not because of that author's mercantilist leanings, but because he could be regarded as a (proto, no doubt) labour theorist of value.[121]

However, from his famous discussion on 'primitive accumulation' in part 8 of the first volume of *Capital*, two different interpretations can be drawn in fact: this economic thinking and policy-making was either regarded by Marx as an illusion which draws upon 'profit upon alienation', or as a rationalisation of the necessary means which had to be carried out during the period of 'primitive accumulation' (see also the discussion of Ekelund and Tollison above).[122] When leaning towards the first of these alternatives, Marx regarded 'profit upon alienation' as the crux of mercantilist thought. In this form it was close to Heckscher's 'fear of goods'. The illusion that wares can be sold in international exchange at a higher price than its actual value amounted to many causes. However, its main source was the confusion between the private economy and the national economy. Thus it was the merchant capitalist's practice of buying cheap and selling dear that was the main propelling force behind this fallacy, he argued. As argued later on, this interpretation is highly questionable as most mercantilists were completely capable of distinguishing between private and national economy. Further, most of them were in agreement that not only foreign trade, but also production was a source of wealth. Notwithstanding, however, this theory has found followers among some Marxist scholars.[123]

However, the other approach offered by Marx leads us in another direction. In order to accomplish a transition from an agrarian 'feudal' to an industrial 'capitalist' economy, peasants must not only be turned into unfree proletarians. A capital must also be created through means of international exploitation – mainly by trade – which later can be invested in industrial production. According to this version, 'the mercantile system' is no longer a mere illusion. On the contrary, it can be fitted to the historical realities of such a period of exploitative 'primitive accumulation'.

Also this theory has had some followers among Marxist scholars.[124] However, set free from strict Marxist clothing, this approach has also been employed in order to illustrate the accuracy of development theory, for example the radical 'development of underdevelopment' thesis. The central theme here is the sense in which mercantilist policies helped to facilitate exploitation through trade. Especially emphasised in this context is the connection between Mercantilism and an oppressive colonial system, favourable terms of trade for European powers, unequal exchange, aggressive trade policies, as well as the explicit policy, only to import certain raw materials while exporting industrial wares worked up from own or foreign raw materials.

While only hinted at in many works, this interpretation appeared in a mature form with the Italian scholar Cosimo Perrotta.[125] He insists that the favourable balance theory 'really' was what Johnson conceptualised as a 'labour balance theory'. Thus the main concern of Mercantilism was industrial development. Its core was the development of national industries by the means of international trade. For Johnson and others, this labour balance theory only emerged after 1660. According to Perrotta, however, it was much older. Especially in the form of a general denunciation 'of the importing of luxury goods and also in frequent calls to import raw materials in exchange for manufactured goods' it harked back to the Middle Ages.[126] Perrotta defines this doctrine in the following way:

> The country gains in the exchange if the value of the matter imported is greater than that of the matter exported, whereas it loses if the labour put into the product imported is greater than put into the product exported.[127]

So depicted, Mercantilism becomes more or less another term for import substitution. According to this modern theory, the establishment of industry will give rise to value, adding production and more employment. Hence, according to Perrotta, the mercantilists already in the seventeenth century had a clear picture of the importance of a process, which development economists critical of free trade, such as Raúl Prebisch and Gunnat Myrdal, stressed three hundred years later:

> that in international trade there is an unequal advantage for the parties involved which is dependent on the value in use of the commodities exchanged, or to be more precise, on the different productive potentials of their value in use.[128]

Furthermore, according to Perrotta, the mercantilists were aware that a higher productive potential in the form of 'modern' industry provided the more developed country with a technological monopoly, which could be used for exploitation or improved terms of trade.

With Perrotta we seem to have done a full circle. Thus his interpretation fits well with both the conclusions of the historical school and Heckscher. Also in Perrotta's version, Mercantilism becomes state building by economic means: a promotion of growth and economic modernisation in an international competitive *milieu*. Also, to some extent, it becomes equal to protectionism. Furthermore, as a policy to promote domestic production in order to substitute import, it goes back to the Middle Ages – and has appeared occasionally ever since. Such an interpretation of Mercantilism as a timeless political figuration would of course have both abhorred Heckscher (for political reasons) as well as pleased him (for theoretical reasons).

The return of Schmoller?

Despite the talk of red herrings and the rejection of any historical existence of a coherent mercantilist theoretical system, the term continues to be used by historians. To be more exact, many avoid the label as best they can while they still refer to it in practice. Hence when the development economist Erik Reinert, in his influential *How Rich Countries Got Rich ... and Why Poor Countries Stay Poor*, says that '... the mechanisms of wealth and poverty had, during several historical periods been better understood than they are today', we can easily understand what he is referring to. Hence he especially mentions Antonio Serra's *Breve Trattato* (1613) – by earlier interpreters classified as an early mercantilist text – as providing a clear analysis on 'underdevelopment' and 'development' as Perrotta talked about. But unlike him, however, Serra explicitly mentions Schmoller as a great inspiration. It is in fact his analysis of the political economy of the seventeenth and eighteenth centuries which more than anything guides Reinert through his book.[129] However, he does not use the term Mercantilism a single time in his text.

Eschewing the concept of Mercantilism while still implicitly referring to it has in fact been a common strategy during the last decades among historians.[130] For example, Istvan Hont in his seminal work *Jealousy of Trade: International Competition and the Nation-State in Historical Perspective* (2005) only mentions the word in passing. However, when he identifies foreign navigation as 'an affair of state' in order to bolster the power of the state, he comes close to Schmoller. The identification of Mercantilism with 'bellicose' political economy during the seventeenth and eighteenth centuries is also emphasised by Sophus Reinert and others.[131] Neither Hont nor S Reinert believes that Mercantilism was a coherent economic theory, but they still find use for it. For example, S Reinert opposes the view that mercantilists were Chrysohedonists who imagined that only money was wealth. But both Hont and S Reinert fall back on an interpretation close to Schmoller's when they regard Mercantilism basically as a system of economic policy in favour of the nation state in a situation of fierce international competition for power and wealth.

As to be expected, Schmoller's return has not been appreciated by everybody. Hence Steven Pincus, in a recent contribution to the debate, emphasised the conflicting views between a Tory and Whig position concerning wealth and the role of the state in order to achieve such an end, also regarding the different views on the relationship between 'power and plenty'.[132] First, such an undermining of the thesis of a coherent mercantilist policy pursued by a powerful English (later British) state has a pedigree in earlier works on commerce and empire carried out by Robert Brenner and others. Hence Brenner points out the close connection during the Commonwealth between radicals such as Samuel Hartlib and 'radical policies of Empire' and an 'aggressive approach to commercial policy'.[133] Without doubt this split between what later became Tories and Whigs was a profound one and crucial in order to understand British policies on commerce well into the late eighteenth century. Second, also, criticism against Schmoller falls back on the often-articulated view that the state before the end of the eighteenth century – not least in Britain – was too weak in order to pursue a coherent economic policy of its own. Hence Michael J Braddick, Paul Stern and others have questioned whether one can even talk of a functioning state at all during this period, and even less so of an 'absolute state'.[134] The tools for such a power were simply not at hand, and different parts of the state – including communities and corporations of various kinds – carried out policies which sometimes ran counter to themselves. The notion of such a pre-industrial 'porous' weak state with low authority has also been used in many others contexts.[135]

Rethinking mercantilism – but in what direction?

In a recent edited work on Mercantilism, its editors Stern and Carl Wennerlind suggested 'rethinking Mercantilism' but not necessarily abandoning the concept. They return to the view – sound as it is – that Mercantilism was not a coherent 'theory' or even policy. But what was it, then? The editors suggest that we should broaden the concept and 'rethink' it in a wider sense. The mercantilists were not economists in our sense of the word, they state. Neither were they necessarily speaking about 'economics' or even 'economic policy' in a modern sense. Hence their approach to what we acknowledge as 'economic' problems 'was inseparable from its seventeenth and eighteenth century European ideological context and controversies in ways of thinking about the universe, the natural world and the body politic'.[136] Some of them were modern, yet some of them also looked back to Aristotle, we hear. A cornerstone of Mercantilism was a project of improvement, and 'modernisation' sprung from a wide set of Baconian reformers – including 'naturalists, colonial officials, directors of joint-stock companies, politicians, preachers and even pirates'[137] – very much grouped around the so-called Hartlib circle from the mid-seventeenth century.

However sympathetic, such a liberal definition seems to also have its problems. Heckscher also liked, as we saw, to think about Mercantilism as 'conception of a society', but he rapidly gave up this project (his part 5 in *Mercantilism* on this subject is certainly no more than a torso). Perhaps he thought that such a definition was too wide and could encompass almost anything. Hence, if we 'rethink' Mercantilism in this sense, the danger is obvious that we dilute it to a point where it has no use value at all.

In this book I will instead insist – as mentioned in the previous chapter – that Mercantilism at its core was a series of discussions that tried to grapple a rapid developing world of commerce and the effects it had on polities and communities in Europe during the Early Modern period. It was a world of strife *within* empires and old political formations as well as *between* what later became nation states in order to establish power and recognition. Such a definition does not necessarily presuppose that states were coherent powers. Instead, the building-up of such strong bodies was almost everywhere an important intention of the ideas and policies put forward (by merchants, politicians or project makers); Schmoller talked about Mercantilism as part of a 'programme' to build a nascent national state. My definition does not exclude the possibility that ideas about commerce, national wealth and the relationship between power and plenty, to a high degree, were influenced by discourses which we today would not define as 'economic'. Clearly no definite borders existed between discourses, for example, concerning the natural world and commerce, as we will see further on in the book. But that does not mean that we are unable to spot how a specific discussion on commerce and how to achieve power and wealth by means of commerce emerged from the sixteenth century onwards.

Notes

1 Author unknown, 'Mercantile system'. In: *Palgrave's Dictionary of Political Economy*. London and New York: MacMillan & Sons 1894.
2 C Wilson, *Economic History and the Historians*. London: Weidenfeldt & Nicholson 1969, p. 50f. See also C Wilson, 'Treasure and trade balances: further evidences'. *The Economic History Review*, 2nd ser., vol. IV (1951–2).
3 D C Coleman (ed.), *Revisions in Mercantilism*. London: Methuen 1969, p. 105.
4 J A Schumpeter, *History of Economic Analysis*. London: George Allen & Unwin 1954, p. 337.
5 R Schaeffer, 'The entelechies of mercantilism'. *Scandinavian Economic History Review*, vol. XXIX: 2 (1980).
6 A Lovejoy, *The Great Chain of Being*. Boston, MA: Harvard University Press 1936.

7 Schumpeter, p. 338

8 J Viner, *Studies in the Theory of International Trade*. London: George Allen & Unwin 1937, pp. 1f. This was even more strongly put by M Blaug in his classical *Economic Theory in Retrospect*. Homewood, IL: Richard D Irwin Inc. 1968.

9 R E Eagley (ed.), *Events, Ideology and Economic Theory*. Detroit, MI: Wayne State University Press 1968.

10 W Letwin, *The Origins of Scientific Economics: English Economic Thought 1660–1776*. London: Methuen 1966. For a common view, see R E Ekelund Jr and R F Hébert, *A History of Economic Theory and Method*. New York: McGrawe-Hill 1997, ch. 1.

11 G Schmoller, *The Mercantile System and its Historical Significance*. New York & London: Macmillan & Co 1896, p. 2.

12 Schmoller, p. 50.

13 Schmoller, p. 59.

14 Schmoller, p. 61.

15 Schmoller, pp. 50f.

16 W Roscher, *Geschichte der National-Oekonomik in Deutschland*. Munich, Germany: R Oldenbourg 1874; E von Heyking, *Zur Geschichte der Handelsbilanztheorie*. Berlin, Germany: Puttkammer & Mühlbrecht 1880.

17 See also K Tribe, 'Mercantilism and the economics of state formation'. In: L Magnusson (ed.), *Mercantilist Economics*. Boston, MA: Kluwer 1993; J Viner, 'Power versus plenty'. In: D C Coleman (ed.), *Revisions in Mercantilism*. London: Methuen 1969, p. 62; Judges, pp. 48ff. For a more recent contribution along the same lines, see E Reinert, *How Rich Countries Got Rich … and Why Poor Countries Stay Poor*. London: Constable 2007.

18 G M Koot, 'Historical economics and the revival of mercantilist thought in Britain ca. 1870–1920'. In: L Magnusson (ed.), *Mercantilist Economics*. Boston, MA: Kluwer 1993. See also G M Koot, *English Historical Economics, 1870–1926: The Rise of Economic History and Neomercantilism*. Cambridge, MA: Cambrige University Press 1987.

19 Koot, 1987; see also A Kadish, *Historians, Economists and Economic History*. London: Routledge 1989, ch. 7; L Magnusson, *Tradition of Free Trade*. London: Routledge 2004, pp. 64f.

20 See Koot, 1987; Kadish, 1989.

21 T E C Leslie, *Essays in Political and Moral Philosophy*. London: Longman, Green & Co. 1879.

22 See Kadish, 1989, ch. 6.

23 See Koot, 1987.

24 A V Judges, 'The idea of a mercantile state'. *Transactions of the Royal Historical Society*, 4th ser., vol. XXI (1939). It was also published in D C Coleman (ed.), *Revisions in Mercantilism*. The citation is here from p. 53 of this book.

25 Refers to A Toynbee, *Lectures on the Industrial Revolution in England*. London: Rivingtons 1884.

26 W Cunningham, *Politics and Economics: An Essay on the Nature of the Principles of Political Economy, Together with a Survey of Recent Legislation*. London: Kegan, Paul, Trench & Co. 1885, p. 135.

27 W Cunningham, *The Growth of English Industry and Commerce in Modern Times, Part II: The Mercantile System*. Cambridge, UK: Cambridge University Press 1882, pp. 13ff., 380ff.

28 W Cunningham, 'Adam Smith und die Merkantilisten'. *Zeitschrift für die Gesamte Staatswissenschaften*, vol. XL (1884).

29 See also L Magnusson, 'Eli Heckscher and his mercantilism today'. In: R Findley *et al.* (eds), *Eli Heckscher, International Trade and Economic History*. Cambridge,

MA: MIT Press 2006; L Magnusson, 'Eli Heckscher and Mercantilism: An intro-duction'. In: E Heckscher, *Mercantilism*, vol. I, London: Routledge 1994.

30   The review of Heckscher's *Mercantilism* by T H Marshall appeared in *Economic Journal*, vol. XIV (1935), pp. 718f.

31   H Heaton, 'Heckscher on mercantilism'. *Journal of Political Economy*, vol. XIV: 3 (1937), pp. 386f.

32   M Bloch, 'Le mercantilisme, un état d'ésprit'. *Annales*, vol. VI (1934).

33   Heaton, 1937; Bloch, 1934.

34   J Viner, 'Power versus plenty'. In: D C Coleman (ed.), *Revisions in Mercantilism*, London: Methuan 1969, pp. 64ff.

35   Heaton, 1937.

36   E Heckscher, *Mercantilism*, vol. II, London: Routledge 1994, pp. 184, 266.

37   See, for example, 'Den ekonomiska historiens aspekter'. In: E Heckscher, *Ekonomisk-Historiska Studier*. Stockholm, Sweden: Bonniers 1936.

38   E Heckscher, *Mercantilism*, vol. I, London: Routledge 1994, pp. 28f.

39   See L Magnusson, 'Eli Heckscher and mercantilism'; R Henriksson, 'Eli F Heck-scher: The economic historian as economist'. In: B Sandelin (ed.), *The History of Swedish Economic Thought.* London: Routledge 1991.

40   J Viner, 'Early English theories of trade part 1 and 2'. *The Journal of Political Economy*, vol. XXXVIII (1930). These two articles were reprinted in his book, *Studies in the Theory of International Trade.* London: George Allen & Unwin 1937.

41   Heckscher, I, p. 20.

42   Heckscher, 'Den ekonomiska historiens aspekter'.

43   Heckscher, I, p. 27.

44   Heckscher, I, p. 24.

45   Heckscher, I, p. 20.

46   Heckscher, I, p. 268.

47   Heckscher, II, p. 347.

48   See Heckscher, II, p. 118.

49   Heckscher, II, p. 138.

50   Heckscher, II, p. 261.

51   Heckscher, II, p. 285.

52   E Heckscher, 'Revisions in economic history'. *Economic History Review*, vol. VII: 1, 1936–7. Also in D C Coleman (ed.), *Revisions in Mercantilism*, p. 32.

53   Heaton, 'Heckscher on Mercantilism', p. 379.

54   J Viner, 'Early English theories of trade'. *Journal of Political Economy*, vol. XXXVIII (1930), p. 249.

55   Viner, p. 250.

56   Viner, p. 265.

57   Viner, p. 260. On p. 259 explicitly he attacks Jones for making a distinction between a 'balance of bargain' and 'balance of trade' stage of development.

58   Viner, p. 270.

59   Viner, p. 404.

60   J Viner., 'Review of Heckscher's mercantilism'. In: *Economc History Review*, 1st ser., 1935, pp. 100ff.; J Viner, 'Power versus plenty under mercantilism'. *World Politics*, vol. I (1948). This last article has also been published in D C Coleman (ed.), *Revision in Mercantilism*, 1969.

61   Viner, 'Power versus plenty under mercantilism', 1948, p. 65.

62   Viner, p. 67.

63   Viner, p. 71.

64   See the work by P W Buck, *The Politics of Mercantilism.* New York: Henry Holt & Company 1942, which undoubtedly is written from such a perspective.

65 As we saw, a chapter on Keynes was added to volume II of the posthumous edition by E Söderlund.
66 On the history of economic history, see L Magnusson, 'Introduction'. In: L Magnusson, *Twentienth Century Economic History*, vol. I, London: Routledge 2010.
67 A V Judges, 'The idea of a mercantilist state'. In: Coleman, pp. 35f.
68 D C Coleman, 'Eli Heckscher and the idea of mercantilism'. In: D C Coleman (ed.), *Revisions in Mercantilism*, p. 116. This article first appeared in *Scandinavian Journal of Economic History*, vol. V: 1 (1957). See also C W Cole, 'The heavy hand of Hegel'. In: E M Earle (ed.), *Nationalism and Internationalism*. New York: Columbia University Press 1950.
69 Coleman, 'Eli Heckscher and the idea of mercantilism', p. 117.
70 Coleman, 'Mercantilism revisited', p. 791.
71 Schumpeter, p. 143.
72 T W Hutchison, *Before Adam Smith. The Emergence of Political Economy, 1662–1776.* Oxford: Basil Blackwell 1988, pp. 4f.
73 See L Magnusson, 'Is mercantilism a useful concept still?' In: M Isenmann (hg), *Merkantilismus. Wiederaufnahme einer Debatte.* Stuttgart, Germany: Franz Steiner Verlag 2014.
74 A W Coats, 'Mercantilism, yet again!'. In: P Roggi (ed.), *Gli economisti e la politica economica.* Naples, Italy: Edizione Scientifiche Italiane 1985, p. 35.
75 R C Wiles, 'The development of mercantilist economic thought'. In: T Lowry (ed.), *Pre-Classical Economic Thought.* Boston, MA: Kluwer 1987, p. 148.
76 Coleman, 'Eli Heckscher and the idea of mercantilism', p. 111.
77 Wilson, *Economic History and the Historians*, p. 48. See also G N Clark, *The Seventeenth Century.* Oxford: Oxford University Press 1947, p. 27.
78 Wilson, p. 64.
79 This is a main conclusion drawn in C Wilson, *Profit and Power.* Cambridge, UK: Cambridge University Press 1957.
80 See C Wilson, 'Treasure and trade balances: the mercantilist problem'. *The Economic History Review*, 2nd ser., vol. II (1949).
81 E Heckscher, 'Multilateralism, baltic trade and the mercantilists'. *The Economic History Review*, 2nd ser., vol. III: 2 (1950).
82 C Wilson, 'Treasure and trade balances: further evidence'. *The Economic History Review*, 2nd ser., vol. IV (1951–2), p. 242. After this Heckscher – not in a position to do this himself – was defended by J M Price, 'Multilaterialism and/or bilateralism: the settlement of british trade balances with the north, c 1700'. *Economic History Review*, 2nd ser., vol. XIV (1961). Price here rather convincingly argued that the need for bilateral specie settlements for example with the North can only have been of minor importance during most of the seventeenth century.
83 Wilson, 'Treasure and trade balances: some further evidence', p. 54.
84 J D Gould, 'The trade depression of the early 1620s'. *The Economic History Review*, 2nd. ser., vol. VII (1954), p. 82.
85 J D Gould, 'The trade crisis of the early 1620s and English economic thought'. *The Journal of Economic History*, vol. XV (1955), p. 123.
86 R de Roover, *Gresham on Foreign Exchange.* Cambridge, MA: Harvard University Press 1949.
87 B Supple, 'Currency and commerce in the early seventeenth century'. *The Economic History Review*, 2nd ser., vol. X (1957), p. 244.
88 Supple, p. 251. See also his conclusions in *Commercial Crisis and Change in England 1600–1642*, 1959, pp. 226ff.
89 Supple, *Commercial Crisis*, p. 228.
90 Supple, *Commercial Crisis*, p. 251.

91 R W K Hinton, *The Eastland Trade and the Common Wealth in the Seventeenth Century*. Cambridge, UK: Cambridge University Press 1959.

92 On this see L Magnusson, *State and the Industrial Revolution*. Abingdon, UK: Routledge 2009, pp. 45f.

93 Coats, 'Mercantilism, yet again!', p. 34.

94 J M Keynes, *The General Theory of Employment, Interest and Money*. [1936] London: Macmillan 1973, pp. 333f.

95 Keynes, p. 335.

96 Keynes, p. 335.

97 Keynes, p. 335.

98 Wilson, *Economic History and the Historians*, p. 48. See also Viner, *Studies in the Theory of International Trade*, p. 55.

99 Keynes, p. 341.

100 Keynes, p. 348.

101 C Wilson, *Economic History and the Historians*. London: Weidenfeld & Nicholson 1969, pp. 48f.

102 For example de Roover, *Gresham on Foreign Exchange*, p. 287.

103 Heckcher, *Mercantilism*, vol. II (Söderlund ed.), p. 347.

104 Heckscher, *Mercantilism*, vol. II (Söderlund ed.), pp. 342f.

105 For a positive restatement of Keynes's interpretation, see D Walker, 'Keynes as a historian of economic thought'. *Research in the History of Economic Thought and Methodology*, vol. IV (1986). This author, however, surely goes too far in hailing Keynes for his '... major service for the history of economic thought. Thus Walker for example suggested that Keynes '... correctly interpreted their reasoning regarding the balance of trade and he correctly identified and explained their concern with the adequacy of consumption and investment spending' (p. 28).

106 For example Keynes, pp. 333, 336f.

107 H D Vickers, *Studies in the Theory of Money 1760–1776*. Philadelphia, PA: Chilton Company 1959, p. 21.

108 Vickers, p. 25.

109 S R Sen, *The Economics of Sir James Steuart*. London: G Bell and Sons 1957, p. 98. Another obvious reference is P Chamley, 'Sir James Steuart: inspirateur de la Théorie generale de Lord Keynes?'. *Revue d' économie politique*, vol. LXXII (1962), pp. 303f.

110 W D Gramp, 'Liberal elements in English mercantilism'. *Quarterly Journal of Economics*, vol. LXVI (1952), p. 471.

111 Grampp, p. 472.

112 R E Ekelund and R D Tollison, *Mercantilism as a Rent-Seeking Society: Economic Regulation in Historical Perspective*. College Station, TX: Texas A & M University Press 1981, p. 5.

113 Ekelund and Tollison, pp. 6, 21, 28, 147.

114 Ekelund and Tollison, pp. 19, 21.

115 Ekelund and Tollison, p. 28.

116 Ekelund and Tollison, p. 153.

117 Coats, 'Mercantilism, yet again!', p. 31. For another critical intervention, see S Rashid, 'Mercantilism as a rent-seeking society'. In: L Magnusson (ed.), *Mercantilist Economics*. Boston, MA: Kluwer 1993.

118 Ekelund and Tollison, p. 154.

119 R E Ekelund and R D Tollison, *Politicized Economies: Monarchy, Monopoly and Mercantilism*. College Station, TX: Texas A & M University Press, p. x.

120 Ekelund and Tollison, p. 17.

121 Marx even called Petty 'his old friend'. See *Theories of Surplus Value*, vol. I, p. 354.

122 This analysis is put forward in ch. 24 of Marx, *Capital: Die Sogenannte ursprüngliche Akkumulation*. K Marx, *Das Kapital*, vol. I, Berlin, Germany: Dietz Verlag 1957, pp. 751ff.

123 M Dobb, *Studies in the Development of Capitalism*. London: Routledge & Kegan Paul 1967, pp. 209 ff.

124 For example, L Herlitz, 'The concept of mercantilism'. *Scandinavian Economic History Review*, vol. XII (1964).

125 See C Perrotta, 'Is the mercantilist theory of the favourable balance of trade really erroneous?' *History of Political Economy*, vol. XXIII: 2 (1991); C Perrotta, 'Early spanish mercantilism: the first analysis of underdevelopment'. In: L Magnusson (ed.), *Mercantilist Economics*. Boston, MA: Kluwer 1993. See also his full-length study, C Perrotta, *Produzione e lavoro produttivo. Nel Mercantilismo e nell' illiministo*. Lecce, Italy: Galatina 1988.

126 Perrotta, 'Is the mercantilist theory of the favourable balance ofttrade really erronous?', pp. 318, 322.

127 Perrotta, p. 321.

128 Perrotta, p. 313.

129 E Reinert, *How Rich Countries Got Rich ... and Why Poor Countries Stay Poor.* London: Constable 2007, p. 7.

130 For an extended discussion, see Magnusson, 'Is mercantilism a useful concept still?'.

131 S Reinert, *Translating Empire: Emulation and the Origins of Political Economy.* Cambridge, MA: Harvard University Press 2011.

132 S Pincus, 'Rethinking Mercantilism: Political Economy, the British Empire, and the Atlantic World in the Seventeenth and Eighteenth Centuries'. *William and Mary Quarterly*, 3rd ser., vol. LXIX: 1 (2012).

133 R Brenner, *Merchants and Revolution: Commercial Change, Political Conflict, and London's Overseas Traders, 1550–1653.* Princeton, NJ: Princeton University Press 1993, p. 598.

134 M J Braddick, *State Formation in Early Modern England, c. 1550–1750.* Cambridge, UK: Cambridge University Press 2000; P Stern, 'Companies, monopoly, sovereignty and the east indies'. In: P Stern and C Wennerlind (eds.), *Mercantilism Reimagined: Political Economy in Early Modern Britain and its Empire.* Oxford: Oxford University Press 2013.

135 L Magnusson, *Nation, State and the Industrial Revolution*, ch. 2.

136 Stern, p. 4.

137 Stern, p. 7.

3   Plenty and power

In his *History of Economic Analysis*, Schumpeter preferred using 'consultant administrators' over 'mercantilists' to identify writers between the sixteenth and the eighteenth centuries who published tracts, pamphlets and treatises on trade, commerce, money and finance, as well as how to achieve increased political power through 'economic' means. However, besides consultants and bureaucrats, this group also included merchants, financiers, project makers and occasionally academic persons from the learned world. They were sometimes of high rank, but also of low order, and could be found in most countries in Europe during this period.[1]

The reason for Schumpeter's choice can be easily acknowledged. According to him the consultant administrators were a far cry from being real economic theorists. Instead they were mainly practical men with an agenda to serve the state or some particular interest group. To the extent they invented 'theory' at all, they did so in the form of running businesses, at best as a result of a learning process. Their aim was to solve problems and find the best solutions to issues and problems that their masters paid them for. Moreover, such masters were not only representatives of the state in a modern sense, as we have discussed. They could also be representatives of private interest groups, corporations and other bodies who struggled for recognition, power and plenty during the Early Modern period.

However, we must be more distinct concerning the historical context in which they all were situated. It was a world of nascent state making – a transition from territorial to national state power as Schmoller formulated it[2] – in which princes and kings as well as parliaments and corporations strived to have the upper hand. But it was also an era of deepening international competition in order to capture valuable commerce and trade – within Europe and overseas. In this power struggle many had stakes – governments and companies. Private gain was thus mixed with public endeavours in a complex manner not easily disentangled.

However, since the late medieval period, it was well understood that the economic strength of a country (or a prince) also implied a plentiful political and military position. The acute importance to have control over territory in order to gain income from taxes had been learned early by princely and other rulers. Moreover, it was an important element in the thinking of the Italian republican school during the Renaissance. Niccolo Machiavelli's patriotic discourse, as we know, dealt with not only republican values as a basis of a good governed virtuous state, but also the ability to control territory with the aid of conscripted soldiers.[3] Somewhere in time between Machiavelli and Giovanni Botero at the end of the sixteenth century a common understanding arose that 'good government' also included economic policies of a particular kind. Hence virtuous government no longer was a mere precondition for wealth and plenty. It was also the other way around: good government relied on a prosperous economy.[4]

However, political power (private, corporate and princely) was exceedingly from the sixteenth century interpreted as being based upon international competition over commerce and trade routes. This also implied that a prince who could capture important trade routes would have an upper hand in times of military conflict and political power struggles. Moreover, increasingly a view emerged that it was an 'interest of state' to establish an own industry in order to work up raw materials instead of sending them out to foreign lands. Through this, many more hands could be employed and there were great profits to be harvested by industrious manufacturers and clever merchants. Moreover, through increased taxation and duties of different kinds, the coffers of the state would be better provided for with money. Hence a country which flourished with manufactories could also house great maritime and military prowess.

In England during the seventeenth and early eighteenth centuries the insight that commerce and manufactures were a means for princely power – combined with interest group backing by rent-seekers of a kind discussed by Ekelund and Tollison – was named 'jealousy of Trade' by, for example, Hume.[5] Moreover it was focussed on emulation; in the seventeenth century particularly with regard to the Dutch Republic.[6] All of Europe watched with awesome wonder how this tiny republic, hardly yet recovered from its bloody war of liberation against the Habsburgs, had risen to prosperity and power during the seventeenth century. Most impressive, according to contemporary observers, was undoubtedly that this small tract of land was able to house such a plentiful population. However, as a great population was perceived as a cornerstone of political power and military strength, the achievement of the Dutch republic was not only looked upon with respect. It also became an example which several states sought to learn from and copy.

Then how had this rise to prosperity been achieved? In *England's Treasure of Forraign Trade* Mun expressed his admiration in a vocabulary which had emerged already at this time:

> [F]or it seems a wonder to the world, that such a small Countrey, not fully so big as two of our best Shires, having little natural Wealth, Victuals., Timber, or other necessary ammunitions, either for war or peace, should notwithstanding possess them all in such extraordinary plenty, that besides their own wants (which are very great) they can and do likewise serve and sell to other Princes, Ships, Ordance, Cordage, Corn, Powder, Shot and what not, which by their industrious trading they gather from all the quarters of the world.[7]

Thus it was surely not because of an exceptionally productive agriculture that this nation had grown so much in plenty and want. According to Petty – the economist and political arithmetician:

> it is hard to say, that when these places were first planted, whether an Acre in France was better than the like quantity in Holland and Zeeland; nor is there any reason to suppose, but that therefore upon the first Plantation, the number of Planters was in Proportion to the quantity of Land.[8]

Much of the same was pleaded by the merchant–writer Henry Robinson in 1649:

> That is that Trade whereby our Neighbours, the *Hollanders* and *Zeelanders*, so much increase both their Navigation and their wealth, their Owne *Territories* are so straight and barren, as would neither food nor set the twentieth man a worke, in which respect they are necessitates to be industrious, and get themselves a living, by becoming Purveyors to other Nations.[9]

Instead, it was commonly agreed upon that it was trade and industry which had brought the Dutch republic to its present wealth in men and power. In 1744 Sir Matthew Decker estimated that: 'Trade maintains in Holland seven times more People than the Land deprived of it could subsist'.[10] Some 60 years previously Child seemed clear about the key to the Dutch success: 'The prodigous increase of the Netherlanders in their domestick and foreign Trade, Riches and multitude of Shipping, is the envy of the present, and may be the wonders of all future generations'.[11] Furthermore, according to Barbon: 'The Greatness and Riches of the United provinces, and States of Venice, consider'd with the little Tract of ground that belongs to either of their Territories, sufficiently Demonstrate the great Advantage and profit that Trade brings to a Nation'.[12]

When William Temple published his well-known *Observations Upon the United Provinces of the Netherlands* (1673), the Dutch and the English were at war for the third time in a decade. He dwelled upon his country's enemy in the following fashion:

> Tis evident to those, who have read the most, and travel'd farthest, that no Country can be found either in this present Age, or upon record of any Story, where so vast a Trade has been managed, as in the narrow compass of the Four Maritime Provinces of this Commonwealth: Nay, it is generally esteemed, than there does to all the rest of Europe.... Nor has Holland grown rich by any Native Commodities, but by force of Industry; By improvements and Manufacture of all Foreign growths; By being the general Magazine of Europe, and furnishing all parts with whatever the market wants or invites.[13]

According to Temple, who served as the English Ambassador to the Dutch Republic in 1668–72 and again in 1674–9, the Dutch had emerged as successful tradesmen because of their sound political institutions – their free 'constitutions and orders':

> [A]s Trade cannot Arise without mutual trust among Private Men; so it cannot grow or thrive, to any great degree, without a confidence both of Publick and Private Safety, and consequently a trust in Government, from an opinion of its Strenght, [*sic*] Wisdom and Justice.[14]

Furthermore, the liberal Dutch constitution admitted and encouraged the immigration of non-conformist dissenters. Many able traders and skilled manufacturers were able to as a result establish themselves in the Dutch lands. This in turn provided an important precondition for an open and competitive commercial atmosphere. In the same fashion the anonymous author of *Britannia Languens* (most probably the London lawyer William Petyt) stated in 1680: 'In this the Dutch have a further advantage upon us, since they allow free Ports, free Trade, and all other National Freedoms to Forreigners; whereby their People of all sorts, their Navigation and Stocks of Trade, have increased continually'.[15]

However, Temple also mentioned a second cause behind the Dutch miracle: a great population. He said:

> I conceive the true original and ground of Trade, to be, great multitude of people crowded into small compass of Land, whereby

all things necessary to life becomes dear, and all Men, who have
possessions, are induced to Parsimony; but those who have none,
are forced to industry and labour.[16]

Hence, a great population according to Temple served as a necessary
condition for the rise of trade and industry as it made people more
industrious and parsimonal. As a next step, naturally, more industry
and trade made further growth of population possible. For Holland this
spiral process of population and economic growth had led to that 'no
other known country in the world, of the same extent, holds any proportion with this in numbers of people'.[17] In the 1620s, Mun had pro-
claimed much of the same:

> As plenty and power doe make a nation vicious and improvident,
> so penury and want doe make a people wise and industrious: con-
> cerning the last I might instance divers Commonwealths of Chris-
> tendom, who having little or nothing in their own Territories, do
> notwithstanding purchase great wealth and strength by their indus-
> trious commerce with strangers, amongst which the United Prov-
> inces of the Low Countreys are now of the greatest note and fame:
> For since they have cast off the yoke of the Spanish slavery, how
> wonderfully are they improved in all humane policy?.[18]

Moreover, the success story of the Dutch Republic was fitted into a
historical conjecture which stressed the civilising functions of trade.
According to Child, for example, only trade and increased communication would serve to cultivate 'the unsociable Tempers of many bar-
barous People'. By and large, thus, trade and commerce created the
very preconditions for a commonwealth by providing a mental framework of mutuality and cooperation:

> Thus we see how a great part of the People of this nation, who
> have no Propriety in the Soil thereof, yet cultivated and Improving
> the same to the best advantage and applying the produce thereof,
> to be employed in manufactures and transferring the same from
> one to another in a way of Traffick and Commerce obtain a dis-
> tinct and peculiar interest in the General Wealth of the Nation.[19]

The conclusion to draw from the Dutch case was thus that riches were
the cornerstone of its phenomenal rise as a great power during the
seventeenth century. Hence power and plenty went hand in hand. For
example, when Child in 1693 discussed the effects of the English
Navigation Acts he explicitly stressed 'that Profits and Power ought
jointly to be considered'.[20] Furthermore, Davenant propounded that the

aim of economic inquiry in general 'had always been and shall ever be to show how the wealth and Strength of England is to be secur'd and improv'd'.[21] In another tract he asked:

> Can a nation be safe without strength? And is power to be secured but by riches? And can a country become rich any way, but by the help of well-managed and extended traffique?'.[22]

As ultimately Davenant was inclined to say a straight 'no' to such questions, so too Roberts a half century earlier had stated that 'for that which produceth Riches doth consequently also beget strength and safety'.[23]

Almost a century later the prolific writer Malachy Postlethwayt, most known for his *Universal Dictionary of Trade and Commerce* (1751–5) would still talk about the necessity of having 'commercial schemes of power'. His main principle was that 'the more our internal as well as external traffic shall be promoted, the wealthier and more powerful will be the state'.[24] This was so important that he provided the following bellicose proposal to his government: 'That the great object of a maritime nation should be, to take advantage of any rupture with another trading state, to destroy their shipping and commerce, and to cut off all resources for naval armaments'.[25]

Thus, at the same time as plenty was a precondition for political and military power, the latter created more trade and plenty. Also this could be fitted to a historical account common during this period, which was probably most accurately formulated by Davenant when he said that trade was first entertained 'by little states that were surrounded by neighbours in strength much superior to them'. Due to a lack of national power, small countries had often been attacked by greater nations, and as an effect their commerce had withered away: 'one battle swept away what had been gathered by the industry of many ages'.[26] Thus trade necessitated power – but at the same time power was a function of plenty and trade.

Fishing in others' waters

Without doubt one often-explicated story at the time why the Dutch went from rags to riches was because of its 'free' and liberal institutions. The theme that commerce and industry best flourished in republics was often repeated in various versions during the seventeenth and eighteenth centuries. For example, in a tract which was printed in at least four editions after 1729, Joshua Gee over many pages discussed the issue of best government for stimulating commerce and trade. He admits that they best seem to thrive in republics, but also under the rule of kings especially where 'penetrating wise Princes came to see into the fruitful Womb of Trade'.[27] Gee presents a number of rulers from Salomon and Alexander the Great to 'Lewis' XIV of France and indeed also Czar Peter of Muscovy. His general message is that a prince who 'make[s] Search after able Men to regulate and improve their Trade will carry it away from those that disregard or neglect it'.[28] Others were less convinced that monarchs of this kind would be good for a flourishing trade in the long run. Hence the author of *Britannia Languens* (Petyt?) in 1680 points out that neither the Dutch Republic nor absolutist France could compete with a constitutional kingdom as England. In an absolute monarchy, he says, 'the Fate of the whole depends upon the Prudence of the Monarch'. And as we know that kings, as all mortals, are 'transported by Passions and otherwise liable to Mistakes' trade might suffer. In a republic, however, there is always the danger of anarchy. Hence a 'constitutional Monarchy with a balance between king and parliament provide[s] the best ground for commercial success'. In his reasoning there are clear links to Machiavelli. He, for example, argues that in a constitutional monarchy people fight in wars for patriotic reasons instead of pay.[29]

Another story of common usage was that the Dutch were more parsimonious, worked harder and used aggressive methods in order to snatch the trade of others. In the 1620s, for example, Mun emphasised how the Dutch had been able to out-compete the English herring fishermen and ousted them from the North Sea. It was on this basis, according to him, that the Dutch monopoly of the trade between the Baltic and the North Sea had developed during the early seventeenth century. 'The Fishing in his Majesties seas of England, Scotland and Ireland is our natural wealth', he says. But instead the Dutch

> draw yearly a very great profit to themselves by serving many places in Christendom with our Fish, for which they return and supply their wants both of forraign Wares and Mony, besides the multitude Mariners and Shipping which they hereby are manintain'd.[30]

The same has happened to 'Our Fishing plantation likewise in the New England, Virgina, Groenland, the Summer islands and New Found-Land'. In the same way the Dutch competed with England, Portugal and Spain over trade routes and cargo in the South Sea and other places. Almost everywhere, Holland gained an upper hand and was able to out-compete the others, Mun argued. This had to be stopped – even if necessary by aggressive methods. The importance of the fishing trade for England was also emphasised by other writers at the time. Hence Robinson in 1641 obviously regarded it as equally important as the trade with East India when he wrote:

That unlesse the fishing imployment and East India traffique be followed and enlarged, other Nations will gaine upon us, our trade infallibly decline daily, and the whole State with the same speede and paces post on to poverty and utter ruine.[31]

Several later commentators – including Heckscher – have gazed over the extent to which the seventeenth century viewed international trade as a zero-sum game.[32] More than a mere reflection of a static view of trade, this attitude was an outcome of the aggressive atmosphere of the late seventeenth century. Thus what one country might gain in profitable trade routes, others had to lose. Even Davenant and Barbon, highly sceptical of the favourable balance of trade slogan, were obsessed by such a view of the world. Many more examples can be given. Thus, for example, Child in the 1690s discussed at length the 'trades lost' especially to the Dutch during the seventeenth century. His list of such lost English trades included the Russian trade, the Greenland trade, the salt trade from St Vuals in Portugal, the white herring trade, the trade for Spanish wools from Bilbao, some parts of the East India trade, the trade for China and Japan and 'the trades of Scotland and Ireland', which 'the Dutch have begreaved us of'.[33]

Robinson, merchant and administrator, was even more precise on this point. He wrote in 1649: 'That the greatest Trade of one Countrey hath a capacity of undermining, and eating out the lesser Trade of any other Countreys'. This was of course dire as 'That what Nation soever can attaine to and continue the greatest Trade, and number of shipping will get and keepe the Soveraignty of the Seas, and consequently, the greatest Dominion of the World'.[34] And with regard to Britain, he believes,

> Tis well knowne, that even till within these Ten Yeares our Trade was famous amongst all knowne Nations and at the same time, our Ships at Sea, as dreadful to whomever became our Enemies but as neither our Trade, nor consequently our shipping were improved to be quarter of what they might have been, even so some other Nation had then advantage, and did get ground upon us, in such manners that in but some yeares longer they continues proportionably to gaine upon in Trade, Riches, Marriners and Shipping.[35]

That Robinson referred particularly to the Dutch ('the Hollanders and Zealanders') can be of no doubt.

Such often-told tales – truthful or not – in which international commerce was looked upon more or less as a zero-sum game formed the basis of discourses, which Hume one century later called 'jealousy of trade'.[36] However, for the English, the fear of being snatched from its former prosperous commerce by the Dutch slowly shifted over to another perceived threat: to be outcompeted in its trade with textile and other wares by France. This became especially pertinent in the 1670s. In a very influential tract from 1673, Samuel Fortrey, a bailiff in the Great Level of the Fens and a member of the King's privy council, emphasised how much England had lost by its trading with France. It was especially the import of luxury goods and wine that had turned the balance of trade against England, he wrote. But this 'overbalance' (in favour of France) had become even more threatening because of the protectionist Colbert system and its heavy duties on manufactured goods (textiles mainly) from abroad. So what could England do? The answer that the French borders must be opened and that this could only be achieved by a great fleet and success in war lay easy at hand.

However, yet another answer to this query was slowly gaining ground: that increased competition could be met by lower prices on export.[37] Against the protectionist duties of the French this might not be very effective at first. However, in other parts of the world and in the long term it would surely increase exportation, it was argued. In principal export prices could be lowered by two methods. The first was to keep wages as low as possible. Such an argument was commonplace among many writers especially from the end of the seventeenth century. However, as noted elsewhere, we should not mistakenly automatically believe that this meant poor workers ought to be starved. For example, the writer Postlethwayt argued in line with the substance theory of wages formulated in the nineteenth century that low prices of provision was the key to low wages. Therefore he dedicated a lot of space, for example in his collection of papers named *Britain's Commercial Interest* (1757), to argue for ways and measures to improve agriculture in his native country – but also to use Ireland, Scotland and the so-called plantations abroad for deliverance of cheap foodstuffs. Hence to render 'the price of the necessaries of life no more than half, or even one third what it is at present ... (t)his will inevitably reduce the general price of labour, that being regulated by the necessaries of life'.[38] Moreover, this would, according to Postlethwayt, lead to it being possible to 'fabricate our staple, and other new invented manufactures at lower rates' and eventually 'abundantly extend our exportation'.[39]

Hence, as argued by Hont, discussions between economic pamphleteers and writers in England, such as Davenant, John Pollexfen and John Martyn, from the 1690s onwards must be seen as different reactions to the strategic issue how increased price competition on the world market ought to be tackled by Britain. (Hont explicitly draws similarities to the present discussion on the effects of so-called offshoring.[40]) Could a wealthy country with high wages really compete with cheap imports from low-wage countries? As a Tory free trader (the phrase was coined by the economic historian Ashley one hundred years ago[41]), Davenant looked upon the future of Britain as the *entre-pote* of cheap calicoes and other wares from India and other formal or informal British colonies and plantations. Much money would then be earned by working up such fabrics for re-exporting. Added to this, much profit could be accrued through shipping and Britain serving as a financial intermediate in international trade. Moreover, according to Davenant, the keeping up of an economic empire was a necessary pre-condition for English wealth and power. Hence, without saying no to formal colonies (plantations), he was close to putting forward a pro-gramme of free trade imperialism of a kind which became popular 150 years later.[42] However, another reaction (also easy to relate to con-temporary debates) was to say that Britain would have more to gain to protect itself from the inflow of cheap wares and by what has later been recognised as import substituting activities, namely, to develop an own domestic industry which would employ a multitude of poor labourers. We will return to this strategy when we in the next chapter discuss different interpretations of the favourable balance of trade 'theory'.

Yet another response during the eighteenth century was to develop the argument that the inflow of cheap products was not a problem as long as the rich country with higher wages increased its productivity in order to sell wares more cheaply than others. Most probably the first to explicate (in 1613) more thoroughly that trade and industry – in contrast to agriculture – could expand by means of increased produc-tivity and increasing returns to scale was an Italian from the south of the peninsula, the Calabrese Antonio Serra (we will return to him soon).[43] The importance of higher productivity by introducing new labour-saving technology was suggested by Martyn in 1701[44] and later on developed by Josiah Tucker, Hume and Smith. By any means this was the response that would win the day in the long run.[45] Through Ricardo, Robert Torrens and others, this suggestion was developed to become part and parcel of the modern theory of comparative advantage.

* * *

We have so far briefly dealt with some reactions from the British Isles to this world order of commercial rivalry and competition, which emerged during the sixteenth and seventeenth century. However, also elsewhere in Europe rulers as well as other powers felt the necessity to react – and they did so in various ways. The key for understanding what different consultant administrators in Early Modern Europe said and wrote (to speak once again of Schumpeter) can only be understood in their particular contexts and must be related to their position in the international competitive struggle for power and influence.

The Kingdom of Naples

What was for Temple and others in England an envy of the Dutch was in Naples the envy of the great trading cities of Venice and Genoa. While Venice and Genoa together with Florence emerged as rich and prosperous, the kingdom of Naples in southern Italy seemed to have fallen behind during the sixteenth century. Ruled by Spanish princes, Naples experienced a social and economic crisis at the end of the sixteenth century: death and famine spread horror in the countryside, and trade was stalled. The kingdom of Naples, which included most of southern Italy as well as Sicily, was totally dominated by agriculture, and its export was in the form of grain and other foodstuffs. Most other things were imported and by the end of the sixteenth century the public debt was staggeringly high.[46] Something of a 're-feudalisation' hit the peasantry, and share-cropping practices made them *de facto* serfs to their lords through life-long debt arrangements.[47]

Pondering from his jail in the Vicaria prison in Naples over the issue why Naples was so poor and Venice so rich, Serra, a Calbrese born in the small city of Cosenza, wrote down his analysis in the form of a small tract *Breve Trattato delle cause che possono far abbondare Li Rengni d'oro & argento*, which was published in 1613. We know little of him or why he was sent to prison. It has been speculated that he wrote the tract – it was dedicated to his ruler the 'most illustrious and excellence Lord Don Pietro Fernandez de Castro' (Spanish viceroy and seventh count of Lemos 1610–16) – in order to be released, but whether his tract pleased his lordship or instead made matters even worse we simply do not know.[48]

More than two centuries later List hailed Serra's 'Breve' as the very 'first special work on Political Economy' and many others have agreed.[49] Moreover, a tradition has been invented which points at Serra as the anticipator of List's national system of political economy – challenging the 'cosmopolitan' political economy of Smith and his followers – as well as the forerunner of modern import substitution theory.[50] This is not necessarily unfounded but at the same time it must be emphasised that, in order to fully understand Serra, we must place him in his own intellectual *milieu*. This to a large extent was influenced by a discourse which – as we saw – expanded Machiavelli's political analysis of good government and how to achieve grandness (*grandezza*) to also include economic means and policies.

With this in mind a reference point to Serra's analysis of the plights of Naples is Giovanni Botero (1544–1617). He was a Piedemontese priest, diplomat and writer, who lived most of his life in Milan when he was not at diplomatic duties abroad. Botero wrote immensely and was highly critical of Machiavelli's 'unchristian' views especially explicated in *The Prince*. Yet he was part and parcel of the post-Machiavellian turn in Italy from politics to economics, as we discussed earlier, in which a great number of writers could be included. Hence Francesco Guicciardini in his *History of Italy* (1537–40) as well as the Neapolitan duke Carafa, who according to Schumpeter already in the mid-sixteenth century argued for more trade and manufactures to make the state rich.[51]

Also Botero in his most famous work *Della ragion di stato* (1589) presents recommendations of good government by economic means, which were not at all unknown at the time in the Italian discussion: that in order to prosper in wealth and power a state must have a great population, ample resources, a well-managed agriculture, many crafts and manufactures and so on.[52] With regard to foreign trade, Botero pointed out that the ruler 'must ensure that money does not leave his country unless this is quite essential'.[53] And further in a fashion that comes close to what Mun would repeat more than half a century later, he writes:

> In order to know exactly how much he may put aside without harming his people a ruler must know in detail how much money leaves his state in payment for the merchandize which enters it, and how much is made or taken in payment for the goods which leave it, and to contrive that the sum laid aside is never greater than the receipts over payments. When less is received than paid, the prince should make no attempts to save, for it is impossible, and to try to do so is to invite ruin.[54]

In order to cover the importation of necessities and luxuries as well as the import of money (silver) Naples must develop a 'favourable balance of trade' in goods, Serra emphasised. Furthermore it should be the task of the prince to fulfil this crucial task, for example, by creating manufactures. Without doubt Serra's discussion on the necessity of a favourable balance of trade became a much discussed topic later on, not least in England in the seventeenth century.[55] It is also important to note that Serra's treatise is perhaps even more interesting from another point of view. It was written as a polemic against Marc Antonio de Santis, who in *Discorso intorno alli effetti che fa il cambio in regno* (1605) explained the shortage of money in the kingdom of Naples as a consequence of unfavourable exchange rates. Now in his treatise Serra instead pointed out – which really echoed the discussion some years later in England between Malynes, Mun and Misselden – that the shortage of coin ought rather to be explained by an unfavourable balance of trade. As Mun later on would insist upon, the low exchange rate was only a secondary consequence caused by 'real' factors.[56]

In Naples economic Machiavellianism did not end with Serra, of course. Southern Italy remained far behind in terms of manufacture and trade, and the whole peninsula suffered when the orbit of commerce and economic activity gradually moved from the Mediterranean to the Atlantic Sea during the seventeenth century. At some point during the 1750s the mathematician and custodian of the Medici estates in Naples Bartolomeo Intieri came across a rare copy of Serra's tract from 1613. Intieri was a leading intellectual and in a seminal contribution the Italian historian of ideas, Franco Venturi, named him 'the source of the Neapolitan Enlightenment'.[57] Belonging to this group was one Antonio Genovesi (1712–69), who in 1754 became the first professor in economics and commerce in Naples and Italy – at a time when there were only three chairs in Prussia (Halle, Rinteln, Frankfurt an der Oder) and two in Sweden (Uppsala, Turku) that had anything to do with teaching economics. Genovesi taught and published immensely on economic issues, particularly commerce and the role of good government for economic prosperity. One of his first works, *Storia del commercio della Gran Brettagna scritta da comment John Cary* (1757–8), in three volumes constituted in fact a history of commerce of England which emphasised the role of protection for the establishment of domestic industry and manufactures. This was a programme which he wholeheartedly exhorted also with regard to his own country.[58] As Sophus Reinert has shown, this text had its origin in one of the Bristol merchant John Cary's publications, *Essay on the State of England in Relation to its Trade, and its Taxes, for Carrying out the Present War against France*, first published in 1695. Then the text went for a grand tour of Europe, being translated and published in French by Georges-Marie Butel-Dumont in 1755, then by Genovese and finally turning up in Cameralist clothings translated into German by Christian August Wichman in 1788. As Reinert vividly points out, for every translation the book became ever more bulky (Cary's original of less than 200 pages grew to 1000 pages in the hands of Butel-Dumont, and with Genovesi to 1500 pages). It also became more detailed concerning country-specific matters and – not surprisingly – less close to the original.[59]

Somebody who also held Serra in high esteem was Ferdinand Galiani (1728–87). Also a Napoletanian, Galiani was appointed secretary to the Neapolitan embassy at Paris, a posting which he held for ten years before returning to Naples to become a councilor of the tribunal of commerce, and in 1777 administrator of the royal domains. In many respects Galiani was a great innovator. Already at the age of twenty-two he had published a treatise *Trattato della Moneta* (1751) in which he outlined a theory of value based on utility and scarcity, which has been said was not surpassed in analytical rigour until Stanley Jevons.[60] Stationed in Paris it is perhaps not peculiar that Galiani was well versed in the French economic discussion within the group of the *economistes* and the Physiocrats. But he also read the works of British philosophers and economists. At the age of fifteen he had already translated John Locke's *Some Considerations of the Consequences of the Lowering of Interest and Raising the Value of Money* – of which he was highly critical. However it was in French that he published his most well-known economic work, *Dialogues sur le commerce des blés* (1769), in which he intervened in the heated French controversy concerning the grain trade, which broke out in 1764 after the promulgation of the new liberalisation measures. Here he took a middling position between freedom of trade and regulation claiming that economic policies had to take into account the peculiar institutional and historical conditions of different nations in order to work properly.[61] However, by most later interpreters Galiani is regarded to be a mercantilist. But put more precisely, perhaps, he was influenced by the general economic discussion at the time particularly in Paris – being a militant anti-Physiocrat.[62] Even more so his general thinking on economic policy had its roots in a discourse which emanated in sixteenth-century Naples and from Serra's *Breve Trattato.*

Spain

Although Naples had a habit of importing rulers from Spain, the latter from 1500 onwards was an empire which did not share the problem that Serra from his solitude prison had tried to solve: how a country without mines of silver or gold of their own could become prosperous. Spain was instead amply provided for with bullion shipped over from the Americas in cargos protected by a potent naval fleet. However, already in the late sixteenth century it was well known that a stream of bullion had not only brought riches to Spain, but also implied important problems that were carried with it.[63] According to conventional doctrinal history, Martin de Azpilcueta in 1556 formulated the famous so-called quantity theory of money. However, as Arthur Monroe pointed out long ago, in a general sense this theory was well known even earlier than that. Thus it was hinted at by Copernicus and certainly also prominent scholars from the Salamancan school, such as Francisco de Vitoria, Domingo de Soto and Tomas de Mercado (a group to which also Azpilcueta belonged).[64]

What they expected was that a great inflow of silver and gold should lead to money falling and goods rising in value. Hence the so-called price revolution was a well-known phenomenon among contemporary Europeans. When the price level increased in Spain, this meant domestic wares became dearer and imports cheaper. As a consequence domestic industries as well as the agriculture suffered from cheap foreign competition.[65] In England in 1720 for example Erasmus Philips in a tract criticising the increase of public debt described Spain as a case of 'money without trade'. As such it 'like stagnated water' was of 'little use to Proprietor'. Moreover,

> Spain is a living Instance of this Truth, the Mines of Peru and Mexico made that People think themselves above Industry, an Inundation of Gold and Silver swept away all useful Arts, and a total Neglect of Labour and Commerce has made them as it were the Receivers only for the rest of the World.[66]

The controller of public finance for the Habsburg throne in the 1550s, Luis Ortiz, struggled hard to find remedies against the puzzle that a great empire overflowing with bullion could fall into poverty.[67] He came up with a classical remedy: to hinder Spaniards to export their money and buy foreign goods. Perhaps this did not exclusively render him, as Perrotta believed, the title 'the first European mercantilist'.[68] Ordnances prohibiting such exports and imports were well known already in the Late Middle Ages, as we know. However, it is without doubt clear that Ortiz – just as Serra in Naples – strongly promoted protectionist measures in order to achieve industrial development. Spain should not buy manufactured goods from abroad, he stressed. Nor should it ship out its raw materials, but instead see to it that they were worked up in domestic manufactories. As long as this did not occur, Ortiz emphasised, Spain would remain 'underdeveloped'.[69]

After Ortiz several other Spanish writers took the same position, including Francisco Martinez de Mata, Sancho de Moncada and Benardo de Ulloa who in the mid-eighteenth century strongly recommended domestic production in his work *Restablecimento de las fábricas y commercio espanol* (1740) – a highly telling title in this context.[70] Best known outside Spain is perhaps Gerónimo de Uztáritz born in Sant Sebastian in the kingdom of Navarra in 1670 (d. 1732). As commercial advice to King Filip V he was well ordered especially on the practical side of trade and commerce.[71] From his long stay in Brussels in the 1690s – where he also married – he also learned about the mores of northern Europe, especially the successful trade of Dutch cities and the manufactures of Brabant and other areas. He was most probably also familiar with the contemporary French and English literature on issues such as trade and manufactures.[72] Despite its title, his most important work, *Theoretica y practica de commercio y de Marina* (1724), did not deal exclusively with trade. Rather, it contained a complete programmeme on how to make Spain more economically prosperous. He discussed how a beneficial tax system should be designed, how the population could increase and more manufactories be inaugurated. For this latter purpose he promoted – in a well-known manner – that raw materials should be worked up by domestic industry instead of being exported. As harmful *commercio danoso* he condemned the practice to export money in order to import foreign manufactures. However, foreign trade which carried out manufactured goods in order to be traded for raw materials he honoured as a *commercio util*.

Hence the Spanish 'consultant administrators' (it is most probably the Spanish case which explains why Schumpeter used this label) came to the same conclusions as the Napoletanians: in order to grow rich a state had to establish its own manufactories, avoid the import of manufactured goods and stop the export of unwrought wares and raw materials. For Naples the main problem seemed to be an underdeveloped agriculture with feudal-like institutions. Spain shared to some extent the same problem: the Spanish countryside was overpopulated with poverty-stricken peasants. But to this was also added the dilemma of empire. Through conquest Spain had established an order which implied a great inflow of bullion from the American colonies. However, commerce had not made Spain rich and more powerful. The inflow of gold and silver from the colonies ('the plantations', as they were called in England) had rather led to rising prices and wages, which made Spain less competitive in relation to northern Europe. Everywhere in contemporary literature – both in Spain and elsewhere – it was a common complaint that the Spaniards had become lazy, neglecting their farms, estates, manufactories and crafts. But obviously, like King Midas, they could not live on silver and gold alone. This insight – as we will see later – was picked up by most writers on the relationship between commerce and prosperity during the coming centuries.

France

Also for France the epithet 'consultant administrators' can be used as a description of some of the mercantilist writers during the seventeenth century. After half a century of religious and political turbulence the country once again found civil peace at the turn of the seventeenth century under the auspices of Henry IV. As a consequence of the long period of bitter internal warfare, agriculture, trade and manufactures were all in sorry conditions. However, from this date, a period of restoration emerged which would bring increased economical and political strength to France during the regime of Lous XIV's minister of finance, Jean Baptiste Colbert (1619–83). From the early seventeenth century, this work of restoration was largely carried out by a *dirigiste* state. Especially after Colbert's rise to power in 1661 this policy became more expansionist. It especially focussed on the beneficial role of colonies and the increased control over profitable trade routes. However, especially during the first half of the seventeenth century, this policy can clearly be characterised as a form of 'policy of provision' – to use Heckscher's vocabulary.[73] It aimed to make France more self-sufficient with both ordinary consumer and luxury wares (especially silk). It submitted the principle that nothing should be bought from foreigners that might be achieved or manufactured in France. Hence it saw no advantage in foreign trade for its own sake. Rather, the main task of foreign trade would be to bring in silver and gold. Most of the other wares should be obtained within France itself.[74]

In principle, such recommendations were not especially new at this time or restricted to France. As in England, governments in France at least back to the late fifteenth century had emphasised that bullion should not be allowed to leave the country and instead stressed the principle of self-sufficiency. Moreover, they had banned the export of raw materials as well as the import of luxury items. Additionally, they strived to encourage shipping among other things.[75] Therefore, upon such a footing, a 'policy of provision' was more forcefully applied than ever before in France during the seventeenth century.

This contrasted radically with current affairs in England. Certainly, although the ban of bullion export gradually was lifted in England in the mid-seventeenth century, protection was nevertheless retained to a large extent (see further p. 174). In the form of an aggressive Navigation Act (1651 etc.) directed against the Dutch it may even be said that it was more forcefully applied than ever before. In France during the last decades of the seventeenth century there was some intense agitation for a policy that encouraged own manufactures and discouraged import of foreign manufactured wares. However, at the core, there were important dissimilarities between French and English policies. In England a main emphasis of trade policy was to encourage more export in order to increase employment. Hence the leading idea was that only a growing international market could provide for England's wealth. In France the tone was strikingly different – at least up until Colbert. At the beginning of the century – as we will see – writers like Antoine de Montchrétien would rather emphasise that France was so rich in natural and other resources that she could be self-sufficient:

'Vos Maistez possedent un grand Estat, agreable en assiete, abondant en richesses, fleurissant en peuples, puissant en bonnes et fortes villes, invincible en armes, triomphant en gloire. Son territoire est capable pour le nombre infini de ses habitants'.[76]

Hence in France the economic discussion during most of the seventeenth century was encapsulated within a spirit of economic nationalism and self-sufficiency. We will in what follows discuss the development of such a discourse with the help of three different authors and then return to a more general discussion on France.

The first of these writers is Jean Bodin (1520–96), although he belongs to an earlier period. The famous political thinker Bodin is seldom thought of as a mercantilist. Nevertheless, he is highly interesting from the point of view of thinking and writing on economic issues which emerged in France from around 1600. In this sense, this great civic humanist writer was clearly a forerunner to an *economie politique* that found its mature expression with de Montchrétien. However, he also differed quite a lot from him, as we will see.[77]

Bodin is best known by economists for presenting an early version of the quantity theory of money in his reply to the *seigneur* M de Malestroict – but as we have argued this principle was known among Spanish writers even earlier.[78] In a short pamphlet dedicated to King Charles IX, Malestroict had explicated the view that the current inflation in France was only apparently caused by a rise of prices. Instead, the real cause behind the inflation was the frequent debasement of coin undertaken by kings. Bodin, however, insisted that a real process of price rising was taking place. It was mainly caused by an increased inflow of precious metals to Europa and France from America. In this context he presented the famous maxim that stated: 'The principal reason which raises the price of every thing, wherever one may be, is the abundance of that which governs the appraisal and price of things'.[79]

Like authors from other nationalities, he stressed that as a nation without own mines France must trade in order to acquire gold and silver. However, as he pointed out, trade with foreigners should not be restricted to only that. Thus in contrast to a later generation of French economic writers Bodin was not promoting self-sufficiency as a general goal. Bodin believed that trade with foreigners instituted civilisation. A friendly intercourse with other nations through trade was part of God's plan:

Et quand bien nous pourions passer de telles marchandises, ce qui nést possible du tout: mais grand ainsi sercit que nous en aurions à revendre, encores deverions nous tojours trafiquer, vendre, achepter, échanger, prester, voire plutost donner une partie de nos biens aux estrangers, et mesmes à noz voisins quand ce ne sercit que pour communiquer et entretenir une bonne amitee entre eux et nous.[80]

Thus, Bodin on the whole felt that it was far better to make friends with foreigners than to wage war against them.[81]

However, the issue is more complex than that. On the issue of self-sufficiency he was in fact quite ambivalent. Thus when he dealt with practical economic problems of the state in his political work *Les Six livres de la republique* (1589), he especially stressed the need for France to develop its own manufactures. More domestic production meant more employment for French workers, he argued. In this context he did not only recommend duties on imported manufactures; also exports should be taxed, he suggested. His argumentation was of the typical 'policy of provision' vein: namely that a great export of salt, grain and wine would make these wares scarce and expensive in the native country. Some exportation of such commodities was certainly necessary in order to bring in gold and silver. However, he was not afraid that export duties would make such wares more difficult to sell to foreigners. Even if the price of French salt was tripled this was no problem, he argued: 'l'estranger ne laisse pas d'achepter au triple pour en avoir, quoy qu'il couste'.[82] Hence, we can safely draw the conclusion that he did not believe in the price elasticity principle. Instead, what he in fact argued for was that the good French wares should be sold at almost any price.[83]

The second author is Barthélemy Laffemas (1545–1611), a true consultant administrator in Schumpeter's sense of the word. His rise to political might have began when he was appointed tailor and *valet de chambre* to Henry IV. Standing at the height of power he was appointed *Controlleur Général du Commerce* in 1602, a position that in practice put him in charge of the already quite state-controlled French manufacturing sector. His chief ambition was to establish more manufactures and, not the least due to a certain ruthlessness, he seemed to have been successful in his task. However, when Henry IV died in 1610 the political career was over for our *valet de chambre.* The year thereafter he died quite unnoticed.[84]

Besides being a shrewd politician, Laffemas was a vivid writer on economic subjects. In a number of pamphlets, most of them published in 1600–4, he presented a whole programme for how the French economy should be made to grow and prosper. Much of his texts were produced when Laffemas served as the president of the *Conseil du Commerce* 1602–4. Thus in his many tracts he presented schemes and suggestions as well as defended them against angry opponents. The commission seemed to have worked very ambitiously. According to Cole, who closely studied its minutes, 'the commissioners held more than a hundred and fifty meetings, delved into every sort of commercial and industrial question, interviewed inventors, workmen, entrepreneurs, made recommendations to the king, set large undertakings going and approved or disapproved a considerable number of ventures'.[85]

Most of of Laffemas' commission efforts were directed to the issue of how to establish a flourishing silk manufacture in the country. However, it also discussed how horses could be better bred, how the linen manufacture should be improved, a manufacture of fustians established and so on.[86] It is often stated that Laffemas was influenced in his thinking by Henry IV's finance minister, Maximilien de Béthune, duc de Sully (1560–1641). But in contrast to Laffemas, Sully's main interest had been in agricultural improvement. However, he was close to him in promoting self-sufficiency. Jérome-Adolphe Blanqui's prompt statement about Sully highlights this very clearly: 'All consumption of foreign products seemed to him a larceny committed against France'.[87]

However, especially in a number of tracts published in the year 1600, he presented a general framework into which his practical suggestions can be fitted.[88] What this framework more exactly amounted to is clearly indicated already if we look at the full title of an even earlier pamphlet:

'Les trésors et richesses pour mettre l'estat en splendeur et monster au vray la ruine des francois par le trafic et négoce des estranger: et empescher facilement les petits prozes en toute vacation; voir comme la justice des consuls doit etre supprimée, et autres belles raisons. Le tout pour le bien de ce royaume' (1598).

Hence, Laffemas was full of moan and groan from the then wretched situation of trade, industry and agriculture in France. It was especially the freedom for foreign merchants to come and go as they pleased which had lead to this sorry state, he pointed out. However, instead of contributing to national wealth and power, also the domestic merchants by partaking in a commerce which impoverished France played an important negative role. Thus, France sold her raw materials and let gold and silver flow out of the country in order to buy foreign luxury items. Thus, by ruining itself France contributed to the prosperity of Italy, Flanders, the German states and England, he emphasised.[89]

In order to replace this wretched order Laffemas sought to establish a nationalist economic programmeme. Hence, all forces should be enjoined to establish for example silk manufactures so that only a minimum of such wares would be imported from abroad. The principal wares worth taking from foreign parts were gold and silver and for this purpose France must export manufactured goods, he pointed out.

Hence, as we can see, Laffemas is preaching what might seem as a common gospel of this period. Poverty and want has been caused by an outflow of money from the country, he said. Therefore, his main concern is to keep as much bullion as possible within France. For gold and silver are the 'nerves' of a kingdom: 'the true matter and substance which maintains the state against … enemies'.[90] At the same time, it is important to note that he nowhere even came close to formulate a favourable balance of trade thesis. Moreover, while he admitted that foreign trade was of importance for a state – but then mainly for bringing in gold and silver – his main ambition seems to have been to promote self-sufficiency. Quite definitively, however, Laffemas must rather be regarded as an exponent of a moderate 'policy of provision' view than as a mercantilist.

Then at last we come to someone we have already mentioned a couple of times, Antoine de Montchrétien (1575?–1621). This poet, adventurer, rebel and hardware manufacturer (certainly no consultant administrator) is best known for the only book he published which dealt with economic matters. It was called *Traicté de l'OEconomie Politique* (1615) and was the first title in which the phrase 'political economy' is mentioned.[91] However, it has been commonplace among later scholars to disregard this book and its author as of 'little merit' or even as a 'piece of overrated trash' (Ashley).[92] We have already argued that this, at least from a historical perspective, is a completely mistaken proposition. Thus in fact de Montchrétien's *oeconomie politique* profoundly influenced the economic debate in France for a century and more.[93] Thus Ashley seems to have been most appalled by de Montchrétien's borrowings and plagiarisms from authors such as Bodin and Laffemas. However, this is to a large extent an anachronism, as such borrowings were extremely common during this period. Literary texts were for common usage and to cite without mentioning the original source was not looked upon as an act of injustice at this point in time.

This is not to say that there, for modern readers, might not be much to feel uneasy about in de Montchrétien's text. For in his *Traicté* the author presents himself as an extreme French patriot full of aggressive avenge for anything foreign. It is not only that foreign merchants were compared with 'sang-sues qui l'attachent à ce grand corps' of France.[94] These were said to overcrowd every public place in France with their *visages innconnus* and their *d'acents barbares*.[95] In fact, there was nothing that he did not accuse foreigners of. For one thing, they were corrupt,[96] and they cheated away precious monies by dishonest tricks. Hence, if France did not expel them in great numbers, they would rob her clothes and leave her in shambles.

It is true, of course, that de Montchrétien's text is not 'a methodical disquisition on economic theories after the fashion of nineteenth century writers, but rather a rambling, discursive treatment of various phases of business, commerce and government'.[97] However, what else could be expected for this period? More interestingly the significance of de Montchrétien's work lies in that it, to a much greater extent than Laffemas, emphasised that France could and must reach self-sufficency. France had ample agricultural and other natural resources. Her population was large and industrious. The author's patriotic zeal seemed to have no limits:

> Si c'est une extreme subject de contentement à vos peuples de se voir nés et eslevés en la France, c'est à dire au plus beau, plus libre, et plus heureaux climat du Monde, vostre gloire ne doit estre moindre d'y temir un Empire que l'on peut avec raison appeller l'incomparable. Car la france seute se peut passer de toute se qu'elle a de termed voisines, et toutes les termes voisines nullement d'elle.[98]

Like Laffemas, de Montchrétien especially stressed the importance of establishing manufactures through which France could support herself. In this context he especially highlighted the need to support the metal craft industry – perhaps not so surprising as de Montchrétien at the time when he wrote *Traicté* was in the hardware business at Ousonne sur Loire. Moreover, in order to make the manufacturing industry prosper, all foreign import must be banned. This was important for both the textile and the metal industry, he pointed out. However, de Montchrétien wanted to go even further. As we saw, his aim was to ban or at least put up severe restrictions for foreign merchants to live, work and trade in France. Drawing heavily upon Bodin, he strongly advocated duties on both export and imports.[99] French raw materials such as wheat, wine, salt, wool and so on, should in fact be hindered to leave the country. He even stressed that it would be good if foreigners bought fewer French wares. Then there would be more left for the French themselves.[100] 'Ce royame est si fleurrisant, si abondant en tout que l'on peut desirer, qu'il n'a que faire d'emprunter rien de ses voisins', he said.[101] That foreign export was particularly important in order to bring in silver and gold, de Montchrétien copied from Laffemas. However, in other respects, it was better if France kept to herself and lived off her own resources. To achieve this great goal only two problems stood in the way: the many foreigners in France and a certain idleness of the French population. The outrooting of these obstacles should be the main objective of state regulation and economic policy, he emphasised.

De Montchrétien also had a wider aim with his work. Through critically examining Aristotle, Xenophon, Plato and other ancient authorities, he discussed how the Aristotelian conception of economy (household-ing) ought to be combined with a (modern) conception of politics and at the same time further developed in a new societal and historical context. De Montchrétien stressed the relationship between state and economic performance. He believed that men are mainly motivated by the desire for private gain. However, he did not trust in any natural force which would see to it that the aim for selfish profit may lead to the common good. On the contrary, a strong state must regulate this selfishness, so that it in the end might bring wealth and happiness to the nation.[102] Hence with his definition *oeconomie politique* he aimed at something more than the classical authors: to define economics as householding in a new era where economic means had become important for political and military power.

The economic policies proposed by Laffemas and de Montchrétien in the beginning of the seventeenth century came alive especially during the era of Colbert. As noted, this policy emphasised self-sufficiency as a central goal. Foreign trade was not looked upon as something that by itself would render economic growth and increased prosperity. For some, as little foreign commerce as possible was the best alternative. Others would recommend a regulated trade which promoted the import of raw materials and export of manufactured goods. If English mercantilists sometimes would describe foreign trade as a zero-sum game where one nation only could win what the other lost, this view was carried to its extreme by Colbert and his followers. As so often emphasised, Colbert believed that the number of trade routes was limited and that political strength and skill in war decided how these routes were distributed among the powers.[103] The German historian Moritz Isenmann has drawn attention to how the French finance minister used the concept *guerre d'argent* to describe the con-temporary order of different states competing for commerce. More-over, he also presented a 'natural order', which defined how much international trade a certain state should be allowed to carry. It should be defined by the length of each country's coastline, he mused. Being more or less constantly at war with the Dutch Republic, and later Britain, this plea to higher orders gave him of course a good argument when defending his king's aggressive policies.[104]

At the same time things began to change. At the very end of the seventeenth century a new economic discourse was introduced in France – in stark opposition to the Colbertism of the previous period, including the policies of Cardinal Richelieu some decades previ-ously.[105] Certainly, in their critique against Colbert and his policy of protectionism and self-sufficiency, the so-called *economistes* did not go as far as to argue for the abolishment of all forms of trade regula-tions or all exclusive privileges to establish manufactories. Rather they drew attention to the causes and factors that might stimulate an increase in wealth in a country: industry of course but most of all agriculture. At the same time they had much less to say about the role of commerce and foreign trade. For the Physiocrats in the mid-eighteenth century such trade was sterile and did not contribute to wealth creation at all.

Among the many *economistes*, we will only mention two (occasionally referred to as mercantilists): Jean-Francois Melon and Charles Dutot.[106] Both were certainly influenced by the contemporary English discussion concerning commerce and a favourable balance of trade as explicated by authors like Davenant and other 'Tory free traders' in England around the seventeenth century (see further p. 177). Particularly for Melon, also Mandeville served as a great inspiration. Furthermore, both had been involved in the spectacular schemes of John Law and were clearly influenced by him.[107] Especially Dutot discussed the concept of the balance of trade, which he called the *Barometre de commerce* in a critical way – as in England, as we will see.[108] Both he and Melon stood far from the Colbert system and its attitude towards foreign trade. Being one of the most cited and translated economists of the first three-quarters of the eighteenth century, Melon was a firm believer in free trade and defended consumption of luxuries because it brought employment. Thus he believed that a high level of demand was necessary for a prosperous commonwealth. He vigorously criticised the notion that wealth was money: 'Il est peut-etre nécessaire de d'etruire ici l'erreur de ceux qui croient le pays abondants en mines d'or et d'argent sont les plus riches'.[109] However, he was not altogether negative towards regulations of import and export. Thus he pointed out that it is usual in his country to forbid 'toute exportation des matiéres premiéres, nécessaires pour faire travailler des manufactures'.[110] However, he was not totally convinced in the wisdom of this rule. There are so many exceptions to be made, he said. And a favourable balance between exports and imports can in the last instance only be obtained as a consequence of 'la concurrence advantageuse sur les autres nations'.[111]

However, in France the opposition to Colbert is most often connected with earlier authors such as Boisguilbert and Vauban. Sebastian le Prestre de Vauban (1633–1707), the great field marshal and fortification expert, is in this context mainly known for his projects to introduce a novel tax system in France. Thus, especially in his *Projet d'une Dime Royale* (1707), he envisaged ideas that would be more fully expressed by Richard Cantillon and the Physiocrats.[112] Pierre Le Peasant de Boisguilbert (1646–1714), however, in a number of works around 1700, especially in *Le Détail de la France* (1695) and *Factum de la France* (1705), developed a system-like view of the economy, which later on would be used by writers such as Richard Cantillon and the Physiocratic school. The idea of the economy as almost a self-equilibrating natural order was used as an argument against the *dirigisme* of an earlier period.

As often stated, Boisguilbert was heavily influenced by Jansenism and perhaps most profoundly by the *moraliste* philosopher Pierre Nicole (1625–95).[113] Like Nicole (but also like Pufendorff and some of the contemporary English writers), Boisguilbert believed in equilibrium and that men, in a commercial society, were fundamentally interdependent. Production and consumption, the forces of supply and demand, were dictated by natural causes as well as providence. Money was only a medium of exchange, and there existed no pressing need to secure as much money as possible. Like Nicole, Boisguilbert argued that, although men were self-interested creatures and full of cupidity, their private vices could be tamed and regulated to procure public benefits. Here of course one can find a clear passage to later writers such as Mandeville and Cantillon. However, we cannot dwell further on these undoubtedly exciting themes in this context. With Boisguilbert and the turn of the eighteenth century, a different economic discourse was undoubtedly born in France – and for an enthusiast as Marx the emergence of Boisguilbert signalled the birth of 'classical political economy' via the French *economistes* and the great Scots.[114]

The German countries

In perspective, early state formation in the German-speaking part of Europe seemed, in contrast to its neigbours in the west and south, to have less to do with the capture of international trade and commerce. Over the centuries, the Holy Roman Empire had been carved up between princes, feudal lords, bishops and magistrates of towns. In the early sixteenth century, it housed several hundred more or less independent political bodies mixed in a complicated manner with cords of loyalty and kinship. Between them they also competed – and fought in wars – for greater recognition and power. Only Austria, which was the homeland of the Habsburg dynasty monopolising the position as emperor of the Holy Roman Empire from the late Middle Ages, was a state of considerable size. However, it shared its land-locked geographical position with the majority of the smaller states and constituencies. To increase or capture foreign commerce was thus not the first priority for the average German prince or ruler. Instead power and income would much more rely on internal resources. Hence it is not surprising to find that German consultant administrators were mainly interested in extending the tax base of their realms, either through increasing the tax burden of citizens (the extensive strategy) or by trying to develop agriculture as well as introduce a better regulative order concerning trade and handicrafts (the intensive strategy). Also of course to establish own manufactories in order to avoid importation of luxury wares as well as weapons and metals. Moreover, the Thirty Years' War (1618–48) implied a devastating blow to the German economies and polities, with armies marching back and forth pilfering, plundering and killing. It took well into the next century for Germany to recover, and by then a new growing state with great ambitions had emerged in the North: Brandenburg-Prussia.

In standard textbooks concerning the history of economic thought and doctrines, it is often taken for granted that Cameralism was a kind of German *Sonderweg* or native version of Mercantilism – or the mercantile system – rooted in its peculiar history, as well as geographical position in Europe.[115] The idea of a German *Sonderweg* in this context goes back at least to Roscher's grand opus from 1874, *Geschichte der National-Oekonomik in Deutschland.* In his book he starts out with lamenting the situation in the German territories after the Thirty Years' War.[116] Out of this turmoil, the first task was to establish territorial states built on law, order and stable taxation. Out of this grew different 'schools' of economic thought and (particularly) policy and practice. This story was even more so emphasised by Schmoller. In his short treatise as we saw *The Mercantile System and its Historical Significance* (1884), he propounded that the German *Sonderweg* of Mercantilism was caused by the underdevelopment of Germany, its late formation of development to establish territorial states and its commercial dependence upon England (and France). Hence its distinctive variety of Mercantilism – also here regarded as a system of selfish economic policies in a word of combating national powers – originated not from 'whether a mercantilist policy was necessary and desirable; about that there was agreement and properly so'. What differed instead was Germany's landlocked position, its political anarchy and still underdeveloped economy.[117]

However, it is unfruitful to press the issue of a German *Sonderweg* too far. Surely, also other such special cases could be identified, as in Italy, Spain, France and of course also England. Moreover, it is not very helpful to name such a German *Sonderweg* Cameralism. There are several reasons for that. First, like Mercantilism, also Cameralism is a very much contested concept.[118] In an often-cited *passus*, Albion Small more than a hundred years ago described Cameralism as 'primarily a theory and a technique of government'.[119] Moreover, 'the cameralists were not primarily economists', he stated. Instead they were a sort of 'political scientists' and 'servants of the state'.[120] Also in Keith Tribe's definition of Cameralism state interest is a central point. However, he regards Cameralism as a type of 'administrative economics' emerging in Prussian universities after 1720.[121] Last, André Wakefield regards more broadly Cameralism as some kind of common discourse mainly developed during the eighteenth century but he extends it far beyond being merely a 'university science'. Moreover, it was not 'economics' and 'administrative economics' in any narrow sense: 'German Cameralists existed at the nexus between science and economic development (and were) ... proponents of the notion that one could promote development through the systematic application of the natural and human sciences'.[122] Hence Wakefield's cameralists include a whole range of individuals from university teachers in cameral science strict to natural scientists in different fields, inventors and cranks experimenting in chemistry and mineralogy, as well adventure seekers and perhaps even simple rogues. Thus, there are large differences between the various interpretations that are not easily combined, besides perhaps the important role they all give to the state in order to create economic prosperity. But conversely that power is a cornerstone for economic wealth and plenty. In different versions we have already traced such thinking in other countries during approximately the same time. Hence, the argument for a very special German *Sonderweg* is not very strong.

Second, it is not fruitful to use the concept of Cameralism to denote a distinct kind of economic thinking and writing in *all* German states, say from the seventeenth century up until the nineteenth century.[123] Surely we must be more distinct than that. Already Roscher pointed out the big differences between different *Länder* and regions within the large territory of the Holy Roman Empire.[124] When the term Cameralism is used, it mainly refers to northern Germany, most particularly Brandenburg-Prussia. Hence to a large extent the construction of an all-encompassing German *Kameralismus* is a construction of later times, when it became useful to link it to German unification after 1870 and the rise of authoritarian political regimes.

Third, there are good reasons to be more specific about the timing of Cameralism. As Tribe has suggested, it did not really emerge – as a distinct discourse – until the eighteenth century and should perhaps also be reserved for a kind of university teaching which emerged especially in Prussia from the 1720s, which included economics but also law, administration, the natural sciences, and so on, in order to promote economic development, a stable political order and perhaps also general *Glucksahligkeit*. Moreover, it was mainly used in plural as the Cameral sciences to denote that it included a number of different but interrelated disciplines and discourses.

Hence, in order to understand Cameralism properly, we most probably should start in 1727, when two chairs in a new discipline were inaugurated in Halle and Frankfurt an der Oder by King Friedrich

Wilhelm I of Prussia. The chair in Halle to which Simon Peter Gasser was appointed held the title *cameralia oeconomica und Policey-sachen*, and the chair in Frankfurt *Lehrstuhl für Kameral-, Ökonomie und Policeiwissenschaften*. Gasser had previously been a professor in law at Halle and achieved the title *Kriegs – und Domänenrat*. Dithmar, however, was a historian. The same year as he was appointed, he wrote an introduction to his new subject. It would become a standard textbook for a long time to come: *Einleitung in die Oeconomischen-, Polycey- and Cameral-Wissenschaften* (1727).

In his book, Dithmar mainly dealt with a description of the contemporary Prussian administrative, financial and police system. During the seventeenth century 'police' was mainly connected with the means to restore power and security.[125] However, for Dithmar it meant something more. *Policey* was the means by which a paternal state provided for the welfare of its subjects.[126] Or according to Kurt Wolzendorff: *Policey* should serve the principle of general welfare.[127] Apart from this, Dithmar's textbook also contained a section for 'economics'. However, his definition of economics was mainly the old Aristotelian one depicting householding. However, as would become a standard during the eighteenth century, Dithmar spoke of two forms of *Oeceonomie*: special *Haushaltung*, which dealt with the individual, and general householding, which prescribed the rules by which society at large would preserve and hopefully also enlarge its material resources. Dithmar himself had not much to say about 'general *Oeconomie*'. However, later on, during the eighteenth century this section would tend to grow with each new writer on the subject. And during the next century, it would form the bulwark of a specific German form of economics, *Nationalökonomie*.

Indeed perhaps the main leading character of the Cameralists during the eighteenth century was the notorious adventurer Johan Heinrich Gottlieb von Justi (1717–68): the 'great systematiser' and *Volländer* of Cameralism, according to Anton Tautscher.[128] Starting a career as an academic teacher, he taught first at the Theresianum Knights Academy in Vienna, after which he moved to Erfurt and Leipzig and was appointed Director of Police in Göttingen in 1755. Two years later, after having to flee in haste out of a window because of some shady business, he went to Copenhagen to work for the Danish minister Bernstorff. After moving again, this time to Berlin, he was in 1765 appointed Prussian Inspector of Mines, Glass, and Steel Works. In 1768, he was imprisoned, accused of embezzling government funds. After being released in April 1771, he moved back to Berlin where he died the following year. Justi's main aim can be best summarised from one major text, his *Staatswirtschaft* (175).[129] His teaching and writing was centred around the concept of *Gluckseligkeit*. A good state, he said, must have such good arrangements and structure 'that everyone may enjoy a reasonable freedom, and by his diligence may be able to attain those moral and temporal gods which the demands of his social station make necessary for satisfactory living'.[130] Thus it is the plight of a good state to see to that *Gluckseligkeit* can be achieved through good *Polizei*. Moreover, Justi's book sticks to the old formula of dividing up the subject into the sciences of police, Cameralism and economy.

Another leading cameralist writer in the eighteenth century was the professor in *Polizei- und kameralwissenchaften* in Vienna, Joseph von Sonnenfels (1733–1817). Clearly both Justi and Sonnenfels were influenced by Enlightenment ideas. Both stressed that the main goal for what Justi called the economic *Polizei-wissenschaften* was to understand the principles by which the wealth and happiness of a state was regulated.[131] However, neither Sonnenfels nor Justi was ready to draw any individualistic conclusions from such enlightenment ideas. Rather, foreign authorities like Adam Ferguson were referred to in order to argue for the need of a paternalist state.[132] *Gluckseligkeit* could not be achieved by a free intercourse between independent individuals, they argued. To this extent, Justi and Sonnenfels became spokesmen for an enlightened authoritarianism – not peculiar perhaps when we consider their background.

Among the cameralists we must also mention two Italians, Cesare Beccaria (1735–94) and Pietro Verri (1728–97), both situated in Milan and thus Austrian citizens. Later interpreters of doctrinal history regarded themas great innovators and forerunners of much more modern economics. Like their contemporary Galiani, they founded their analysis of the economic process upon a subjective basis.[133] Schumpeter even baptised Beccaria as the 'Italian Adam Smith' and found in him a number of analytical inventions. Verri he particularly hailed as an inventor of the constant-outlay demand curve, and his anticipation of Jevon's phrase 'calculus of pleasure of pain'.[134] Where did they pick up such innovative thought? It has been stated that a clearly drawn line existe between them and a scholastic tradition which harked back to the late medieval period. Thus Odd Langholm has emphasised that for example Galiani's strong insistence on a subjective analysis of value and price was clearly influenced by fourteenth- century Schoolmen such as St Bernardino of Siena and St Antonious of Florence. Via Bernardo Davanzati's important *Discourse Upon Coins* (1588) and the writings of Geminiano Montanari,[135] this thinking would inspire the eighteenth-century economic discussion and in this sense also contribute to the formation of modern economics.[136]

However, at the same time we must stress the strong connections with Cameralism as it was written and thought in Germany and Austria in the eighteenth century. The professional history of Beccaria is highly typical from this point of view. As Milan was part of Austria in the eighteenth century, economics as an academic subject largely took a cameralist direction. Thus, when Beccaria received his chair in Milan in 1768, it was in 'Cameral science'. However, in his inaugural lecture he described his subject in a perhaps not too orthodox fashion when he said that it compromised 'the principles of public economy and commerce, in those sciences which furnish the means of increasing the riches of a state, and applying them to the most useful purposes'.[137]

We have already noted that it makes little sense to speak of Cameralism as an encompassing school before the eighteenth century. Thus when Roscher in his *Geschichte der National-Oekonomik in Deutschland* spoke of the early seventeenth century as the 'beginning of a systematical science of Economics ("Volkwirtschaftslehre") in Germany', he emphasised a variety of discourses and traditions.[138] Hence during the seventeenth century the bulk of literature dealing with economic subjects – trade, money, finance, taxes and so on – were still not moulded into the cameralist format it received later. Moreover, the German discussion during the sixteenth and seventeenth centuries can to a large degree be described as an echo of the contemporary English, Italian, Spanish and French discussion. Thus for example Jacob Borniss – the first systematiser of economic discourse in Germany according to Roscher – in a work such as *Tractatus politicus de rerum sufficienta in republica et civitate procuranda* (1625) discussed the nature of money and coin and the need for a state to have much bullion. He described money as the *Nerv der Dinge* for a state. In order to gain more bullion it was necessary for a state without own mines to export to gain more money. However, raw materials should never be exported if this could be avoided. They should instead be worked up in manufactures and when finished be exported.[139] From this Roscher would draw the conclusion that Borniss was a mercantilist.[140] And it is certainly true that Borniss can be placed alongside such authors as the Italians Botero and Serra, de Montchrétien in France and Thomas Smith in England. As T Simon recently emphasised the differences between Colbert, the English mercantilists and the *produktionsorientierten Kameralismus* should not be exaggerated.[141] Most certainly their geographical situation and other circumstances made them sometimes think differently to their counterparts in other countries. However, they also, to a large extent, reacted and took positions in a new international order of commercial rivalry and power struggles.

According to Roscher, an older 'mercantilistic' trend in Germany during the seventeenth century was replaced by a *polizeilisch-cameralistisch* trend during the eighteenth century. Only in the middle of this century did this discourse mature into a more definitive form –

a policey, oeconomy and commercial science. Thus for the period after
the Thirty Years' War Roscher emphasised the emergence of three different traditions in the German states: a moral philosophical, *rein wissenschaftliche*, economic discourse connected with the names of
Pufendorff and Conring; a *praktisch-progressive* tradition in Austria;
and, third, a *praktisch-conservative* tradition in most parts of middle
and south Germany.[142] Especially that the 'mercantilist' trend did not
follow the example of England and transform itself during the eighteenth and early nineteenth centuries into something akin to classical
political economy Roscher regarded mainly as a consequence of
German backwardness. Thus the failure to establish a science of trade
or a forceful *economie politique* in Germany was explained as a consequence of the persistence of a fragmented Germany after the Thirty
Years' War and the cementation of small state politics. Within such a
political, social and cultural context, the emphasis was put on 'economic administration' in a rather narrow sense. Hence economy
became the art of private and general householding, policei the way to
run small states and Cameralism the art of finance.[143] The prominent
influence of old *Hausvater* literature perhaps also played some part in
this. Nevertheless, it was this situation Roscher referred to when he so
pertinently emphasises that 'Germany could not have had a Boisguill-
bert as it had no Colbert'.[144]

However, now we will return to the seventeenth century before
Cameralism became part of university curriculum and discuss a
number of writers who are related to what is our main concern in this
chapter: to trace the different responses to an age of nascent state
making and the combination of political aims and ends with economic
means and ends.

Ludvig von Seckendorff (1626–92)

For Roscher von Seckendorff was the most typical of the Middle-
German *praktisch-conservative* writers. As a *Hofjunker* to the duke
Ernst von Gotha, he wrote a most influential work, *Der Teutsche
Furstenstaat* (1655). Furthermore, he was promoted to *Geheimer
Hof- und Kammerrath im Verwaltungsdienst* and later on became chancellor. Thereafter he moved to Sachenzietz where he in Duke Moritz's
service received the title *Kanzler und Constistorial-Präsident*.[145] Obviously, thus, von Seckendorff was well versed in the administrative
chores of small-state Germany. Against this background it is perhaps not
peculiar that for Small he was 'the Adam Smith of Cameralism'.[146]
However, as we have argued, this is at best only partially true.

Small is of course correct when he claims that the aim of *Furstenstaat* was 'to furnish an account of the operative machinery of a typical

German state'.[147] The text is divided into four parts. The first part argues that a good prince must investigate the geographical conditions of his lands in order to know what might be improved. Especially essential in this context were good maps, he concludes. The second part treats the *Verfassung* of the state: how it should be organised, how the well-being of its inhabitants both in moral and material sense should be provided for, and so on. Lastly, the third and longest part is devoted to Cameralism. In this section von Seckendorff lists the revenues open to the ruler and how his income might be improved.

With reference to the second book, which dealt with the administration of the state, von Seckendorff emphasised that the ruler should not be an autocrat and rule as *eigenwillige Herrschaft*. Thus he was not in any sense a representative of a more modern absolutism, Roscher stressed.[148] He was much more old-fashioned, rather a paternalist of the old school who postulated that *Salmonische Regierungsweisheit* was the imperative of a pious and civic prince. With the help of God, the prince must rule in order to preserve morale and peace in his state, as well as provide for the welfare of his subjects.[149]

Thus in *Furstenstaat* von Seckendorff at some length discussed the preconditions for moral government and princely dignity. A good ruler must be true to himself as well as to others. He must stick to his laws and obligations. He must respect hereditary dispositions and accept the customs of his people. In short, von Seckendorff's second book was really a handbook in how to govern a small state.[150] He focussed especially on the economic organisation of the state and its productive potentials. Thus he, for example, proposed that in order for the state to prosper it must increase its population, improve its agriculture and establish manufactories. However, when Roscher provides von Seckendorff with an embryo of a 'mercantilist system', somewhere between Sully and Colbert, he is not far off the mark.[151] *Der Furstenstaat* certainly contained a number of observations which fitted well into the general economic-political thinking of this day. But, first, his reference was the small princely state – and not a great state like France. Second, not to any degree did he refer to the mercantilist discussion about foreign trade and wealth as for example carried out in England. Like Borniss before him, von Seckendorff strongly suggested that in the *Furstenstaat* all raw materials should be worked up instead of exported. With regard to money the author did not, however, share the contemporary fear that it might become too scarce. Instead, he was more worried about the loss of population than a drain of coin. His main concern in this context was that good coin in exchange with foreigners must not be traded for worse and debased coins.[152] He was also suspicious of too large an import – but mainly because it brought in luxury items harmful to the morals of the population. Lastly, his third book on the revenues and incomes of the prince included observations with regard to taxes, and how the prince's *Domänen* should be organised in order to yield maximum income. Here, however, von Seckendorff's discussion was clearly fixed within the tradition of the *Hausvater* literature and the Aristotelian concept of economy as householding. The *Domänen* of the prince was here to a large extent treated as his own private property.

Johann Joachim Becher (1635–82)

Nothing illustrates so well the diversity of the German economic literature during the seventeenth century than when we after von Seckendorff turn to Becher. To begin with, his main reference point was Austria. During his hectic life he travelled a lot, but if he had an anchor point it was certainly Vienna. During the seventeenth century, Austria was the only great state within the Holy Roman Empire, and to live there instead of in one of the small states certainly made a difference. Moreover, while von Seckendorff seems to have led a rather comfortable life making a steady career as a small-state administrator, Becher explored several callings during a rather short lifetime but did not gain success in any. As a young man with no learned background – an *Autodidakt* according to Roscher[153] – he tried his luck within the natural sciences. He became a teacher of medicine and a physician, and he carried out experiments trying to make gold. Hence, at the court of Leopold I in Vienna, Becher was acknowledged as an alchemist. He seems also to have been the originator of the famous so-called phlogiston theory.

During the 1660s Becher frantically toured the different *Kurfürstenhofen* in the empire trying to attain their authorities for some new scheme or plan. Becher was certainly a man who sought opportunity where he could find it. But he was seldom very successful. One reason was that he was often ahead of his time. Thus he involved himself in a colonisation project of Guyana under the auspices of the *Kurfürst* of Bayern. Furthermore, for the count of Hanau, he made up a detailed plan to colonise the area between Orrinocco and the Amazonas. Nothing came out of this, of course. Besides, he outlined plans for new industrial and manufacturing projects, for example with the *Kurfürst* of Mainz. In Vienna, where he stayed during most of the 1670s, he became the head of the *Manufakturhaus* supported by the emperor. At the same time he projected the building of the Rhein-Donau canal – another wild scheme which failed. At the end of the 1670s he seemed to have fallen in disfavour with the emperor. He settled in London where he died in 1682.[154]

Although Becher wrote abundantly, his sole 'economic' work is the *Politische Discurs von den eigentlichen Ursachen des Auf- und*

Abnehmens der Städt, Länder und Republicken, published in 1668. It is remarkably different than von Seckendorff's work. For one thing Becher was much less paternalistic in an old-fashioned sense. Instead, his discussion of the state and its origin closely reflected the contemporary moral philosophical discussion. In this context he even pointed out that men were *sociable* animals and society a 'natural' construct emerging as a consequence of this inherent sociability. His definition of a state was also quite up to date: he saw it as 'a populous, self-supporting community'.[155] This community, in turn, could be depicted as a system of reciprocal relationships:

> When the members of a community arrange their affairs so that the one lives from the other, the one can earn his piece of bread from the other, yes that the one plays his support into the hand of the other, that is the right community.[156]

Certainly, Becher did not draw any *laissez-faire* conclusion from this. Such a reciprocal order would not arise spontaneously, he emphasised. On the contrary, it must be instituted and consciously regulated so that it might serve the welfare of all. Thus he was very much against an order in which: 'Each is left to get his living as he may; whether he is ruined and ruins a hundred others with him, or he prospers, with the common gain or loss, prosperity or adversity, no one asks any questions'.[157]

Furthermore, he strongly emphasised that a community only could be strong if it housed a great population. He put forward the maxim that: 'The more populous a town is the mightier it becomes'.[158] Also, there must be a right proportion between the three main orders of people: peasants, craftsmen and merchants (*Kaufleute*). These three orders corresponded to three different sectors of the economy: (a) the primary sector (food and raw materials), (b) the secondary sector (manufactured goods) and (c) the tertiary sector (distribution, capital). Moreover, if a 'true' proportion between these sectors was instituted, nobody would have to starve and everything would be kept in good order. To some extent this could certainly be regarded as a plea for a planned economy. And as such it would have a tremendous influence upon the economic and political discussion during the next century, especially in Germany but also in neighbouring countries like Sweden and Denmark.[159]

Thus without doubt, Becher, in comparison to for example Seckendorf, was much less interested in the prince than in the community and its people. Becher did not deny the importance of a strong state, of course. But he was mainly interested in other topics. This seems highly pertinent if we look at the structure of his main economic work, for the bulk of *Politische Discurs* mainly deals with matters of commerce and trade. Thus the long Part 2 of the text discusses how commerce and trade was organised in Germany and how it could be improved. In general, he proposed the principle of free trade: 'Wares should be freely transported in and out of the country ... in order to best and honestly support individuals with housing, cloth and drink'.[160] This fitted in rather badly with his vision of a planned economy, of course. He therefore proposed a significant restriction to this principle of freedom. Thus free trade may rule only if it did not infer with the goals of *Volksreichheit*, *Nahrung* and *Gemeinschaft*, he pointed out.[161] It was in this context that he brought in his famous distinction between *Monopolium*, *Polypolium* and *Propolium*. All these forms implied great threats to a well-organised trade. Thus, '*Monopolium* obstructed the rise of a great population, *Polypolium* threatened the existence of business, and *Propolium* good order in the community'.[162] With *Polypolium* Becher referred to a situation where there were too many competitors on the scene, and the term *Propolium* alludes to forestalling and cornering of necessities.

In *Politische Discurs* we also find many references to the general discussion of the role of trade and commerce for economic growth and modernisation. Mainly for this reason, Becher has often been referred to as a true mercantilist. It is quite true that he seemed well acquainted with the British literature and discussion. It was in this context that Roscher, furthermore, emphasised the impact a trip to Holland had upon him before writing the *Discurs*.[163] However, as Roscher also pointed out, Becher was not a mercantilist of a kind which confused wealth with money.[164] Instead, for Becher, wealth lay in production. Furthermore, a well-ordered productive sector stimulated an increase in consumption. Consumption in its turn was the centre and source of the well-being in a country. However, he believed that 'money was the soul and nerve of the Land ('*das Geld gleichsamb die Nerve und Seel eines Landes ist*'). Consequently, it should be kept in the country.[165] Roscher interprets Becher's point as to rate money as a form of *Verlag* capital. Hence, with a great *Verlag* it was possible to employ many workers and increase the riches of the country.[166]

In the end we cannot avoid the question whether Becher was a mercantilist, a cameralist or perhaps both. To some degree – as argued before – this question is anachronistic as Cameralism as a distinctive discourse had really not yet come into existence. Nevertheless, Becher together with Hörnigk and Schröder (see below) are most often referred to as a group of 'Austrian cameralists'.[167] However, at least Becher was clearly no direct *Vorlaufer* to the peculiar form of systematic *Staat-Intervensionismus*, which provides the key to the later Austrian cameralists' works (for example, Justi and

Sonnenfels). As we saw, his perspective was different. To this effect he was much closer to being a mercantilist. Hence, he was profoundly influenced by English mercantilist writers and the discussion regarding the role of trade and commerce. Even more pertinently, however, he was a synthesizer who used English discourses on trade, new works in moral philosophy, and so on, and put it all together in a quite original form. However, his attempt in this direction was hardly followed in Germany. Increasingly, instead, the cameralist tradition won over.

Philipp Wilhelm von Hörnigk (1640–1714)

It is certainly true that the German states had no Colbert.[168] However, if that had been the case, von Hörnigk was probably the closest to becoming an Austrian de Montchrétien. Born in Frankfurt am Main, von Hörnigk was promoted to a doctoral degree in law at Ingolstadt in 1661. Thereafter he served under Leopold I in Vienna for a substantial number of years. During this period he also became Becher's brother-in-law. In 1690 he entered the service of count Lamberg, *Furstbischop* in Passau, as *Geheimsekretär*. At Passau he achieved nobility position as a *Freiherr*.[169]

Hörnigk's most famous work, *Österreich über alles wann es nur will* (1684), must be regarded in the context of war and the national humiliation inflicted upon Germany during this time. Without any real resistance Louis XIV of France had seized Trier and Strasbourg in 1684. The same year the Turks stood before the gates of Vienna. Hence, Hörnigk's tone was aggressive and nationalistic. 'The slyness of the French ... has corrupted everything', he said ('Die List der Franzosen hat fast Alles in ... zerruttnung gebracht').[170] Hence for the future Hörnigk looked forward to a *rechschaffenen Krieg* with the *hochfärtiger* nation of France.[171] However, Austria's weakness was her own fault, he argued. Thus she had sold most of her wealth to foreigners. *Fremmende kaufleute* had for example seized and made a monopoly of her important linen trade. They paid workers such minimal wages that they were hardly able to subsist.[172]

However, as Hörnigk argued, Austria was able to change this 'whenever she wanted'. In this context Hörnigk presented a programme for national recovery, which resembled de Montchrétien's for France. His main solution was to establish economic and administrative means by which Austria could provide enough national independence and *Subsistenz in ihrem eigenen Haus*.[173] In order to establish such self-sufficiency Hörnigk presented a list of nine principles which must be followed strictly. Upon these a sound *Lands-Oeconomie* should be based, he argued. These *Hauptregeln* were:

1   a thorough investigation of the production potential of the country must be carried out, especially the possibility to achieve gold and silver;

2   to work up raw materials in *fabricatur*;

3   to find the right means to increase the amount of people which can contribute to the *Verarbeitung* of raw materials;

4   see to that gold and silver, as far as possible, is not transported out of the country;

5   watch over that the *Lands-Inwohner* mainly use wares of their own produce ('dass sie sich an ihren einheimischen Gutern begnügen');

6   in this context also that all *Missbrauch* of foreign wares must be averted and, to the extent importation is necessary, they must be exchanged for other wares and not money;

7   mainly manufactured goods shall be exported;

8   if export of raw materials ('im land gefallene überflussige Guter') takes place they must only be exchanged for gold and silver; and

9   no wares should ever be imported which can be produced within the country.[174]

It is only logical, of course, that Roscher found this programme mercantilist.[175] Without doubt, in form and content it was closer to the programme for self-sufficiency connected with de Montchrétien in France than what seventeenth-century English economic writers of trade and commerce had propounded. Seen in its proper context, Hörnigk's real aim with his nine *Hauptregeln* was to outline for Austria what he saw as the thrust of Colbertism. With such a programme for increased independence, the French seemed to have succeeded very well. However, could it not also be used in an Austrian context? Why should this great nation remain a second-class state ruled by foreign economic interests? It is in such a context we must regard Hörnigk's book, which became an instant success and reached several editions over the following century. We must also notice that we with Hörnigk, as with Becher, seem far distanced from von Seckendorff's provincialism as well as from the old *Hausvater* literature. Instead, Hörnigk launched a programme for a specific form of economie politique, *Lands-Oekonomie*. During the eighteenth century it became integrated into the General *Oeconomie* section of a science of policey, economy and Cameralism.

Wilhelm von Schröder (1640–88)

Also Schröder served under Leopold I in Vienna. In fact, he was appointed director of the *Manufakturhaus* in Vienna after Becher. However, after the Turks in 1683 burnt down this institution, which aimed to be a centre of industrial innovation as the great Gobelins works in Paris established by Colbert, it was never rebuilt. During his last years, Schröder served as *Hofkammerrat* in Zips in Hungary; his biography does not so far suggest anything unusual. However, Schröder was also a learned man. He studied Law first in Jena and then in Amsterdam. Before presenting his dissertation in Jena in 1663, he had been in England, where he socialised with such leading figures as Thomas Hobbes, Petty and Boyle. Since his visit he was also a standing member of the English Royal Society.[176]

Thus, among the threesome Becher, Hörnigk and Schröder the last of the Austrians was without doubt the 'most advanced' in learned terms. He was well read in the general scientific, political and moral discussion at the time and had a first-hand knowledge of the contemporary English economic discussion. In political terms he was a stern believer in the absolute monarchy and spoke with admiration of Ludwig XIV.[177] In *Disquisitio Politica vom absoluten Fürstenrecht* – a supplement to his famous *Fürstlischen Schatz und Rentkammer* – he outlined the divine right of rulers in such an extreme fashion that it incited von Seckendorff to name von Schröder *a homine perverso* both in person and writing.[178] However, at the same time, von Schröder pointed out that with divine right followed obligations. Thus, he emphasised, 'the prosperity and welfare of the subjects is the foundation upon which all happiness of a prince as ruler of such subjects is based'.[179]

Von Schröder's reputation as an early cameralist mainly stems from his work *Fürstliche Schatz- und Rentkammer* (1686). His viewpoint here is, as Roscher noted, *rein fiskalisch.*[180] He argued for the inauguration of a chamber of treasury in most of the book and according to which principles it should be administered. He suggested that it would be divided into two: a *Collegia*, which collected the incomes, and a *Collegium*, which had the task to find out new sources of revenue for the prince. It is especially when discussing the latter institution that he revealed a profound knowledge with regard to contemporary ideas on how a country could be made rich through trade. Thus he, for example, emphasised the 'old truth' that: 'A country becomes richer the more gold it can bring forth ... and the poorer when gold is carried out of the country'.[181] Thus a state must export in order to bring in bullion and money. However, in line with many of the English discussants, he regarded money mainly as a beneficial *pendelum commercii*: 'by an increased use of money many more people can be supported and trade multiplicated'.[182] Trade and commerce were thus a necessary precondition for increased growth and development – and not only a necessary evil in order to bring in money for a country which had inadequate supplies of its own. In fact, he regarded trade – *commercium* – 'the most principal mean by which a country can grow richer'.[183]

As a principle, von Schröder stressed that trade should be free. But at the same time he supported the need for protectionist measures especially related to the establishment of manufactures. In fact, von Schröder was a great friend of manufactures. In this context, he mainly referred to the French example, but he was quite aware of the English. However, he seems to have been hesitant to import a formal favourable balance of trade 'theory'. This disinclination he in fact shared with most other German authors during the seventeenth and eighteenth centuries. They in fact seldom made explicit references to such a balance. Certainly, they might have believed that an inflow of money by means of an 'active' balance of trade was beneficial. But they would seldom elaborate this idea.[184] They seem to have been more concerned with other things: self-sufficiency, good government, a greater population and domestic manufactures.[185]

* * *

Hence, in different countries, a literature emerged from the late sixteenth century in which power and plenty were regarded as intertwined phenomena – in Italy, Spain, England, France, Germany as well as other countries. All over Europe, writers from different corners of society (not only consultant administrators) promoted protective measures to bolster the establishment of manufactures, inaugurated laws which prohibited the export of precious minerals and raw materials, encouraged the export of finished wares and so on. On this basis, a common stock of ideas of how to achieve national wealth and power successively emerged from the late medieval period and experienced a definite breakthrough during the sixteenth century. All of these discussions were set in a wider context of a contest for power which focussed on international commerce but also the establishment of manufactures and own production. However, it is important to note that although many 'unit ideas' regarding economic growth and modernisation appeared from country to country, the national framework of the discussion tended to be quite different. Especially in the German continental states the economic policy was less framed in order to achieve a favourable balance of trade through international trade than to establish manufactures and a 'modern' economic institutional structure. Reformers here were more defensive in their proposed methods. They pursued economic and administrative reforms in order to catch up with the leading countries, especially the Dutch Republic and England.

Moreover, it was such a programme for power and plenty that was the common theme rather than an abstract adoration of money, a confusion of wealth with money or even a trust in a specific doctrine, the favourable balance of trade. In the next chapter, we will deal with this alleged theory.

Notes

1 J A Schumpeter, *A History of Economic Analysis*. London: George Allen & Unwin 1972, pp. 143f.
2 See above p. 19.
3 J G A Pocock, *The Machiavellian Moment: Florentine Political Thought and the Atlantic Republican Tradition*. Princeton: Princeton University Press 1985; Q Skinner, *Visions of Politics, vol II: Renaissance Virtues*. Cambridge, UK: Cambridge University Press 2002, chs 3, 5, 6.
4 On these Italian developments, see S A Reinert, 'Introduction' to A Serra, *A Short Treatise on the Wealth and Poverty of Nations*. London: Anthem Press 2011.
5 D Hume, 'On the Jealousy of Trade'. In his *Essays: Moral, Political and Literary*. Indianapolis, IN: Liberty Fund 1987.
6 On the role of emulation in general during this period see S Reinert, *Translating Empire: Emulation and the Origins of Political Economy*. Cambridge, MA: Harvard University Press 2011. Also I Hont, *Jealousy of Trade: International Competition and the Nation-State in Historical Perspective*. Cambridge, MA: The Belknap Press of Harvard University Press 2005.
7 T Mun, *England's Treasure by Forraign Trade* (1664). New York: Augustus M. Kelley 1986, p. 74. As we will see later this text was actually written in the 1620s but not published until almost 40 years later when Holland and England were about to go to war again (the Second Anglo–Dutch War started in 1665).
8 W Petty, *The Political Atonomy of Ireland* (1691). Here cited from *The Economic Writings of Sir William Petty*, vol. 1, Cambridge, UK: Cambridge University Press 1899, p. 250.
9 H Robinson, *Briefe Consideraions Concerning the Advancement of Trade and Navigation*. London: Matthew Simmons, Aldgate Street 1649, p. 6. Reprinted in L Magnusson (ed.), *Mercantilist Theory and Practice: The History of British Mercantilism*, vol. I, London: Pickering & Chatto 2008, pp. 165f.
10 M Decker, *An Essay on the Causes of the Decline of the Foreign Trade*, (1751 4th ed.). New York: Augustus M. Kelley 1973, p. 109.
11 J Child, *Brief Observations Concerning Trade and Interest of Money*. London: Elizabeth Calwert 1668, p. 3.
12 N Barbon, *A Discourse of Trade*. London: Tho. Milbourn 1690, preface.
13 W Temple, *Observations Upon the United Provinces of the Netherkands* (1673). Cambridge, UK: Cambridge University Press 1932, pp. 128f.
14 Temple, p. 131.
15 Unkown author, *Britannia Languens or a Discourse of Trade*. London: Tho. Dring 1680, pp. 73f.
16 Temple, p. 129.
17 Temple, p. 131.
18 Mun, pp. 73f.
19 J Child, *A Discourse of the Nature, Use and Advantages of Trade*. London: Edmund Bohun 1694, pp. 8f.
20 J Child, *A New Discourse of Trade*. London: Edmund Bohun 1693, p. 93.
21 C Davenant, *An Essay Upon the Probable Methods of Making a People Gainers in the Ballance of Trade*. London: James Knapton 1699, p. 6.
22 C Davenant, *An Essay on the East India Trade*. London 1697. Cited from *The*

Political and Commercial Works of that Celebrated Writer Charles D'Avenant, vol. I, London: R Horsfield 1771, p. 86.

23 L Roberts, *The Treasure of Traffike or a Discourse of Foraign Trade.* London 1641, p. 55.

24 M Postlethwyat, *Britain's Commercial Interest Explained and Improved*, vol. I, London: D Browne *et al.* 1757, pp. ix, 2.

25 Postlethwyat, II, p. 347.

26 C Davenant, *Discourse on the Public Revenues and on Trade, Part II* (1698). Cited from *The Political and Commercial Works of that Celebrated Writer Charles D'Avenant*, vol. I, London: R Horsfield 1773, p. 350.

27 J Gee, *The Trade and Navigation of Great Britain Considered.* London: A Bettlesworth and C Hitch 1729, p. xxxiv.

28 Gee, p. xxxiv.

29 *Britannia Languens*, p. 465. (In J R McCulloch (ed.), *Classical Writings on Economics*, vol. I, London: William Pickering 1995.)

30 Mun, pp. 9f.

31 H Robinson, *England's Safety in Trade Encrease.* London: Nicholas Bourne 1641, p. 49.

32 E F Heckscher, *Mercantilism*, vol. II, London: Routledge 1994, p. 317: 'In spite of the mercantilists' static outlook on economic affairs and the economic system of the world as a whole, they tried with a fanatic zeal to secure, each for his native country, as large as possible a share in the activities of this system, which was regarded as an unchangeable total'.

33 J Child, *A New Discourse of Trade.* London: n.p. 1693, preface.

34 H Robinson, *Briefe Considearions Concerning the Advancement of Trade and Navigation.* London: Matthew Simmons 1649, p. 1. Reprinted in L Magnusson (ed.), *Mercantilist Theory and Practice: The History of British Mercantilism,* vol. I, London: Pickering & Chatto 2008, pp. 165f.

35 Robinson, p. 2.

36 S Fortrey, *England's Interest and Improvement*, London: Nathanael Brook 1773, p. 16.

37 On this see Hont, p. 185f.

38 Postlethwayt, I, p. 2.

39 Postlethwayt, I, p. 3

40 Hont, p. 155f.

41 See further below p. 190.

42 On free trade imperialism and its relation to English political economy, see B Semmel, *The Rise of Free Trade Imperialism Classical Political Economy the Empire of Free Trade and Imperialism 1750–1850.* Cambridge, UK: Cambridge University Press 1970.

43 S Reinert, 'Introduction'. In: A Serra, *A Short Treatise on the Wealth and Poverty of Nations* (1613). London and New York: Anthem Press 2011, p. 65.

44 H Martyn, *Considerations Upon the East-India Trade.* London: A and J Churchill 1701, p. 67.

45 More on this in Hont, pp. 60f.

46 A Calabria, *The Cost of Empire: The Finances of the Kingdom of Naples in the Time of Spanish Rule.* Cambridge, UK: Cambridge University Press 1991.

47 R Villari, *The Revolt of Naples.* Cambridge, UK: Polity Press 1993.

48 On the life of A Serra and the history of his tract, see S Reinert, 'Introduction', pp. 9f. Also see T Hutchison, *Before Adam Smith: The Emergence of Political Economy 1662–1776.* Oxford: Blackwells 1988, pp. 19f.

49 F List, *National System of Political Economy.* Philadelphia, PA: J H Lippincott 1856, p. 410.

50 For example C Perrotta, *Produzione e lavore prodduttivo. Nel mercantilismo e nell' illuminismo Galatina.* Lecce 1988, pp. 110ff. Also L Magnusson, *The Tradition of Free Trade.* London: Routledge 2004.

51 Schumpeter, pp. 162f. For a longer list see S Reinert, 'Introduction', pp. 33ff.

52 G Botero, *The Reason of State* (1589). London: Routledge & Kegan Paul 1956, p. 150.

53 Botero, p. 145.

54 Botero, p. 143.

55 On this see Hutchison, *Before Adam Smith*, pp. 19f.

56 Although it is impossible to trace to what extent this discussion affected the standpoints taken in the early 1620s' controversy in England, it must at least be pointed out that Mun was well acquainted with Italy. He seems in fact to have lived there for some time. See further Chapter 5.

57 F Venturi, 'Alle origini dell illuminismo napoletano'. *Revista storica italiana*, vol. LXXI: 3 (1959).

58 On Genovesi see for example S Reinert, *Translating Empire*, 2011. Also I Hont, *Jealousy of Trade*, 2005.

59 S Reinert, *Translating Empire.*

60 T W Hutchison, pp. 254ff. See also F Ceserano, 'Monetary Theory in Ferdinando Galiani's Della Moneta'. *History of Political Economy*, vol. VIII: 3 (1976).

61 On this discussion see S L Kaplan, *Bread, Politics and Political Economy in the Reign of Louis XV.* (2nd ed.). London: Anthem Press 2012, ch. 4.

62 On anti-Physiocratism, see S Reinert, *Translating Empire*, pp. 177f.

63 See C Perrotta, 'Early Spanish mercantilism: the first analysis of underdevelopment'. In: L Magnusson (ed.), *Mercantilist Economics.* Boston, MA: Kluwer 1993.

64 A E Monroe, *Monetary Theory before Adam Smith.* Cambridge, MA: Harvard University Press 1923, p. 53; Also Perrotta, p. 8.

65 On the price revolution and its effects on the Spanish economy, consult D Fisher, 'The price revolution: a monetary interpretation'. *The Journal of Economic History*, vol. IL: 4 (1989), pp. 883–902, who provides a short summary of the discussion, which started with the seminal contribution by E J Hamilton, *American Treasure and the Price Revolution in Spain, 1501–1650* Harvard Economic Studies, 43. Cambridge, MA: Harvard University Press, 1934.

66 E Philips, *An Appeal to Common Sense: Or Some Considerations Offer'd to Restore Publick Credit.* London: T Warner 1720, p. 2.

67 On Oeriz, see Perrotta, p. 23.

68 Perrotta, p. 23.

69 *Memorial del Contador Louis de Ortiz a Felipe II* (1558). Ed. Manuel Fernandez Alvarez. *Anales de Economia*, vol. VII (1957). See also Perrotta, p. 23; Schumpeter, p. 165.

70 Perrotta. On Mata see M G Moreno, 'Francisco Martinez de Mata (Siglo XVII): Agitador social y economist de la decadencia'. *eXtoikos*, no. 5, 2012.

71 On Uztáriz, see R F Durán, *Gerónomi de Uztáriz (1670–1732). Una Poitica Econonómica para Felipe V.* Madrid: Minerva Eiciones 1999.

72 Durán, pp. 21f.

73 E F Heckscher, *Mercantilism*, vol. II, London: George Allen & Unwin 1955, pp. 84, 104ff.

74 For a general characterisation, see H Hauser, *Les Débuts du Capitalisme.* Paris: Libraire Félix Alcan 1931; P Deyon, *Le Mercantilisme.* Paris, France: Flammarion 1969; C W Cole, *French Mercantilist Doctrines before Colbert*, vols I–II, New York: Richard R Smith 1931 and 1939.

75 For a description, see C W Cole, vol. I, ch. 1.

76 A de Montchrétien, *Traicté de l'oeconomie politique* [1615]. (Ed. Funck-Bretatano 1889). Gèneve: Slatkine Reprints 1970, p. 23.

77 For this connection, see H Hauser's introduction to *La Reponse de Jean Bodin a M. de Malestroict*. Paris: Armand Colin 1932. For a general presentation of Bodin, see N O Keohane, *Philosophy and the State in France*. Princeton: Princeton University Press 1980, chs 4–6.

78 See above p. 67.

79 J Bodin, *Discours de Jean Bodin sur le rehaussement et diminution des monnoyes tant d'or que d'argent et le moyen d'y remedier, et responce aux paradoxes de M. de Malestroict*. Paris, France 1568.

80 H Hauser, *La Response de Jean Bodin a M. de Malestroict* [1568]. Paris, France: Armand Collin 1932, p. 32.

81 *Response de Jean Bodin*, p. 34.

82 *Response de Jean Bodin*, p. 36.

83 J Bodin, *Les Six Livres de la Republique* [1589]. Paris, France 1986, pp. 875ff. Also *La Response de Jean Bodin a M. de Malestroict*, pp. 36ff.

84 On Laffemas, see C W Cole, *French Mercantilist Doctrines Before Colbert*, vol. I, ch. 2; Hauser, *Le Débuts du Capitalisme*, ch. 5.

85 Cole, I, p. 93.

86 For a full account of the work of this commission, see Cole, I, pp. 92ff.

87 J-A Blanqui, *History of Political Economy in Europe*. London: G Bell & Sons 1880, p. 269.

88 Laffemas's six tracts on commerce from 1600 published together with his *L'incredulité ou l'ignorance de ceux qui ne veulant cognoistre le bien & repos de l'estat & veoir renaistre la vie heureuse des Francais*. Paris, France 1600.

89 B de Laffemas, *Les trésors et richesses pour mettre l'estat en splendeur et monstrer au vray la ruine des francois par le trafic et négoce des estrangers...* Paris, France: Estienne Preousteau 1598, pp. 6ff.

90 Cole, I, p. 68.

91 For an account of de Montchrétien's life and works see the foreword by T Funck Brentano to the 1889 edition of *Traicté de l'oeconomie politique*. Geneva, Switzerland: Slatkine Reprints 1970.

92 See W J Ashley, 'Montchrétien' in his *Surveys: Historic and Economic*. London: Longmans 1900, pp. 263f. Also Hutchison, pp. 263f.

93 See J-C Perrot, *Une histoire intellectuelle de l'economie politique*. Paris, France: EHESS 1992, pp. 64ff.; Keohane, pp. 163ff.

94 De Montchrétien, *Traicté de l'oeconomie politique*, p. 161.

95 De Montchrétien, p. 165.

96 De Montchrétien, p. 241.

97 Cole, I, p. 115.

98 De Montchrétien, p. 23.

99 See the notification by Cole, I, p. 146 n. 6 that he here uses almost identical words to Bodin.

100 De Montchrétien, p. 240.

101 De Montchrétien, p. 240.

102 De Montchrétien, p. 65. See Perrot, pp. 64ff. N Panichi is mainly interested in the poetic works of de Montchrétien in her *Antoine de Montchrétien. Il Circolo dello Stato*. Milan, Italy: Guerine 1989. See also Keohane, *Philosophy and the State in France*, pp. 163ff.

103 Hutchison, p. 88.

104 M Isenmann, 'War Colbert ein Merkantilist?' In: M Isenmann (hg), *Merkantilismus. Wiederaufnahme einer Debatte*. Stuttgart, Germany: Franz Steiner Verlag 2014.

105 On Richeliu, see H Hauser, *La Penseée et l'action economiques du Cardinal Richeliu*. Paris, France: Presses Universitaires de France 1944. See also Cole, I, ch. 1, etc.

106 More of this in S Reinert, *Translating Empire*, ch. 3.

107 *Economistes Financiers du dix-huiteme siecle*, Geneva, Switzerland: Slatkine Reprints 1971, pp. 781ff.; J Bouzinac, 'Les Doctrines Economiques au XVIIIme siècle. Jean-Francois Melon'. Diss, Université de Toulouse 1906, pp. 27ff.

108 M Dutot, *Reflexions Politiques sur Les Finances et Le commerce* [1738]. Reprinted in *Economistes financiers du dix-hutieméme siecle*. Geneva, Switzerland: Slatkine Reprints 1971, p. 902.

109 J-F Melon, *Essai politique sur le commerce* [1734]. Reprinted in *Economistes financiers du dix-huitiéme siecle*, p. 669.

110 Melon, p. 703.

111 Melon, p. 707.

112 Schumpeter rejected this. See his *A History of Economic Analysis*, p. 293.

113 Hutchinson, pp. 100ff.; G Faccarello, *Aux orgines de l'économie politique libérale: Pierre de Boisguilbert*. Paris, France: éditions anthropos 1986, e.g. pp. 35ff., 113ff. See also T Horne, *The Social Thought of Bernard Mandeville: Virtue and Commerce in Early Eighteenth-century England*. London: Macmillan 1978.

114 K Marx, *A Contribution to the Critique of Political Economy* (1859). Chicago, IL: Charles H. Kerr & Company 1913, pp. 54f.

115 Palgrave Dictionary: Cameralism. For a longer version of the following pages, see Lars Magnusson, 'Is Mercantilism a Useful Concept Still?'. In Moritz Isenmann (Hg.), *Merkantilismus. Wiederaufnahme einer Debatte*. Stuttgart: Franz Steiner Verlag 2014.

116 W Roscher, *Geschichte der National-Oekonomik in Deutschland*. Munich, Germany: R. Oldenbourg 1874, pp. 219f.

117 Schmoller, p. 76.

118 For a general treatment of the 'cameralistic school', see A Small, *The Cameralists*. Chicago, IL: University of Chicago Press 1909; E Dittrich, *Die deutschen und österreichischen Kameralisten*. Darmstadt, Germany: Wissenschaftliche Buchgesellschaft 1974; K Zielenziger, *Die alten deutschen Kameralisten*. Jena, Germany 1914; G Marchet, *Studien über die Entwicklung der Verwaltungslehre in Deutschland*. Munich, Germany 1885; W Roscher, *Geschichte der National-Oekonomik in Deutschland*. Munich, Germany: R Oldenbourg 1874; K Tribe, *Governing Economy*. Cambridge, UK: Cambridge University Press 1988.

119 Small, *The Cameralists*, p. 1f.

120 Small, pp. viii, xiii, 3, 4.

121 Tribe, p. 11.

122 Wakefield, pp. 20f., 25.

123 See for example older scholars such as Axel Nielsen, who obstinately attempted to see a tradition stemming directly from Aristotle up to eighteentheighteenth-century Cameralism, in *Die Entstehung der deutschen Kameralwissenschaft im 17 Jahrhunderts* (1911). Frankfurt am Main, Germany: Verlag Sauer & Auberman 1966, pp. 63f.

124 Roscher, p. 237f.

125 See J Bruckner, *Staatswissenschaften, Kameralismus und Naturrecht*. Munich, Germany: Verlag C H Beck 1977, p. 29: 'die innenpolitischen Sicherheit des Staates als Conservierung der landfurstlichen Hoheit'.

126 For a discussion of the *policey* concept, see Bruckner; P Preu, *Polizeibegriff und Staatszwecklehre*. Göttingen, Germany: Verlag Otto Schwartz & Co 1983; K Wolzendorff, *Der Polizeigedanke der modernen Staats* [1918]. Aalen, Germany: Scientia Verlag 1964.

127 Wolzendorff, p. 14.
128 A Tautscher, *Geschichte der deutschen Finanzwissenschaft bis zum Ausgang des 18. Jh., in Handbuch des Finanzwissenschaft* (hrsg von W Gerloff u F Neumark). Tübingen, Germany 1952, p. 411.
129 The full title reads: *Johann Heinrich Gottlobs von Justi Staatswirtschaft, oder systematische Abhandlung aller Oekonomischen und Cameral-Wissenschaften, die zur Regierung eines Landes erfordert werden.* Leipzig, Germany 1755. See E Nokkala, *The Political Thought of J.H.G von Justi.* Leiden, The Netherlands: Brill forthcoming.
130 Cited from Small, *The Cameralists*, p. 330.
131 See Dittrich, *Die deutschen und österriechischen Kameralisten*, p. 105.
132 J von Sonnenfels, *Grundsätze der Policey-, Handlung- und Finanz* [1765]. 5th ed., 1787, vol. I, preface.
133 On Galiani, see above p. 66.
134 Schumpeter, p. 178ff.; Hutchison, pp. 298f.
135 For both of these, see Hutchison, pp. 17f., 254ff. In his monetary treatise from 1588 Davanzati strongly emphasised 'the fundamental nature of an economy as rooted in mutuality' (p. 17) and a subjective origin of price and value. Montanari (1633–87) followed largely in this tradition. For him, 'Money served as a measure of desires.... The values of goods were raised by scarcity and lowered by abundance ... not in absolute terms, but relative to human needs, desires and valuations' (pp. 254f.).
136 O Langholm, *Price and Value in the Aristotelian Tradition.* Bergen, Norway: Universitetsforlaget 1979, p. 144.
137 Cited from Hutchinson, p. 299.
138 Roscher, *Geschichte der National-Oekonomik in Deutschland*, pp. 183ff.
139 See Roscher, pp. 187ff.
140 Roscher, pp. 190ff.
141 T Simon, 'Merkantilismus und Kameralismus. Zur Tragfähigkeit der Merkantilismus Begriffs und seiner Abgrenzung zum deutschen Kameralismus'. In: M Isenmann, *Merkantilismus*, pp. 69, 77f. Simon distinguishes between an English *Handelsorientierter* and a *Produktionsorientierter Merkantilismus* (which then most certainly also should include Serra, Montchrétien and the Spaniards).
142 Roscher, pp. 219ff., 236f.
143 Roscher, pp. 219ff.
144 Roscher, p. 289.
145 On Seckendorff, see Roscher, pp. 238ff.; Small, pp. 60ff.
146 Small, p. 69.
147 Small, p. 69.
148 Roscher, p. 241.
149 The explicit reference to *Volkes Wohlfart* is in his second book, *Der Christen Staat* [1685]. For the reference see Roscher, p. 242. However, he also discusses welfare in ch. 8 of the second book of *Furstenstaat*.
150 For a longer description of this book, see Small, pp. 63ff.
151 Roscher, p. 247.
152 Roscher, p. 248.
153 Roscher, pp. 270f.
154 On Becher, see especially L Sommer, 'Die Österreichischen Kameralisten, II'. (Diss) Vienna, Austria 1925, pp. 1–78; H Hassinger, 'J J Becher 1635–82. Ein Beitrag zur Geschichte der Merkantilismus'. (Diss.) Vienna, Austria 1951; Roscher, pp. 270ff.; Small, pp. 107ff.; Dittrich, pp. 58ff.
155 J J Becher, *Politische Discurs von den eigentlichen Ursachen des Auf- und Abnehmens der Städt, Länder und Republicken...* Frankfurt 1668, p. 50.

156 J J Becher, p. 44. I have used Small's translation here, p. 113.

157 Becher, p. 77. Translation by Small, p. 114.

158 Becher, p. 2: 'Je volckreicher ein Stadt ist, je mächtiger ist sie auch'.

159 For Sweden see L Magnusson, 'Mercantilism and reform mercantilism: The rise of economic discourse in Sweden during the eighteenth century'. *History of Political Economy*, vol. XIX: 3 (1987). For Denmark, see for example K G-E Oxenboell, *Studier i dansk merkantilisme*. Copenhagen, Denmark: Akademisk Forlag 1983.

160 Cited from Becher's *Psychosophia oder Seelenweisheit* (1707) by Roscher, p. 278. 'Freiheit in Zu und Ausfuhr der Waaren, wenig oder keine Imposten darauf, dass sich ein Jeder mal erhrilichen nähren, wie er kann und weiss, und sich in Wohnung, Kleider und Trank möge seinen Willen nach betragen'.

161 Roscher, p. 278.

162 Becher, *Politische Discurs*, p. 25: 'Monopolium verhindert die Populosität, das Polypolium die Nahrung, das Propolium die Gemeinschaft'.

163 Roscher, pp. 277f.

164 Roscher, pp. 275f.

165 Becher, *Politische Discurs*, p. 2.

166 Roscher, p. 276.

167 See for example Dittrich, p. 58.

168 Roscher, p. 289.

169 On von Hörnigk, see Sommer, II, pp. 124ff.; Roscher, pp. 287ff.; K Zielenziger, 'P W von Hörnigk', *Encyclopedia of the Social Sciences*. New York: Macmillan 1951; Dittrich, pp. 66ff. and most recent E Reinert, *How Rich Countries Got Rich … and Why Poor Countries Stay Poor*. London & Constable 2007, pp. 95f., 313f.

170 P W von Hörnigk, *Oesterreich über alles wann es nur will* [1684]. Leipzig, Germany 1707.

171 von Hörnigk, p. 25.

172 von Hörnigk, p. 32.

173 von Hörnigk, pp. 70, 222.

174 von Hörnigk, pp. 33ff.

175 Roscher, p. 292.

176 On von Schröder, see Sommer, II, pp. 79ff.; Small, pp. 135ff.; Marchet; Zielenziger, pp. 33ff.; Dittrich, pp. 62ff.; Roscher, pp. 294ff.

177 Roscher, p. 294.

178 Roscher, p. 294.

179 W F von Schröder, *Furstliche Schatz- und Rent-Cammer…* 1686, ch 1.

180 Roscher, p. 295.

181 von Schröder, ch. xxix, p. 3: 'Das Land wird so viel reicher, als entweder aus der Erden, oder anderswoher Geld oder Gold in's Land gebraucht wird, uns so viel ärmer, als Geld hinausstauft'.

182 von Schröder, ch. xvii, p. 11: '… durch die Verwecheselung des Geldes wird so viel Menschen die Nahrung multipliziert und Handel und Wandel im Schwange behalten'.

183 von Schröder, ch. xlii.

184 For this reason E Dittrich's summary statement seems far from the record (p. 124).

185 On the population issue, see C E Stangeland, *Pre-Malthusian Doctrines of Population* [1904]. New York: Augustus M Kelley 1966, pp. 187ff.

4   The favourable balance of trade

Since Smith it has been emphasised that the 'favourable balance of trade' performs a key role in the formation of a specific mercantilist discourse. According to Smith – as we saw – it served as the theoretical core of Mercantilism, as both a system of thought and practice. As already stated such a position is untenable for a number of reasons. First, as we shall see, this 'doctrine' varied with different writers. Second, it appears in different shapes and contexts in different parts of Europe, and it is unlikely that it was interpreted and understood everywhere in the same way. Third, at least in England, it changed in emphasis and language over time. Hence, at the end of the seventeenth century it had developed into a 'labour balance' or 'foreign paid income' doctrine quite different from earlier versions. Fourth, the idea of a surplus of money or bullion as the key to wealth and power is hardly substantiated by a thorough reading of the relevant contemporary literature.

Admittedly, however, the notion of a favourable balance of trade fitted very well into what we have insisted upon was the kernel of Mercantilism: a series of discourses in Early Modern Europe pointing to the pivotal role played by commerce and trade for power and plenty. Was it thus mainly a metaphor describing the workings of a contemporary mercantile economy, as Bruno Surviranta long ago suggested, something 'good to think with' in the sense that it focussed on the role of foreign trade and commerce for national economic growth and development?[1] The argument here is that it was something more than that. By focussing on the balance of trade economic, writers in the seventeentht and eighteenth centuries sought to find an answer to how the economy worked and how the wealth of a nation could be achieved. In this instance the phrase was historically bound to a specific historical context. However, at the same time, it was involved in a process through which a new language of economics developed – as we will se in the next chapters – that transcended the very notion of its subject matter.

The creation of wealth

In 1930 Viner published his very influential essay on trade theories before Smith. In this article, Viner supported Smith's basic thesis that the main fallacy of the mercantilists had been their identification of money and bullion with wealth. In order to provide factual evidence to support this thesis he cited a number of mercantilist writers who he thought had fallen victim to such a Midas fallacy: Malynes, Misselden, Mun, R Coke, Fortrey, Charles Reynel, Pollexfen and others.[2] He admitted that it was mainly the 'extreme' mercantilist who had made the mistake to identify gold with wealth. But he nevertheless insinuated that Mercantilism, at its core, was a doctrine which honoured 'precious metals as the sole constituents of the wealth of the nation'.[3]

However, this interpretation has been challenged by many.[4] Before Viner, Suviranta for example had been explicit on this point: 'there is no reason to suppose that the wildest mercantilists ever suffered from this delusion ... (t)he mere existence of the fable of Midas was a sufficient safeguard'.[5] Heckscher took a middle position when he, on the one hand, stated that the mercantilists were not so 'absurd' that they propounded 'that there could be no economic value apart from money'. However, he suggested in opposition to himself that they believed 'that money and wealth are equal or something very similar'.[6]

In order to clear up the fog that encircles this issue we must acknowledge that most economic writers, especially between 1620 and 1690, believed that a net inflow of money or bullion was of *special* benefit which could increase the wealth of the Commonwealth. However, there is no indication at all that they, as Schumpeter said, 'confused money with what money can buy'.[7] To this extent the quotations provided by Viner do not provide conclusive proof at all. Most of them are taken out of context and often mean something quite different than Viner suggests.[8]

Hence, as Schumpeter emphasised, among most writers of this period 'wealth was defined ... much as we define it ourselves'.[9] Most certainly, a majority would have agreed with Davenant's dictum that:

> Gold and Silver are indeed the Measure of Trade, but that the Spring and Original of it, in all Nations, is the Natural or Artificial Product of the Country; that is to say, what this Land or what this Labour and Industry produces.[10]

Moreover, they would have felt in concordance with Davenant when he pointed out: 'Industry and skill to improve the advantages of soil and situation, are more truly riches to a people, than even the possession of gold and silver mines'.[11]

Further, for example, Temple believed that the ground of riches was in 'the general Industry and Parsimony of a people'[12] and Fortrey regarded that 'England's Interest and Improvement consists chiefly in the increase of store and trade'.[13] According to Barbon the wealth of a nation lay in the wealth of its people. The inhabitants of a country could only be made rich by 'Industry, Art and Traffick'. Moreover, as he said,

> By Industry and Art the Minerals are dug out of the earth, and made useful: the land made more fertile…. And from the profit of this increase of Stock, the People are paid for their Time, Art and Industry, which makes such Inhabitants Rich.[14]

Furthermore, in the early eighteenth century, the author of the famous tract *Considerations on the East-India Trade* (John Martyn?[15]) outrightly said that 'Bullion is only secondary and dependant, Cloaths and Manufactures are real and Principal Riches'[16]. In this context William Wood also filled in:

> [T]here is scarce any Man, not disabled by Nature or accident, but may by Industry and Pains, earn *more* than would supply his Necessities; and so much as any man gets *more* by being truly Industrious above *that*, so much he enriches himself and Family.[17]

However, it is wrong to assume that such 'anti-bullionist views only belonged to a later period. Mun stated much of the same already in his first tract from 1621: 'that the riches or sufficiencie: of every Kingdome, State or Common-wealth, consisteth in the possession of those things, which are needful for a civill life'.[18] And in his *England's Treasure by Forraign Trade* he remarked:

> For what greater glory and advantage can any powerful Nation have, than to be thus richly and naturally possessed of all things needful for Food, Rayment, War, and peace, not onely for its own plentiful use, but also to supply the wants of other Nations, in such a measure, that much money may be thereby gotten yearly, to make the happiness compleat.[19]

Moreover, the view that Peter Chamberlen, the physician nowadays most known for his attacks on London midwives for their alleged ignorance, propounded in his plea for more help to the poor in 1649 in *The Poor Man's Advocate* that 'the Wealth and Strength of all Countries are in the poore; for they do all the great and necessary workes, and they make up the maine body and strength of Armies' was without doubt shared by most at this time.[20]

We can thus safely draw the conclusion that the 'error' of confusing money with wealth seems not to appear in the main body of mercantilist literature at all. Not even in the tract *Britannia Languens* (1680), mentioned in earlier chapters, as a matter of fact – which Schumpeter wrongly stated. This exception to the rule Schumpeter explained away by referring to the 'poor performance' of the author and that all 'schemes of thought' have a tendency to produce 'freaks' once in a while.[21] However, already from the outset the author of *Britannia Languens* (Petyt?) makes it very clear that he will only deal with the form of 'National Gain' which was brought forward 'by Forreign Trade'. His silence on other forms of national gain does not, of course, exclude his possible perception that riches and wealth could consist also in things other than money and bullion.[22] And although he insisted that 'Poverty is but the privation of Treasure', he in fact at the same time stressed that increased treasure can only be achieved by the 'industry of the people'. And he said: 'People are therefore in truth the chiefest, most fundamental, and precious commodity, out of which be derived all sorts of Manufactures, Navigation, Conquests, and solid Dominion'.[23]

Economic writers at the time generally spoke of two forms of national 'riches': 'natural' and 'artificial'. Thus in typical fashion Mun remarked that natural riches 'proceedeth of the Territorie it self' and the other form 'dependenth on the industry of the Inhabitants'.[24] For Roberts the 'riches of an estate or nation' consisted in 'naturall' and 'arificiall' commodities or wares and in the 'profitable use and distribution, of both by Commerce and Traffike'. Under the title 'naturall commodities', he comprehended 'such wares ... as either the earth naturally & originally afford, or such as by the labour of land is brought forth'. As 'artificiall wares and commodities' of a country he particularly alluded to 'the manufactories of all commodities'.[25]

By and large this distinction was kept by many other writers on similar topics.[26] Besides showing that most of them did *not* define money as the sole form of wealth or riches, this distinction is also important from another point of view. Thus although most mercantilist writers put trade and manufactures in the forefront, they did not altogether neglect the importance of 'naturall' riches. On the contrary, several spoke of the important role of a well-organised agriculture for increased wealth and trade. From this point of view the general picture of Mercantilism as totally nonchalant towards agriculture – and as such the antithesis of the 'agricultural system' of the Physiocratic school later on – gives the wrong impression. Thus for example Roberts over several pages in his *The Treasure of Traffike* (1641) addressed the question how the natural riches of the kingdom should be improved, including agriculture. Although the 'riches of the earth' were 'the fountaine and mother of all the riches and abundance of the world', they were most often utterly neglected. Thus, further according to Roberts, landlords and husbands must:

> take the paines, either by industry, improvement and care, to increase those their demesnes and estates, either by planting, cleansing, or manuring a waste or barren piece of ground, or by drayning a marshy bogge, or the like, and thus to inrich themselves by a faire advancement of their own.[27]

Postlethwayt (usually considered a typical mercantilist), fifty years later, would be even more explicit on this issue when he wrote:

> Every essential object of traffic and commerce, requisite to the sustenance and convenience of human life being produced by the earth, the more our land in general shall be improved, and the greater quantity thereof shall be beneficially cultivated, the greater will be the plenty of land productions amongst the people.[28]

Hence for most writers 'wealth' or 'riches' consisted of material objects capable of satisfying our 'external happiness'.[29] They were brought forward and increased by means of labour, art and industry. Quite apart from that, money was regarded as wealth in the form of a store of value – 'the Wealth of this Kingdom in general, as the Money therof' of which Petty spoke.[30]

Instead money or bullion most often was identified as 'treasure' by economic writers.[31] Sometimes they would also talk about 'the stock of money'[32] or the 'National Stock of Treasure'.[33] An extreme example we find in the periodical *The British Merchant*, where the concept 'capital stock of bullion' was used.[34] Also the concept 'riches' and sometimes also 'wealth' was spoken of in terms of money or bullion. This is clearly so with for example Mun, Cary, Pollexfen and Decker.[35]

However, it is most probable that they also would label other items which create 'external happiness' as 'wealth'. Some were clearly explicit in this respect. Thus, for example, Child, Davenant, Temple, Wood and Barbon – as well as Dudley North and Hume – would include more than money or bullion as 'wealth' or 'riches'.[36] Furthermore, Barbon warned for the false 'supposition ... that Gold and Silver are the only Riches'.[37] Also Child was aware that money itself was not wealth but rather that 'Gold and silver [was] being taken for the measure and standard of riches'.[38]

Hence, the concepts 'riches' and 'wealth' referred interchangeably to money and/or to other items as well. Sometimes an author was apt to use both references in the same text. Hence Mun in *A Discourse of Trade* (1621) spoke of wealth as 'ready money', whereas a little later on he stated that 'the riches or sufficiency of every Kingdome, State or Commonwealth, consisteth in the possession of those things, which are needful for a civill life'.[39] Lastly, 'stock' could sometimes also be used in order to designate a 'stock of money'. Most often, however, authors would mean something more specific when they used the concept of 'stock'. As this usage is crucial in order to better understand the balance of trade doctrine, we will return to it in a short while.

Definitions of this kind have caused much confusion among those interpreters who seek coherence in 'mercantilist doctrines'. First, we must take account of the 'language' problems that appear when we seek to translate seventeenth-century usages of words into our current vocabulary. As Rashid has pointed out, concepts like wealth and riches had a somewhat different meaning then than they have today. Hence concepts such as wealth or plenty and power were often used together in a confusing way. Postlethwayt even said that money was 'the sinews of commerce as well as war'.[40] Also, such a radical 'Tory free trader' as North would define 'wealth' as 'plenty', but also as 'bravery' and 'gallantry'.[41] Hence it is clear that before the nineteenthth century words which later on acquired meaning within a theoretical structure of economics still retained much of their 'non-economic' connotations. Obviously, no such coherent structure of an independent subject of economics had yet appeared, and thus economic writers during this period tended to use words and concept which sometimes carried highly ambiguous meanings for both themselves and their audiences.

Second, this ambiguity might also have underpinned the kind of analytical problems – stressed by Schumpeter – that haunted the discourse on economic issues up until the eighteenth century.[42] As Viner rightly pointed out, analytical 'error' is part of the intellectual history of any age and can surely not be explained away by referring only to a certain economic environment or the specific logic of a certain period, the 'intellectual climate' and so on.[43] However, such 'errors' must also be related to a specific conceptual and intellectual framework. Hence, as we will see, the economic discussion for example in England from the early seventeenth century onwards constituted a process in which new concepts and analytical tools were developed. They were utilised in order to understand the creation of wealth, the relation between production and want and between exchange and trade balances. It was in the form of end results of such intellectual processes that concepts like 'stock', 'wealth' and so on, gradually acquired well-defined connotations connected to a theoretical structure. Before this occurred, however, the concepts that writers used were equivocal perhaps mainly because they were not correlated to one specific discourse.

Hence, it is as difficult for this period to determine what writers meant when they used the concept of 'stock', as it is to interpret correctly the concepts of 'riches' or 'wealth'. Clearly, also this term was understood differently by various writers. Some seem to have defined 'stock' as some form of capital in monetary form. Others defined it more widely to include also what we today would call the National Product (GDP). Hence, in order to confuse matters further, for example Davenant talked of 'stock of wealth' as the 'superlucration arising' where the 'Annual income exceeds the Expence' (i.e growth of National Product).[44] Obviously he, as well as many other authors, had difficulties in drawing a clear distinction between stock and flow concepts. Without doubt this was also an important factor behind the confusion of how 'wealth' and 'riches' ought to be understood. Sometimes these concepts were used to denote an increase in money or the national income (flow) and at other times to describe a 'stock' of the same items.

Furthermore, as with 'stock' the concept 'national gain' would sometimes refer to the inflow of money made possible by a favourable balance of trade and sometimes to an increase of national income achieved by value-added exportation of worked up manufactured goods. For example, the account made by Gee in the early eighteenth century acutely illustrated the difficulty that many mercantilist writers had both with the phenomenon and conceptualisation of national income and expenditure. Gee presented a number of proposals in his book on how to increase the national profit by 'many Hundred thousand Pounds yearly'. First, he believed that the nation would gain 400 000 pounds through import substitution. For example, instead of wearing French woollens 'and other manufactures of France', English manufactures of 'fine Lace, velvets, silver and gold stuffs' should be encouraged. Second, he explained, 200 000 pounds may be gained by using 'Muslins and other fine Manufactures' from India rather than importing the same items from France. Third, Gee believed that 300 000 pounds might be saved by taking Hemp and Flax from the plantations, that is, the English colonies in northern America.[45]

So far, the gains Gee has spoken of were clearly related to a saving of bullion and can thus be regarded as logical from the point of view of a stylised favourable balance of trade standpoint. His suggestions how to increase the inflow of bullion such as in the above-mentioned case extended over several pages. However, in his calculus he also referred to another kind of 'profit', which he believed ought to be reaped for the benefit of the nation state. Thus he suggested, for example, that 400 000 pounds might be gained by Britain through 'Regulating our Trade from the Plantations … in obliging all Ships that come to Portugal, the Streights, & c. to come to England, and lay out their Money here'. Hence, he seemed to think that, through this regulative order, income and *demand* in the mother country would be raised by the same sum. Lastly, he calculated that 1 250 000 pounds might be gained: '

> Supplying the North of England, Scotland and Ireland with plenty of Hemp and Flax from our Plantations, would give Employment to a Million of People supposed to be now out of Work, allowing each earned one Penny a Day, and accounting 300 Working Days a Year. [46] (=1 250 000 pounds).

The example of Josiah Gee clearly portraits the analytical and conceptual problems which haunted early eighteenth-century writers when they discussed national income and wealth. Thus, how Gee's 'gains' in employment and demand might be added together with his saving or gains of bullion, made possible by import substitution in order to make up the yearly profit of the nation, is really not so easy to comprehend.[47]

* * *

In the next chapter we will see how the concept 'a favourable balance of trade' came to use in the discussions concerning the trade crisis in England after 1620. According to Suviranta the first author to 'almost' have formulated the concept was the officer of the Mint in London, Richard Ailesbury, in 1381. However, he did it in a negative way warning for an unfavourable balance: 'It must be ascertained that no more foreign merchandise come within the realm than the value of the merchandise of this country that goes out of the realm'.[48] Almost two hundred years later the anonymous author (perhaps Thomas Smith, see below Chapter 5 note 62) of the famous *Discourse of the Common Weal* (1581) made the following recommendation of exactly the same kind: 'we must always take hede that we bie no more of strangers than we sell them'.[49] In print the term 'balance of trade' appears first in the famous pamphlet discussion between Malynes, Misselden and Mun. Before that most probably it was used in the discussions within the group lead by Sir Lionel Cranfield.[50] Moreover, on 21 May 1615 he provided a report, which has the title 'balance of trade'.[51] Moreover, the year thereafter F Bacon uses the concept in a report of his own 'Advice to Sir George Villiers' (the Duke of Buckingham). He uses it in print the very first time in the third edition of his *Essays* (1625).[52] By then it was already a contested concept defined in a different fashion by the two sides in the pamphlet debate (see below p.133).

Still the economic literature in Britain dealing with trade, commerce, plenty and power during the rest of the seventeenth and up to the mid-eighteenth century would be pertinently centred around this long-lived concept of a balance of trade, the horrors of having a negative one and the benefits of an 'overplus' (a much more common word than 'favourable' in the literature). The orthodox view was for example formulated in a pamphlet from 1641:

> The Purchase and price of Lands in this Kingdome, doth rise and fall by no other ways and meanes (for the common benefit) then by the profit or losse which is made by the over or underbalance of our Forraigne Trade, that is to say, when we bring in and consume yearly a lesse value in Forraigne wares, than we export in our Owne Commodities, we may rest assured that the difference is brought in and doth remaine to us in so much Treasure.[53]

More than one hundred years later, Postlethwayt still formulated the phrase in its most simple form: 'The difference that results from the exports and imports during a certain time, compared, is called the balance of trade'.[54] One can wonder why it remained for so long. Was it once again merely because 'it was good to think with'? Against this background I will address some of the attempts that have been presented in order to interpret the concept 'favourable balance of trade'. As we will see, some of them are perhaps more relevant than others.

Money in the king's coffers

It can be stated firmly that very few English writers explicitly at least argued for the need to accumulate precious metals in order for the prince or state to have a financial reserve in liquid form. In fact, as also Viner noticed, there is hardly any mention at all of the king's treasure in this literature. Consequently, his enrichment is scarcely at all used as an argument for a favourable balance of trade.[55] Mun, however, seems to have been an exception to this rule. In *England's Treasure by Forraign Trade* he says that that a positive balance may 'enable the King to lay up the more Treasure out of his yearly incomes'.[56] However, the main favour a positive balance can create is an increase of the 'Kingdome's stock', he continues. Moreover, the prince should not lay more taxes on his subjects than the profit from the balance of trade would admit to: 'the gain of their Forraign Trade must be the rule of laying up their Treasure', he said.[57] Thus his message was clear: a ruler must be parsimonious with his treasure. If he takes out more taxes than the national gain will present him 'he shall not only Fleece, but Flea his subjects'.[58] Hence, the notion that the increase of taxes shall be held in check by the factual enlargement of the national income cannot to any extent be taken as proof that Mun regarded the enrichment of the king's treasure as a motive for a positive balance of trade. If the nation stock is enlarged by a favourable balance of trade, also the king can be a winner, but he is not the main gainer.

Beside a small number of authors mentioned by Viner,[59] the argument that a favourable balance of trade ought to enrich the king's treasure with bullion also appeared in *Britannia Languens* (1680). According to its author, the increase of treasure enabled the king to 'lay up mighty Stores' and build 'a great Fleet'. He looked with envy at the French king, who for this reason was able to withstand 'in a War with near 20 Princes and States'.[60] It was especially for the purposes of war that a great Treasure was required: 'if the National Treasure be much greater, it will support the charge of a War much longer'.[61]

In a more general form this view was certainly also shared by many other writers in Europe at the time. Indeed it was a leading theme that plenty and power were closely knit together during this period of intense competition for power and recognition. For example, the widespread expression that money or trade 'is the sinews of war'[62] certainly pointed in this direction. As we have seen, still in 1757 Postlethwayt used the expression that money was 'sinews of commerce *and* war'.[63] However, the increase of the king's treasure was only one contribution trade could bring in order to bolster national power and war. Also, a great trade would lead to the enlargement of a state's naval force as well as to an extended import of necessary provisions. Increased trade and treasure would also breed the very 'vehicles', according to the author of *Britannia Languens*, 'which carry out men of daring Spirits, might, Thought and Abilities into the Conquests of Forreign Countries'.[64] By a favourable balance of trade the nation would prosper and its population grow. Through foreign commerce, income rose and employment increased. However, only in a few cases was the argument explicitly used that the enlargement of the Crown's treasure was the main objective of a favourable balance of trade. Moreover, William Potter in 1650 argued for usage ('revolution') of money instead of hoarding as a means to achieve wealth in these terms: 'The Multiplication of Money amongst any People doth through the Revolution thereof draw in so much Commodity amongst them ... as their Estates in other things do soon exceed such multiplied stock of Moneys according to the aforesaid proportion'. He here argued against the ruler's wish to hoard money for their own use in order to carry out wars or for other puposes.[65]

The favour of inflation

Another suggestion has been that mercantilist writers supported a favourable balance of trade because they saw an advantage in higher prices.[66] The underlying theoretical foundation for this is of course the so-called specie–flow mechanism formulated by Hume and others during the mid-eighteenth century, which predicted that a trade surplus would lead to rising prices in the receiving country.[67] But as already Viner noticed, 'There were very few price inflationists among the English mercantilists'.[68] Most of the mercantilists, in fact, explicitly argued against higher prices. The contention was that high prices would imply diminished foreign demand and shrinking export shares. Thus it is clear that the principle of price elasticity was recognized by most mercantilist writers. For example in 1623, Misselden in his polemical tract against Malynes in 1623 had left his previous inflationism and now explicitly warned against too-high prices for English cloth (see Chapter 6). Thus the argument, he stated, 'That the Dutch could not subsist without our English cloth … is false'.[69] The same caution was repeated over and again in mercantilist literature. Mun for example thought that 'we must strive to sell as cheape as possible' when a high price might cause 'a less vent in the quantity'.[70] Furthermore, Davenant proposed that woollen manufactures in England should 'be wrought cheaply' in order 'to enable us to command the markets abroad'.[71] Also other authors such as Jacob Vanderlint, Decker and Locke insisted that low prices were to the advantage of England.[72] For example, Locke discussed the existence of different elasticities for separate wares in principal terms:

> By the like proportions of Increase and decrease, does the value of Things, more or less convenient, rise and fall in respect of Money, only with the difference, things absolutely **necessary** for Life must be had at any Rate; but Things **convenient** will be had only as they stand in preference with other Conveniences.[73]

It is indeed difficult to find writers who in principle would disagree with this. Certainly, Malynes and his followers argued for improved terms of trade and can thus to some point be said to have been inflationists. According to their view, more money in the country would lead to higher export prices, better terms of trade and more favourable exchange rates.[74] Likewise, Misselden in his first pamphlet, where the influence from monetarists such as Malynes was still clearly visible, stressed that 'it is much better for the Kingdome, to have things deare with plenty of Money, whereby men may live in their severall callings, then to have things cheape with want of money'.[75] However, in Misselden's case the argument for high prices was put in a context where he did not directly discuss the influence of prices on foreign demand. Thus it is not clear whether he in fact reflected upon the relationship between price levels and foreign demand at all. Perhaps he for some reason just forgot to connect these two variables. Whatever reason there might be, other authors as well have neglected to pay attention to this affiliation. Thus Fortrey, for example, was contented by stating that 'the only way to be rich, is to have plenty of that commodity to vent, that is of the greatest value abroad'. In this passage, he did not seem to consider that foreign demand had to be rather inelastic if the method to 'sell dear and buy cheap' would at all be applied.[76]

Perhaps as many have noted it is paradoxical that writers propagated for low prices while at the same time adhered to some version of the favourable balance of trade idea, even more so as most mercantilists were aware of the relationship between prices and the quantity of money. Many of them made explicit references to Bodin and recognised that an increased money supply would lead to a rise of domestic prices.[77] The idea that the inflow of precious metal from the Spanish colonies might lead to a rise of prices found exponents already among sixteenth-century writers. Hence the author of the already mentioned *A Discourse of the Common Weal of this Realm of England* (1581) wrote about the money: 'yt is the varietie and plenty thereof that maketh the price thereof base or high'.[78] Furthermore, in the 1620s, Mun stated that 'all men do consent that plenty of money in a Kingdom doth make the native commodities dearer'.[79] A half century later the author of *Britannia Languens* would fill in that 'the price of Home Commodities … will hold proportion with the quantity of the National Treasure; and will rise or fall as the Treasure does increase or diminish'.[80] Last, according to the stern supporter of a quantity theory of money Locke, there existed a certain 'proportion between … Money and Trade'. Hence if we should, he pointed out, withdraw half of our money stock this would most certainly lead to our 'Native Commodities' selling at half price.[81]

Hence, it seems clear that many writers of economic tracts in England during the seventeenth century supported low prices as well as acknowledged the relationship between a quantity of money and the domestic price level. But the question of course arises how they could still emphasise the need for more bullion in to the country.

Money as liquid assets

In his *Early British Economists* Max Beer particularly stressed that the *rationale* behind the favourable balance of trade 'doctrine' was the alleged need for more money in circulation. 'The contest for the balance of trade was a struggle for liquid assets', he said.[82] Thus the balance of trade formula was at heart an expression of the economical essentials of the time. As England had no silver or gold mines of its own it could only obtain bullion through a net surplus in its export affairs. Thus, according to such a line of argument, with an equal balance of commodities in value terms no gold and silver could be acquired. In order to procure such precious wares, instead, more other commodities must be exported than imported.[83]

Another often-formulated view in this context was that, *by itself*, an increase in the amount of money circulating in an economy served as a stimulus to trade and industry. An easy circulation was as necessary to trade as blood to a living organism, it was often said in contemporary texts (more on this later).[84] Hence a prosperous trade could only be achieved when there was an abundance of money in the country. This reasoning could at least find some support in Bacon's 'Of Seditions and Troubles' in his *Essays*: 'Money is like muck, not good except it be spread'.[85] Almost 150 years later, Postlethwayt would say the same thing in a more dull phrase: 'because it is certain that the nation's home circulation, and consequently procure a greater number of men the means of subsisting comfortably'.[86]

Hence, it became a highly appreciated goal to achieve more bullion. A representative exponent of such a view was the author of the pamphlet *England and East India Inconsistent in their Manufactures*:

> As it hath been Suggested that Gold and Silver is the only, or at least the most useful and best deserving to be called the Treasure of a Nation, and so necessary for the Carrying on of Commerce, that when even plenty of that fails, we may expect that Trade will in great measure fail also; so it may be affirmed that Bartering of Commodities cannot supply the want therof, because it cannot make any quick progress, neither can it be supplied by Credit, because Credit must have its Original and existence from an expectation or assurance of Money.[87]

Hence during this period many would certainly have agreed with for example Decker's dictum that 'Trade always languishes where Money is scarce',[88] or Locke's view of the 'necessity of a certain Proportion of Money to Trade'.[89] However, in reality it is difficult to find the argument spelled out that more money *in itself* quickened trade. From this point of view, Beer's position seems untenable for empirical reasons. In fact, if the need for liquid assets had been such a central issue for the stubborn preservation of the favourable balance of trade 'doctrine', we would have expected authors to be more explicit in this direction. But they were not, in fact. Locke as an example was much more concerned with speedier *circulation* of money than with an enlargement of its quantity. Thus he stated that a country might very well survive with a smaller stock of money as long as its circulation is increased.[90] Moreover, even earlier Mun seemed sceptical to the whole idea that much money in liquid form was necessary for trade. In *England's Treasure*, he remarked,

> Neither it is said that Mony is the Life of Trade, as if it could not subsist without the same; for we know that there was great trading by way of commutation of barter when there was little mony stirring in the world.[91]

Further, for example, Petty made it clear that there could be too much money as well as too little in a commonwealth. It is significance that he used the body metaphor to illustrate his argument: 'For Money is but the Fat of the Body-pollitick, whereof too much doth as often hinder its Agility, as too little makes it sick'.[92] 'The keeping or lessening of Money, is not of that consequence that many guess it to be of', was his further comment. Hence to double the cash money in a nation does not double its wealth. By this token wealth will remain the same although its monetary expression will be doubled.[93]

However, the importance of receiving more money in liquid form was sometimes also claimed with other arguments than that it merely contributed to an increased circulation. Hence, it was suggested during the seventeenth century that a net inflow of money implied an increase of purchasing power. For example, accordingly to *Britannia Languens* an increase of treasure would lead to people having more money in their pockets. This would enable the 'seller' to put out more wares to 'chapmen'. Furthermore, with their 'plenty of money', such chapmen could 'cause a higher and quicker Market for any desireable Commodity'.[94] Albeit the author might be recognised for his originality, he was not always very clear and precise. Thus he does not develop under which conditions more money might lead to increased demand. However, modern theory can without doubt show how inflation, if not too dramatic, can affect aggregate demand beneficially. Our author was certainly not far off the mark if it was this that he hinted at in this context.

A more frequent argument than this, however, often appeared to defend the favourable balance of trade doctrine. How such an alternative idea was developed by Mun has been especially pointed out by Gould.[95] Thus Mun in his *Englands's Treasure*, as well as in his memoranda during the trade crisis of the early 1620s, showed awareness of the close relationship between prices and export volumes. Further, he was attentive to that an import of bullion might lead to souring prices. Against this background, how could he still defend the favourable balance theory? It seems, however, Mun provided the adequate answer himself:

> [F]or all men do consent that plenty of mony makes wares dearer, so dear wares decline their use and consumption.... And although this is a very hard lesson for some great landed men to learn, yet I am sure it is a true lesson for all the land to observe, lest when wee have gained some store of mony by trade, wee lose it again by not trading with our mony.[96]

Certainly this passage can be understood in different ways. What Mun wanted to establish with the sentence 'by not trading with our mony', Gould argued, was that an inflow of bullion would not necessarily lead to a decline of export through a raised internal price level. But this required, according to Mun, that 'the increased stock of bullion was used as liquid capital to finance a greater volume of trade.[97] Obviously, Mun here seems to have identified money with circulating capital – to this we will return soon.

However, it is also possible to interpret Mun in an alternative way that perhaps better fits in with what others said during the same period. Thus, although Mun might have accepted the essentials of the specie–flow argument, he seems *not* to have accepted it as a weighty argument against the favourable balance 'theory'. Instead, he seems to have believed that without an inflow of bullion caused by a favourable balance, trade would stagnate and prices on land fall. The main cause was that trade and industry expanded faster than the velocity of money – the v in the quantity theory of money equation. Given this fact, a steady increase of money was necessary to keep up a certain amount of trade. Hence an increase of money would not have to imply rising prices. Instead, if it did not increase due to a favourable balance of trade, prices would tend to sink. Without doubt, in his text, Mun seems to hint at this possibility. Whether this interpretative framework reflected the reality of the prevailing economic conditions is of course a completely different matter.

It is interesting, however, to notice that the same basic idea also appeared elsewhere in seventeenth-century literature. Thus Vaughan in a treatise, the first which at length analysed the phenomenon of money after Malynes had presented his 'feats of bankers', pointed out that more bullion might be needed whenever the quantity of money did not increase in proportion to the rise of prices.[98] Thus in England a 'rarity of money' had appeared because the 'the things valued by them [i.e. money]' had increased in quantity faster than the quantity of money. This would in turn 'induce a Rarity and Scarcity of these Mettals'.[99] This view was also shared by Vanderlint at the beginning of the eighteenth century. In 1729 he noted with regard to the current situation in Britain: 'Cash amongst them in general is considerably diminish'd as least that it is not increased in Proportion to their Number, and the prices of things'.[100] Without doubt, the relevance of such a situation was the main reason why Vanderlint at the same time could propagate for the favourable balance of trade theory *and* at acknowledge what later has become known as the specie–flow mechanism.[101]

Another variant of this was to say that, if there was not enough money in gold and silver to meet an expansion of selling and buying of goods, bills of exchange might do the job. The role of bills of exchange, especially for the eastland trade in the Baltic waters, was pointed out by Heckscher in his critique of Wilson's insistence of the unique role played by precious metals.[102] The role of bills of exchange in this context was exemplified by Potter's plea for increasing the usage of bills of exchange in a pamphlet from 1650. In this case the full title of the tract says it all: The Trades-mans Jewel or a Safe, easie, speedy and effectual Means, for the incredible advancement of Trade and Multiplication of Riches, Without parting with Money, or any Stock out of their own hands: By making Bills to become current instead of Money, and frequently to revolve through their Hands, with as much Money as the Sums therein mentioned do amount to.[103]

The increase of the kingdom's stock

Another suggestion of Heckscher's was that for many economic writers ('perspicacious mercantilists', as he calls them in this context) money was perceived as a factor of production on the same footing as for example land. Further, according to him, this 'confusion' was easy to understand as capital and credit was always expressed in monetary form. To this might be added a specific historically conditioned factor. During this period most invested capital existed as circulating capital and not in the form of a real, physical capital stock. Hence the 'artificial wealth' or 'stock' which most mercantilists referred to was either bound up in storage of goods or existed as money or credit.[104]

However, as argued, mercantilist writers used concepts such as 'stock', 'the nation's stock' or 'the kingdom's stock' interchangeably in monetary or real terms. According to many writers 'stock' in real terms could only be enlarged if production in physical or value terms rose above consumption. Furthermore, 'stock' in monetary terms could only increase from a net foreign surplus originating from a favourable balance of trade. Or as Postlethwayt formulated it: 'when that balance is against a nation, its [*sic*] amount is a dimunition of the capital stock'.[105] Lastly, both 'surpluses' could be regarded as savings that in turn could be used to further increase the 'natural' and 'artificial' wealth of the nation.[106] That is to say, if gold and silver was not hoarded in the form of plate and so on – a practice often condemned by mercantilist authors.[107]

The idea that a net inflow of money might be regarded as something saved, which later on in the form of 'liquid capital'[108] could be invested in order to enlarge trade, was quite usual at the time. Moreover, against this background the view that consumption of exportable goods should be kept down to a limit was perhaps not so strange. Thus it would not need any reference to some psychological attitude or *mentalité* that lay behind that which Heckscher described as a 'fear of goods'. Without doubt, the dictum that a nation must save in order to export was commonplace within mercantilist literature. Early on, Mun here set the tone when he in *England's Treasure* underlined that we must send 'out as much of everything we can spare or vent abroad'.[109]

However, let us return to the alleged view that a net surplus of money could be regarded as capital. Without doubt such a viewpoint can be spotted in Mun's writings, but it is also hinted at elsewhere. Already in the 1621 pamphlet Mun emphasised that the 'generall stocke of the Kingdome' would be enriched by a net inflow of bullion from the re-exportation of East India goods. This inflow, he said, 'negotiated to the increase of the said stocke, and for the imployment of the Subjects'.[110] Further, in *England's Treasure* he pointed out: 'That as the treasure which is brought into the realm by the ballance of forraign trade is that money which oneley doth abide with us, and by which we are enriched'.[111] What Mun in fact here conveys is that a favourable balance of trade will provide a nation with more capital that may enhance the kingdom's stock.[112] His famous negative analogy of what would happen if a nation imported more than it exported cannot be understood outside this context:

> For in this case it cometh to pass in the stock of a Kingdom, as in the estate of a private man; who is supposed to have one thousand pounds yearly revenue and two thousand pounds of ready money in his Chest: If such a man through excess shall spend one thousand five hundred pounds **per anum**, all his ready mony will be gone in four years, and in the like time his said money will be doubled if he take a Frugal course to spend but five hundred pounds **per annum**.[113]

A likewise negative example can be found in Locke's writings 70 years later. Certainly, it is only if we admit that Locke here refers to money as a form of capital that the following argumentation will make any sense: 'If such a Trade as this be managed amongst us, and continue Ten years, it is evident, that our Millions of Money will at the end of the Ten years be inevitably all gone from us to them'.[114]

Against this background it was not far-fetched to believe that more money in the form of precious metals added to the kingdom's stock and thus was pivotal for the increase of plenty. But as we have seen this was only one suggestion of many concerning the beneficial influence of a steady inflow of money. The idea that more money was needed in order to expand trade and transactions was another and perhaps even more frequent suggestion. Yet another idea was emphasised already by Serra in Naples before the pamphlet war broke out in England in 1623 (see p.138): that a country with no mines must always have a positive trade balance with goods *other* than precious metals as it also needed to import bullion.[115] Arguing about why Venice has grown so rich (in contrast to Naples), he says, in his *Breve Trattato*, that 'the difficulty consists in finding an inflow which is not only sufficient to compensate for the outflow but exceeds it to such an extent that it produces the abundance of money which in fact exists'.[116] This idea in not explicitly mentioned in the English debates in the seventeenth century. However, the fact that England had no mines of its own was mentioned once in a while. Also of course that the only way that England could receive enough money for circulation and in order to keep interest rates low was through a positive balance of trade. The fear that this also could mean that money would lose in value was as we saw feared by some but perhaps not considered as grave as the consequences provided by a negative balance of trade.

Foreign paid incomes

By any means the view that was expressed in the early seventeenth century by Mun and Misselden that defined the balance of trade as a simple 'overplus' of trade leading to an inflow of bullion was steadily losing ground in the economic debates in England during the seventeenth century. Still, someone like Postlethwayt, as we have seen, would still use the formula in 1757 (see p. 108), but there were also traces with him of another version which gradually came to swing, baptised by E A Johnson as a 'labour balance of trade' or alternatively a 'foreign-paid-income theory'.[117] Hence the foreign trade 'balance', which ought to be 'positive', was rather the balance between worked-up commodities on the one hand and raw- and semi-finished wares on the other. Worked-up wares caused employment to rise and factory income to be pocketed by merchants, manufacturers and workers. Thus, foreign trade should be so organised that foreign countries, by importing manufactured goods, 'paid' the exporting country for its wages and profits on stock. As we have seen, this was by no means a new idea. It was prevalent in Italy among neo-Machiavellianists, such as Botero, and in Spain and France already in the sixteenth century. However, in England it is clear that it gained ground especially at the end of the following century. For instance, Wood in 1718 would talk about 'the balance' paid to us 'for the greater quantity of Manufactures we sell than buy'.[118] 'The British Merchant' around the same time tended to reformulate the 'old' balance doctrine in the same manner: a 'Balance' which 'pays to us for the greater quantity of manufactures we sell than buy' thus implied that 'every Country which takes off our finished Manufactures, and return us unwrought Materials to be manufactur'd here, contributes so far to the Employment and Subsistence of our People as the costs of manufacturing those Materials'.[119]

Thus the export of value-added goods implied that foreign nations would pay for the wages and profits of the exporting nation. The more such wares were exported, the more income would accrue to England from Portugal, Spain and other countries. By becoming the manufacturer of the world, England would employ thousands of workers and the great stock would be reimbursed by 'foreign paid' incomes. Hence, if more 'work' is exported than is imported, a nation will gain from its foreign trade.[120]

Without doubt, the interest for such a version of the balance phraseology must be put in a specific political context. We have already seen how 'jealousy of trade' first against Holland but increasingly also France was common in England during the seventeenth century. Additionally, we have seen that economic writers such as Child, Davenant and others at the end of the century sought to find competitive strategies in order to strengthen the position of England against its adversaries. Moreover, in the 1690s the East India Company came into the public eye again. Especially two pamphleteers contributed to a critique of the company: Cary (–1720) and Pollexfen. According to these two partisans of the wool manufacturing interest, the import of cheap Indian calicoes had lead to the ruin of the English cloth industry. However, while Pollexfen seemed satisfied with repeating the old argument that the East India trade brought forward a 'dangerous' net outflow of bullion[121], Cary used other arguments to underscore this point. First, like many others, he pointed towards the difficulty of accounting for a true balance of trade, especially as so much trading was carried out by means of bills of exchange.[122] However, he further stated as a general principle:

The Foundation of our Trade is our Product, and the Improvement
thereof by the Labour of our People; which being Exported and Sold
Abroad brings back in Returns, not only what serves for our more
comfortable and splendid Living, but also great quantities of Bullion,
and other Treasure, which cost us little more than Labour.[123]

And in another context where he spoke of the benefits accruing from
the exportation of manufactured goods, he said:

we export them where they yield a Price, not only according to the
true value of the Materials and labour, but an Overplus according
to the Necessity and Humour of the Buyer: And this adds to the
Profit and encreases the Wealth of the Kingdom".[124]

A last formulation by Cary may suffice: 'the products coming from the
Earth, and the manufacturing of them being an Addition to their Value
by the Labour of the People'.[125]

However, it was especially in the discussion that accrued the peace
of Utrecht and the trade agreement put up between England and France
in 1713 that the idea of foreign paid incomes was further elaborated
on. It was especially the group of authors congregating around *The
British Merchant*, who used this idea as an argument against *Mercator*, a periodical edited by Daniel Defoe. As is well known, Defoe had
been hired by the Tory government to defend the peace and trade
agreement in his publication, which appeared thrice a week. However,
in *The British Merchant*, a group of Whig supporters sternly criticised
this 'hireling writer' and the treaty which he defended so vigorously.[126]
It contained papers written by a large number of authors such as
Charles King, Gee, Theodore Janssen and Henry Martin. But it was
especially in a paper titled 'General Maxims in Trade', written by
Janssen, that the new 'doctrine' was fully spelled out.[127]

According to Janssen, the following trades were not advantageous
to a nation: (1) a trade 'which brings in things of mere Luxury and
Pleasure', (2) a trade which hinders the consumption 'of our own
wares', (3) a trade 'which supplies the same goods as we manufacture'
and (4) 'the importation upon Easy terms of such Manufactures as are
already introduc'd in a country'.[128] As only to be expected, Janssen
and the other writers in *The British Merchant* argued that the trade
agreement with France would lead to all these wasteful results and
more. Moreover, the author of the *General Maxims* presented the following general principle:

That every Country which takes off our finished manufactures,
and returns us unwrought Materials to be manufactur'd here,

contributed so far to the Employment and Subsistence of ouyr People as the cost of manufacturing those Materials.[129]

However, it was when concretely applied in an example – how much Portugal in fact contributed to 'the Prosperity and happiness of this Nation' – that the original aspects of this principle were spelled out:

> To begin with our Trade to Portugal: For the Goods we send to that Country, it is acknowledg'd that our Returns are Wine, Oil, and some other things for our own Use and Consumption; but it is indisputable that the greatest Value of our Returns are Gold and Silver. So much therefore the Portugese pay to the Employment and Subsistence of our People, and for the Product of our Land: so much as this Balance in Gold in Silver, they contribute to the Propsperity and Happiness of this Nation.[130]

Later in the text Janssen also applied the same principle with regard to rents and profits.[131] Thus he concluded:

> For my own part, I know no other way of estimating the Profit or Loss of Trade between two Nations. All that the Labour of the People, the Product of the Lands, and the Gain of the Merchants in one nation, exceed in Value those in the other, is so much Gain to the first, and so much Loss to the second.[132]

This idea, which made it possible to retain the balance concept while in reality furnish it with a new content, was found useful by a number of authors during the following decades. In fact, from *The British Merchant* onwards it became generally acknowledged that a country should sell more of manufactured goods than it bought. Postlethwayt in 1757 called this a general 'maxim' of commerce and divided 'beneficial' from bad trade. And to achieve a beneficial commerce 'is what constitutes the art and science of the administration of *political commerce*', he stated.[133] Further, this 'balance' was paid in income to domestic workers, manufacturers and the landed interest. Thus for example Wood in 1718 pointed out that 'the Country which does not *sell* us so many Manufactures as it *buys* from us, contributes the whole of the *Balance* to the Employment and Subsistence to *our* People, and to the product of *our* Lands'.[134] Another example was Gee, who in a computed 'General Balance' included in his widely read *The Trade and Navigation of Great Britain* (1729), strongly emphasised that England must become a manufactory working up raw materials from its growing colonial empire. By trading with such worked-up wares we will gain a great profit, he said. And he concludes by saying that this meant that England will be able to 'employ our own poor' instead of other countries' poor.[135]

In ordinary history of economics textbooks James Steuart is often mentioned as the last mercantilist.[136] In his *An Inquiry into the Principles of Political Economy* he stated what then had been standard: 'It is therefore a general maxim, to discourage the importation of work, and to encourage the exportation of it'.[137] He believed that trading countries were involved in serious industrial competion. To take this competition seriously was the task of the statesman. In fact, he even stated that 'the abilities of a statesman are discovered, in directing and conducting what I call the delicacy of national competition'.[138] A loss in the balance of labour would in the long run lead to economic and societal decline. In (only) this sense, the old maxim if 'one nation is growing richer, others must be growing poorer' could be held to be accurate.[139] In order to protect a nation from disadvantageous competition, Steuart used something like J S Mill's argument concerning infant industry a hundred years later to press the point that a nation must be free to protect itself from detrimental competition especially when it was later in the process of creating its own industrial base.[140] His main argument was that 'laying trade open would not have the effect proposed; because it would destroy industry in some countries'.[141] Moreover, Steuart did not believe that trade in itself created wealth. In fact, he emphasised that international trade must be reciprocal. Moreover, an inflow of specie was not a true sign that a country gained from its trade with other countries. Instead, 'To judge of the balance of trade is one thing; to judge of the wealth of a nation as to specie is another'.[142] Generally he was for economic freedom and against monopoly. Instead of 'balance of trade' he insisted on the aim of economic policy to provide employment. This is the balance which he was most concerned with: 'In order therefore to preserve a trading state from decline, the greatest care must be taken, to support a perfect balance between the hands employed and the demand for their labour'.[143]

A last example may perhaps suffice. In 1744 Matthew Decker published a popular work which would reach seven editions by 1756. Historians of economic doctrine have mainly recognised this author for his 'free trade' inclinations. Thus for example in *Palgrave's Dictionary* he was greeted as 'one of the most important precursors of Adam Smith'.[144] However, this did not the least stop him from presenting a rather crude version of the balance theory pointing out that 'if the Exports of Britain exceed its Imports, Foreigners must pay the Balance in Treasure and the Nation grow Rich'.[145] He even said with regard to silver and gold that 'the more or less of these Metals a Nation retains, it is denominated Rich or Poor'.[146] However, Decker seems to be divided on this issue. Later on in the text he would point out that raw materials imported and 'improved by the People's Labour at least twice' would thereby increase 'a Nation's Treasure in proportion'.[147]

Although it seemed difficult for Decker to make up his mind, his *Essay* is certainly a very important work. It amounts to one of the last attempts during the eighteenth century to use the balance theory as a point of departure for analysis. It was Decker's aim to present some general principles with regard to trade. Its main focal point was to discuss the causes of a perceived decline of British foreign trade. As we saw, he started out from a conventional favourable balance of trade view emphasising that the ultimate object of foreign trade was to bring in precious metals. This is also shown in his frequent use of literary references. By citing authors such as Gee, Child, Locke, Coke and many others, Decker without doubt considered himself part of a long tradition dominated by speculation over the balance of trade

Moreover, as we saw, he agreed with his older colleagues that, in order for a country to prosper, more manufactures and trade were a necessity. However, with regard to the means by which industry and trade should be augmented, he stood quite far from the *dirigisme* of for example Child. He set his faith in free trade as a general principle and in the need to abandon duties and regulations in order to become more competitive. A proper 'knowledge of the true Nature of Trade', he said, can only lead to the conclusion that 'the cheaper things are, the more of them will be exported, and it is Exportation only that makes a Nation rich'.[148] He even went so far as to write: 'Every Home Commodity in a free Trade will find its natural value'.[149] Furthermore, he believed in low wages, but only in order to have low costs of production and low prices. He cherished a great population but stressed at the same time 'That such as your Employment is for People, so many will your People be'.[150]

Hence, Decker's work is noteworthy for two different but clearly linked reasons. First, it certainly illustrates that it was possible still in the beginning of the eighteenth century to adhere (play lip-service) to a quite orthodox favourable balance of trade doctrine, while at the same time hail free trade in principal terms. Second, Decker is an example of how the recognition of the role of export for economic growth and development during the eighteenth century could lead in the same direction: to promote free trade and argue against restrictions. It is true that promulgators of 'the mercantile system' during the nineteenth century would have found it hard to admit to this alleged paradox. However, those who lived during the eighteenth century must have been much less surprised.

Decline

It is easily at hand to believe that the idea of a favourable balance of trade disintegrated as a mere consequence of an increase of free trade opinions. However, as noted, Decker is a good example that it was possible to combine a free trade position while at the same time keep to at least parts of the old formula. Another illustration of this is Jacob Vanderlint, a Dutch merchant, who in 1734 published a small tract, which we already have cited, *Money Answers to All Things.* As several authors have noticed, Vanderlint's treatise contained a combination of 'orthodox mercantilist views' and free trade principles.[151] His main complaint was an alleged scarcity of money caused by a negative balance of trade. This negative balance was in its turn caused by the high price of 'necessities' originating from a too-low output of agricultural produce in relation to a large population.[152] Like so many others during this period, he thus stressed the important role of low production costs and cost competition. Nor were such free trade aptitudes uncommon even earlier. They were in fact often combined with a mercantilist vocabulary. From this basis it might even be argued that most mercantilists, at least from the end of the seventeenth century, are better described as free traders than protectionists.[153]

However, other authors arguing for increased 'employment' through the means of foreign trade did not use the balance argument at all. Rather, their focus was on the more general benefits accomplished by foreign trade. Thus, as we saw, Child for instance would ignore the favourable balance of trade doctrine altogether and instead stress that trade should be regulated and properly organised: 'To encourage those trades most, that Vent most of our Manufactures, or supply us with Materials to be further Manufactured in England'.[154]

In fact, writers like Child, Davenant, Barbon, North and others would address both technical and more principal arguments against the balance of trade concept. It became in fact increasingly common to argue that, to the extent such a balance existed at all, it was too difficult to account for. Thus, instead, the amount of employment foreign trade could provide was a far better indicator of a favourable trade. Sometimes also it was emphasised that the exchange rates with foreign countries could be regarded as a 'barometer of trade'. Thus they could be used as signs whether foreign trade was advantageous or not.[155] Increasingly, also, a more principal critique would appear against the balance of trade concept. In this context, as we will show in more detail later, Barbon was one of the first who directly spoke of this 'popular notion' as 'a mistake'. It was after all he who first had emphasised 'that there is no such usage as balancing the Foreign Accompts of Merchants, by the Money of Foreign Nation'.[156]

Hence, to the extent the balance discourse slowly disintegrated during the eighteenth century, we must look at other propelling forces than just as a mere consequence of increasing free trade inclinations. In this context a growing uneasiness with the favourable balance of trade formula was certainly more important. As we saw, already in the 1690s several writers had pointed out how difficult it was to make an account of this balance. They found it impracticable in order to decide whether a nation won or lost by its trade.

However, already at this time, a more radical attitude towards this doctrine made itself felt. Barbon is one early exponent of such a critique.[157] Another writer of importance in this context was Dudley North (1641–91), a wealthy merchant of the Turkey Company and a Tory just like Child, Barbon and Davenant. However, it is not likely that his little tract, *Discourses Upon Trade* (1691), was much read at the time. The reason for this is simple: it was supressed for political reasons and most copies in fact were destroyed.[158] Mainly, its purpose was to intervene in the current discussion regarding the currency reform and the regulation of the interest rate that soured high at this time. However, its few pages compromised a radical onslaught on most of the conventional economic thinking of the age. With regard to his method he emphasised the need to establish truths on the basis of empirical investigation. As he argued, most old philosophy had been overtly interested in abstractions and principles *in vacuo*. Furthermore, he regarded trade and economic phenomena as ruled by some simple principles that he explicitly referred to as natural laws. Consequently, he vigorously and in principle charged the idea that interest – as a 'natural' price of the use of money – might be regulated by law. From this point of view he also attacked the notion of a favourable balance of trade. Money is only a medium of which there can be too little and too much, he said: 'This ebbing and flowing of Money supplies and accommodates itself, without any aid of Politicians'.[159] He was even more radical in his treatment of commerce as part of a natural system which not only encompassed one country, but also the whole world: 'That the whole World as to Trade, is but as one Nation or People, and therein Nations are as Persons'.[160]

Thus for North as well as Barbon it was the notion of money as a medium, in fact an ordinary commodity, that made the notion of a stable and long-term surplus of bullion achieved by foreign trade especially untenable. With Joseph Harris some fifty years later this argument had become the commonplace. Nobody at this time would seriously have argued against his view that 'Money finds its own value, according to the whole quantity of its circulation'.[161]

Another argument raised against the balance theory, which became increasingly hard to ignore, was a principle later on known as 'the specie flow mechanism'. We will not here go into a more detailed investigation of how this analytical tool was gradually cultivated. It suffices to say that this mechanism had been in use for quite some time when it was picked up by Hume in his famous essay 'On the Balance of Trade' from 1752.[162] Hence, the proposal that a net outflow of money would lower prices and thus encourage exports and after a time 'bring back the money which we had lost'[163] can already be found in the writings of Barbon[164], Vanderlint[165] and Isaac Gervaise (1680–1739). Son of a French Hugenot immigrant, Gervaise in 1720 published a remarkable tract in which he displayed the economy as a self-regulating order which, left to itself, would find the best means to enrich all partakers in trade and industry. With regard to the specie–flow mechanism he stated:

> When a Nation has attracted a greater Proportion of the grand Denominator [money] of the world, than its proper share; and the Cause of that Attraction ceases, that Nation cannot retain the Overplus of its proper Proportion of the grand Denominator, because in that case, the Proportion of poor and Rich of that Nation is broken; that is to say, the number of Rich is too great, in proportion to the poor so as that nation cannot furnish unto the World that share of labour which is proportion'd to that part of the grand denominator it possesses: in which case all the Labour of the Poor will not ballance the Expence of the Rich. So that there enters in that Nation, more Labour than goes out of it, to ballance its want of Poor: And as the End of trade is the attracting Gold and Silver, all that difference of labour is paid in Gold and Silver, until the Denominator is lessen'd, in proportion to other Nations.[166]

However important analytical inventions of this type might seem to us today, it must be emphasised that a writer like Gervaise was totally unknown during his lifetime and his tract virtually ignored. It was only through the publication of Hume's essay – as we saw – that the specie–flow mechanism became known to a wider public of readers. Moreover, the dismantling of the idea of a positive net surplus of money or capital accruing from foreign trade was only gradually disappearing. The notion of 'foreign paid income' view – that protection was necessary for industry to grow and that the exportation of value-added produce was preferable – stayed much longer. It can be argued whether the case for principal free trade was won in Britain before the 1840s and early 1850s – both as doctrine and practice.[167] Stubbornly also it has reappeared in different shapes since then: as the 'infant industry' argument, in List's critique of a hypocritical Albion denying others the industrial progress itself had achieved through free trade imperialism, import-substitution and so on.

The balance theory in retrospect

We have in this chapter discussed the different uses of the concept of a favourable balance of trade during the seventeenth and early eighteenth centuries. It has underscored our previous conclusion that no real agreement existed during this time with regard to how it should be interpreted. Thus at the same time as this phrase was 'good to think with', it really meant different things to different writers. Although this seems quite obvious, if we study the actual texts, this *factum* seems to have been averted by most interpreters of the mercantilist literature. We can only speculate why this has been so. It is clear that for Smith the view that the favourable balance doctrine reflected a confusion of money and wealth was appropriate not least for polemical reasons. Also for nineteenth-century free traders the notion of an erroneous 'mercantile school' could serve to propel assurance in their own 'system'. However, why such one-cause explanations remain vital even today is more of an enigma. It might perhaps be tempting to look for a robust and simple explanation to a certain phenomenon. But unfortunately the idea that it is possible to detect *one* simple explanation for mercantilist writers' obstinate use of the favourable balance phrase has no empirical support whatsoever. If there is a red herring anywhere in this story it would be found exactly here.

Moreover, it is not only that contemporary explications of the term differed. It is also clear that some of the interpretations exclude each other quite effectively. Hence, the foreign paid income interpretation was often explicitly offered in opposition to definitions that emphasised the role of a net surplus of bullion. This was quite clear with authors such as Child, Barbon, North, Steuart and Davenant. Moreover, it is a complete misnomer, as we saw, to regard such an opposition as a simple outcome of *laissez-faire* versus protectionist tendencies. As we will see in the next chapter, explications of the favourable balance of trade doctrine emerged quite separately from opinions with regard to free or protected trade. Furthermore, the idea that the inflow of money constituted a liquid capital and *if used* enlarged the nation's stock was often presented in opposition to another suggestion which emphasised the positive role of more circulating money as such. Both these interpretations, in turn, were set against other accounts that stressed the role of cheating money dealers or perhaps also the enrichment of the king's treasure as a main policy objective behind the favourable balance. Without doubt terminological differences of this kind stemmed from economics at this time sharing no agreed upon vocabulary. Neither was it a coherent discipline nor field of inquiry separated from, for example, political discourse. Hence writers tended to use concepts and words in various ways. However, change was at hand, and we will in the next two chapters discuss the implications of new ideas concerning a commercial economy that rose especially in England during the seventeenth century.

Notes

1 B Suviranta, *The Theory of the Balance of Trade in England. A Study in Mercantilism.* Helsingfors: Suomal.Kirjall Kirjap. O.y. 1923, pp. 135, 165 etc.
2 J Viner, 'English Theories of Foreign Trade before Adam Smith'. *Journal of Political Economy*, vol. XXXVIII: 3, 4 (1930), pp. 264ff.
3 Viner, p. 264.
4 For different views see for example A Oncken, *Geschichte der Nationalökonomie*, vol. I, Leipzig: Verlag von C L Hirschfeldt, 1920, pp. 154f.; P J Thomas, *Mercantilism and the East India Trade*. London: Frank Cass 1963, p. 3; J Schumpeter, *A History of Economic Analysis*. London: George Allen & Unwin 1972, p. 361; M Bowley, *Studies in the History of Economic Thought*. London: Macmillan 1973, p. 24; M Beer, *Early British Economics*. London: George Allen & Unwin 1938, pp. 190f.; W H Price 'The origin of the phrase Balance of Trade'. *Quaterly Journal of Economics*, vol. XX (1905); F Fetter, 'The Term Favourable Balance of Trade'. *Quarterly Journal of Economics*, vol. XLIX (1935); S Rashid, 'The Interpretation of the "Balance of Trade": A Wordy Debate'. *BEBR faculty working papers*, no. 89–1538 (1989).
5 Suviranta, p. 116.
6 E F Heckscher, *Mercantilism*, vol. II. London: George Allen & Unwin 1955, p. 186.
7 Schumpeter, p. 361.
8 See Viner, 'Early English Theories of Foreign Trade before Adam Smith'.
9 Schumpeter, p. 361.
10 C Davenant, *An Essay Upon the Probable Methods of Making a People Gainers in the Ballance of Trade*. London: R Horsfield 1699, p. 12.
11 C Davenant, *Discourse on the Public Revenues and on Trade*, part 2, London: R Horsfield 169. Here cited from *The Political and Commercial Works of that Celebrated Writer Charles D'Avenant*, vol. I, London: R Horsfield 1771, p. 354.
12 W Temple, *Observations Upon the United Provinces of the Netherlands* [1673]. Cambridge, UK: Cambridge University Press 1932, p. 141.
13 C Fortrey, *England's Interest and Improvement*. London: Nathanael Brook 1673, p. 7.
14 N Barbon, *A Discourse Concerning Coining the New Money Lighter*. London: Robert Chiswell 1696, pp. 48f.
15 Consult Christine MacLeod, 'Henry Martin and the authorship of Considerations upon the East India Trade'. *Historical Research*, vol. 134 (November 1983).
16 Unkown author, *Considerations on the East-India Trade*. London 1701, p. 11.
17 W Wood, *A Survey of Trade*. London: W. Hinchliffe 1718, pp. 1f. See also T Papillon cited by J A Schumpeter, pp. 361f.
18 T Mun, *A Discourse of Trade*. London: Nicholas Okes for John Pyper 1621, p. 49.
19 Mun, *England's Treasure by Forraign Trade*, pp. 71f.
20 P Chamberlen, *The Poore Man's Advocate*. London: Giles Calvert 1649, p. 1. 'Poore' here refers to labourers, not destitute people.
21 Schumpeter, p. 362.

22 For a similar viewpoint see Rashid, 'The Interpretation of the Balance of Trade', p. 6.
23 *Britannia Languens*, pp. 446, 458.
24 Mun, *A Discourse of Trade*, pp. 49f.
25 L Roberts, *The Treaure of Traffike*, p. 7.
26 See for example S Fortrey, p. 7; C Davenant, *An Essay Upon Ways and Means*. London: Jacob Tonson 1695. Here cited from *Works*, I, pp. 1ff.; C Davenant, *An Essay Upon the Probable Methods of Making a People Gainers in the Ballance of Trade*, pp. 12f; Mun, *England's Treasure*, p. 7.
27 Roberts, p. 6.
28 M Postlethwayt, *Britain's Commercial Interest Explained and Improved*, vol. I, London: A Millar *et al.* 1757, p. 1.
29 S Johnson, *A Dictionary of the English Language*, vols. I-II, London: Longman 1827.
30 W Petty, 'A Report from the Council of Trade'. In: C H Hull (Ed.), *The Economic Writings of Sir William Petty*, vol. I (1899). Fairfield, NJ: Augustus M Kelley, p. 213.
31 E Misselden, *The Circle of Commerce*, London: John Dawson for Nicholas Bourne 1623, p. 117; J Child, *A New Discourse of Trade*. London: John Everingham 1693, pp. 135f.; Mun, *England's Treasure*, p. 14; Barbon, *A Discourse Concerning Coining the New Money Lighter*, p. 46 (… bullion … which is treasure …); Mun, *A Discourse of Trade*, pp. 2, 17, 22, etc.; *Britannia Languens*, pp. 390, 416, etc.; J Cary, *An Essay Towards Regulating the Trade and Employing the Poor of this Kingdom*. London: Susanna Collins 1717, introduction.
32 As with Mun, *A Discourse of Trade*, pp. 21, 56.
33 *Britannia Languens*, p. 416.
34 *The British Merchant*, London 1721, pp. 21, 28.
35 Mun, *A Discourse of Trade*, pp. 39f.; J Pollexfen, *A Discourse of Trade and Coyn*. London: Brabazon Aylmer 1697, p. 60; J Cary, *An Essay Towards Regulating the Trade and Employing the Poor*, p. 2; M Decker, *An Essay on the Causes of the Decline of the Foreign Trade* (4th ed.), London 1751, pp. 7f.; *Britannia Languens*, pp. 301f.
36 Davenant, *An Essay Upon the Propable Methods of Making a People Gainers in the Balance of Trade*, pp. 140f.; Temple, *Observations*, p. 141; W Wood; Barbon, *A Discourse Concerning Coining the New Money Lighter*, p. 35; D Hume, *Political Discourses*. Edinburgh: R Fleming 1752, pp. 15ff.
37 Barbon, *A Discourse Conerning Coining the New Money Lighter*, p. 35.
38 Child, *A New Discourse of Trade*, p. 135.
39 Mun, *A Discourse of Trade*, pp. 22, 40.
40 Postlethwayt, pp. 3f.
41 D North, *Discourses Upon Trade*. London: Thos Basset 1691, p. 15. On this see also Rashid, 'The interpretation of the balance of trade'.
42 Schumpeter, pp. 340ff., 352ff.
43 Viner, 'Early English Theories…', pp. 448f.
44 Davenant, *An Essay Upon the Propable Methods…*, pp. 140f.
45 J Gee, *The Trade and Navigation of Great Britain* (1729), Cited from the 4th ed., 1738, pp. 182f.
46 J Gee, *The Trade and Navigation of Great Britain* (1729), Cited from the 4th ed., 1738, pp. 182f..
47 Gee, pp. 182ff.
48 Cited from Suviranta, p. 21.
49 W S [Sir Thomas Smith], *A Discourse of the Common Weal of England* [1581]. Cambridge, UK: Cambridge University Press 1893.

50 C E Suprinyak, 'Trade, Money and the Grievances of the Commonwealth: The Economic Debates in the English Publi Sphere during the Commercial Crisis in the Early 1690's'. Econpapers, repec. org.

51 Beer, *A History of Early British Economics*, p. 138. See also note above.

52 Price op. cit. Also consult A Finkelstein, *Harmony and the Balance. An Intellectual History of Seventeenth-Century English Economic Thought.* Ann Arbor: The University of Michigan Press 2000, pp. 89f.

53 *Decay of Trade; A Treatise Against the Abating of Interest.* London: John Sweeting 1641, pp. 1f.

54 Postlethwayt, II, p. 382.

55 Viner, p. 271.

56 Mun, *England's Treasure by Forraign Trade*, p. 12.

57 Mun, p. 69.

58 Mun, p. 68.

59 Viner, p. 272.

60 *Britania Languens*, pp. 187f.

61 *Britannia languens*, p. 101.

62 This expression was already used by W S [Sir Thomas Smith], *A Discourse of the Common Weal of England* [1581], but most probably written in 1549 (ed. E Lamond). Cambridge, UK: Cambridge University Press 1893, pp. 86f. For the discussion of who the author of this pamphlet was, see the edition of the book published by M Dewar in 1969.

63 See p. 105

64 *Britannia Languens*, p. 187.

65 W Potter, *The Trades-Man's Jewel.* London: Edward Husband and John Field 1650, p. 1.

66 An exponent of such a view is for example M Dobb's *Studies in the Development of Capitalism.* London: Routledge & Kegan Paul 1967.

67 See p. 105

68 Viner, p. 283.

69 Misselden, *The Circle of Commerce*, p. 51. See also pp. 114f.

70 Mun, *England's Treasure*, p. 8.

71 Davenant, 'An Essay Upon the East India Trade', *Works*, p. 99.

72 See for example J Vanderlint, *Money Answers All Things.* London: To Cox 1734, p. 16; Author unknown, *A Discourse Consisting of Motives for the Enlargement of Trade.* London: Richard Rowtell 1645, p. 25; Decker, pp. 31, 40, 48 etc. See further Viner, p. 282 for more examples.

73 Locke, *Some Considerations*, p. 47.

74 See the discussion in Bowley, *Studies*, p. 24 whether or not Locke was a later exponent for the view that an inflow of bullion would lead to embettered terms of trade and could thus be seen as beneficial for a country. This seems quite clearly to be the case. See for example Locke, *Some Considerations*, p. 79, where he discusses the effects of diminishing the stock of money. One consequence will be, he says, that 'in all our exchange of native for Foreign Commodities, we shall pay double the Value that any other Country does, where Money is in greater Plenty'.

75 Misselden, *Free Trade or the Meanes to Make Trade Flourish.* London: I Legatt for Waterson 1622, p. 107.

76 Fortrey, p. 27.

77 See also A E Munroe, *Monetary Theory before Adam Smith.* Cambridge, MA: Harvard University Press, who denies that 'English writers' prior to Locke had adopted the quantity theory. As Viner insists this is certainly not correct and builds on a too-strict definition of this theory. See Viner, p. 288.

78 See W S, *A Discourse of the Common Weal of England*, p. 71.

79 Mun, *England's Treasure*, p. 17.

80 *Britannia Languens*, p. 8.

81 Locke, pp. 77f.

82 Beer, *Early British Economics*, p. 189.

83 Besides Beer this interpretation has been suggested for example by Viner, p. 284 and Heckscher, II, pp. 209ff.

84 See for example Davenant, *An Essay Upon the Probable Methods*, p. 8; and J Cary, *An Essay on the Coyn and Credit of England as they Stand with Respect to its Trade*. Bristol 1696, p. 1.

85 F Bacon, *Essays, Moral, Economical and Political*. Warwick, UK: R Spemmel 1882.

86 Postlethwayt, II, p. 384.

87 J Pollexfen, *England and East India Inconsistent in their Manufacture*. London 1692, pp. 47f.

88 Decker, p. 173.

89 Locke, p. 30.

90 Locke, p. 40.

91 Mun, *England's Treasure*, pp. 16f.

92 W Petty, *Verbum Sapienti* (1691). Cited from *The Economic Writings of Sir William Petty*, part 1, p. 113. See also W Petty, *A Treatise of Taxes & Contributions* (1662). Cited from *The Economic Writings of Sir William Petty*, part 1, p. 35.

93 W Petty, *The Political Anatomy of Ireland* (1691). Cited from *The Economic Writings*, I, pp. 192ff.

94 *Britannia Languens*, p. 8.

95 J D Gould, 'The Trade Crisis of the Early 1620's and English Economic Thought'. *The Journal of Economic History*, vol. XV (1955).

96 Mun, *England's Treasure*, pp. 17f.

97 Gould, p. 131.

98 According to McCulloch, this tract was written 'probably in the interval between 1630 and 1635'. See *A Select Collection of Scarce and Valuable Tracts on Money*. (ed. McCulloch) London: Political Economy Club 1861, p. vi.

99 R Vaughan, *A Discourse of Coin and Coinage*. London: Th Dawks for Th Basset 1675. Reprinted in *A Select Collection of Scarce and Valuable Tracts on Money*, p. 37ff. See also pp. 68ff.

100 Vanderlint, p. 150. See also pp. 155, 160ff.

101 This conclusion seems not to have been drawn in previous literature on Vanderlint. For example, T Hutchison makes a complete muddle of him when he treats him as part mercantilist, part free trader and part Physiocrat (!). See Hutchison, *Before Adam Smith*, p. 129.

102 See above p. 35

103 Potter, *The Trades-Mans Jewel*. Ann Arbor, MI: Edward Husband and John Field 1650. Title page.

104 Heckscher, II, p. 200.

105 Pstlethwayt, II, p. 382.

106 See above p. 35. See also L Herlitz, 'The Concept of Mercantilism'. *Scandinavian Economic History Review*, vol. XII (1964), p. 116.

107 For documentation, see Viner, pp. 293ff.

108 See also E A Johnson, *Predecessors to Adam Smith*. New York: Prentice Hall 1937, p. 78, who talks of 'financial capital' in this context, although the reference to credit arrangements which during this period prevailed within the putting-out form of production is perhaps a more accurate analogy.

109 Mun, *England's Treasure*, p. 15.

110 Mun, *A Discourse of Trade*, p. 25.

111 Mun, *England's Treasure*, p. 21.

112 For a similiar view see Johnson, *Predecessors*, p. 79.

113 Mun, *England's Treasure*, p. 5.

114 Locke, *Some Considerations of the Consequences of the Lowering of Interests*, p. 25.

115 Still in 1757 Postlethwayt would mention this. See Postlethwayt, I, p. 22.

116 A Serra, *A Short Treatise on the Wealth and Poverty of Nations* (1613) (ed. and trans. S Reinert). London: Anthem Books 2011, p. 139.

117 Johnson, *Predecessors*, ch. XV.

118 Wood, pp. 84f.

119 *The British Merchant*, pp. 22f.

120 Probably the most sophisticated version of this 'theory' appears in J Steuart, *An Inquiry into the Principles of Political OEconomy, book II, chapter X. The Works Political, Metaphysical and Chronological of the Late Sir James Steuart*, vol. I, London: T Cadell and W Davies 1805, pp. 289ff. See also E A Johnson, pp. 308ff.

121 See J Pollexfen, *A Discourse of Trade and Coyn*. London 1697, pp. 3, 5ff. At the same time he would say things like: 'Our Product's improv'd by the labour of our people, are the Nations yearly income' (preface, p. 3). The fact that this author could at the same time adhere to this 'modern' principal and defend the favourable balance of trade theory shows the complexity of this whole issue and that the prevalence of this dogma cannot be 'explained' by some simplistic formula.

122 J Cary, *An Essay Towards Regulating the Trade and Employing the Poor of This Kingdom*. London: S Collins for Sam Mabbat 1717, pp. 84f. This edition from 1717 is almost identical to a work he published already in 1695: *An Essay on the State of England in Telation to its Trade, its Poor, and its Taxes for Carrying on the Present War against France*. Bristol 1695.

123 Cary, *An Essay Towards Regulating the Trade*, dedication.

124 Cary, p. 11.

125 Cary, p. 2.

126 *The British Merchant*, vol. I [1721], p. vii.

127 On *The British Merchant* discussion see E A Johnson, *Predecessors of Adam Smith*, pp. 142ff.

128 *The British Merchant*, I, pp. 4f.

129 *The British Merchant*, I, p. 23.

130 Op. cit., p. 24.

131 Op. cit., pp. 35f.

132 *The British Merchant*, I, p. 37.

133 Postlethwayt, p. 368.

134 Wood, *A Survey of Trade*. London 1718, p. 84.

135 Gee, *The Trade and Navigation of Great Britain*, p. 193.

136 This view is challenged by for example A Skinner who points at Steuart's similarity to the Scottish school of Enlightenment, especially concerning his ideas on economic development. See also A Skinner, 'James Steuart', *Economic History Review*, 2nd ser., vol. XV (1962–3), p. 439. See also S R Sen, *The Economics of Sir James Steuart.* London: G Bell & Sons 1957. For different interpretations of Steuart, see also R Tortajada (ed.), *The Economics of James Steuart.* London: Routledge 1999.

137 J Steuart, *An Inquiry into the Principles of Political Economy*. 1767. Here cited from J Steuart, *Works*, vol. II, London 1805, p. 2.

138 Steuart, I, p. 310.

139 Steuart, II, p. 115.
140 On J S Mill and the infant industry argument, see D A Irwin, *Against the Tide. An Intellectual History of Free Trade*. Princeton, NJ: Princeton University Press 1996, particularly pp. 128f.
141 Steuart, II, p. 117.
142 Steuart, II, p. 128.
143 Steuart, I, p. 299.
144 *Palgrave's Dictionary of Political Economy*, I.
145 Decker, *An Essay on the Causes of the Decline of the Foreign Trade*, p. 7.
146 Decker, *An Essay on the Causes of the Decline of the Foreign Trade*, p. 7.
147 Decker, p. 8.
148 Decker, p. 48.
149 Op. cit., p. 49.
150 Op. cit., p. 105.
151 See D Vickers, *Studies in the Theory of Money 1690–1776*. Philadelphia & New York: Chilton Company 1959.
152 His negative attitude of a too-great population was quite unusual at the time and is worth attention. See Vanderlint, *Money Answers All Things*, p. 17. See also C E Stangeland, *Pre-Malthusian Doctrines of Population* [1904]. New York: Augustus M Kelley 1966, chs 7–8. For a recent overview, see T McCormick, 'Population: Modes of Seventeenth-Century Demographic Thought'. In: P Stern & C Wennerlind (eds.), *Mercantilism Reimagined. Political Economy in Early Modern Britain and its Empire*. Oxford: Oxford University Press 2013.
153 See for example Grampp's position above p. 41.
154 Child, *A New Discourse of Trade*, pp. 156f.
155 Especially Decker, pp. 8f.
156 Barbon, *A Discourse Concerning Coining the New Money Lighter*, p. 35.
157 See further p. 196.
158 See entries on D North in *Dictionary of National Biographies* and *Palgrave's Dictionary on Political Economy*.
159 D North, *Discourses Upon Trade*, p. 25.
160 North, preface.
161 J Harris, 'An Essay Upon Money and Coins, I'. In: J R McCulloch (ed.), *Old ands Scarce Tracts of Money*, p. 390.
162 D Hume, 'On the Balance of Trade' (1752). In his *Essays. Moral. Political and Literary*. Indianapolis, IN: Liberty Fund 1985, part 2, ch. 5,.
163 Hume, p. 311.
164 See above p. 196.
165 Vanderlint, *Money Answers All Things*, p. 51.
166 I Gervaise, *The System or Theory of the Trade of the World* [1720]. Reprint Baltimore 1954, p. 7. In his foreword Viner suggests that we by 'rich' shall understand the consumers, and the 'poor' should be understood as the producers.
167 See the discussion in L Magnusson, *A Tradition of Free Trade*. London: Routledge 2004, ch. 2.

5 The 1620s debates

In a pathbreaking study of the emergence of mercantilist thought, the economic historian J D Gould speculated about what would have happened if Mun's *England's Treasure by Forraign Trade* (1663) had been published when it was actually written – in the late 1620s – instead of three or four decades later.[1] As we have seen, Smith hailed Mun for having presented a definitive mercantilist 'manifesto'. And as such, ever since, it has had a profound influence on our understanding of 'mercantilist' thought. Undoubtedly, however, Smith's reading of Mun was biased by the fact that his main text was published in the 1660s instead of the 1620s. Smith, as well as other commentators, has tended to interpret it mainly as a partisan text in favour of aggressive economic policies directed particularly at the Dutch. However, as we will see, this remains half true. Without doubt Mun *was* aggressive in tone, but this does not account for his principal argumentation nor the historical circumstances to which it was directed.

Mun's 'mercantilist manifesto' was published posthumously by his son John Mun. No doubt the first and perhaps most important reason why it was published in 1664 was because of its harsh tone against the Dutch typical of that time. In 1652, after the introduction of the English Navigation Act, the mutual accusations and angry diplomatic notes exploded into open warfare. Up until 1674 England and the Dutch Republic were almost constantly at war. For an English audience, what Mun wrote about the 'Netherlanders' thus had real actuality. In *England's Treasure* he had pointed out that: 'there are no people in Christendome who do more undermine, hurt, and eclipse us daily in our Navigation and Trades, both abroad and at home'.[2]

Second, the publication of Mun's main work must also be regarded as a response to an increased critique of the doings of the East India Company. Hostile charges against this company for exporting bullion had indeed been legion since the beginning of the century.[3] But there were some sudden outbreaks of more intensive criticism – especially during the acute trade crisis in the 1620s and again from the 1660s. At both times a general discontent within the English cloth industry seems to have been the most profound reason behind the outbursts. For example in the 1660s the dissatisfaction was manifested in a flood of pamphlets which depicted protection from cheap Indian calicoes as the only rescue against unemployment and depression.[4]

Third, and last, Mun's text was useful in order to find support for the unfettering of restrictions against the export of bullion that had been a main policy issue during the Restoration period. In 1663 those who wanted free export of money had scored a final victory.[5] The Council of Trade recommended that bullion would be exported freely with the argument that 'Money and Bullion have always forced their way against the several laws; that the trade of the world will not be forced, but will find or make its own way free to all appearances of profit'[6] In particular, the Council further stated, it was necessary for certain trades to carry out money, especially the one to East India. In this context both Mun's first published treatise *A Discourse of Trade* (1621) as well as the later *England's Treasure by Forraign Trade* (1663) were important, of course. In both works Mun defended the export of money in some circumstances by making a distinction between a 'general' and a 'particular' balance of trade.

That Mun's manifesto was used in the political debates of the 1660s undoubtedly has had some far-reaching repercussions. As a consequence, according to Gould, it has been looked upon mainly as a political pamphlet while its analytical and principal side often has been neglected. Moreover, it was only in the political turmoil of the 1660s that its main argument became the distinction between a general and a particular balance, for or against the export of bullion and so on. From the point of view of the 1620s, its central message looks quite different. Viewed from this perspective its main focus was the contemporary depression and trade crisis. More specifically, its aim was to argue against a monetary explanation of the crisis, which had been put forward by Malynes and others.[7] In his *A Discourse of Trade* Mun thoroughly defended the East India Company. In *England's Treasure* his focus was different. It is obvious that Mun here set the task to find some *general* explanations to the acute trade crisis of the 1620s. Moreover, in his search for a true interpretation of the trade and industrial crisis, Mun – together with Misselden – presented a new view and vision of the economic process which he thought would explain the turmoil and misery of the contemporary situation more accurately.

Mun's famous tract is thus a clear example of how texts may attain different meanings within differing discursive frameworks. As we argued in the first chapter, they must be understood in relation to the historical context in which they come to use. In this chapter we will show how the contemporary discussion of the 1620s' crisis gave rise to a specific literature dealing with economic issues which concerned the balance of trade and many have preferred to call 'mercantilist'. That it aroused in such an economic context does not of course delimit its analytical value. On the contrary, in order to better understand and find remedies for the crisis, people like Mun had to rethink how the economy operated. As Supple so acutely puts it, there is surely 'a strategic connexion between economic dislocation and development of economic thought'.[8] As we will argue, this process of rethinking implied the emergence of a kind of analysis quite different from the existing one. To some extent as a consequence of this discussion a new language and view of the 'economy' was born.

The 1620s discussion

In *The Economic History of England* Lipson characterised the 1620s as a period of trade and industrial crisis: 'One of the most memorable depressions in the annals of the English textile industries began in 1620 and lasted four to five years'.[9] The export trade of cloth (especially broadcloth) fell dramatically, many clothiers were brought to the verge of bankruptcy and unemployment was epidemic. Distress was common throughout England, and the authorities feared 'disturbances' and widespread begging and stealing. 'The Unemployed went in groups to the houses of the rich, demanding food and money, and seized provisions in the market place', Lipson wrote.[10] In May 1620 the Privy Council reported that: 'We have of late taken notice ... of the complaints made ... by manie weavers, spinners and fullers of the decay of cloathinge and the great distress thereby fallen upon them for want of worke ...'.[11] Still two years later the Council lamented upon a petition presented

> by the clothiers of the county of Suffolk and Essex complaining that they were disabled from going forward in their trade by reason of the great quantity of cloths lying upon their hands for which they could find no utterance or vent.[12]

The sudden crisis led to the appointment of parliamentary and Crown commissions and committees.[13] The discussion regarding its causes were widespread. According to Mun, among the general public the 'causes of those evils which we secke to schase away' were especially pointed out as: 1) the 'breach of Entercourse by forraine Nations' (foreign debasement of coins), 2) 'the abuse of the exchanges bewixt us and other Countries', 3) the melting down of coin into plate, and 4) 'our Dammage in Commerce with Strangers'.[14] In a memorandum set up in 1621 the crisis was looked upon mainly as a monetary one: as 'a want of money'. It pointed to the following 'causes' for this want:

1   high rate of mint charges which had disfavoured the coining of precious metals;
2   the Statute of Employment had not been effectuated properly in order to prevent the exportation of bullion;
3   the great import of tobacco from Spain;
4   the restrictions of foreigners to enter England;
5   the exportation of money to Ireland, Scotland and East India;
6   the 'restraint' of trade;
7   'the inequality of our gold and silver';
8   too-high (?) customs;
9   'the want of importation of silver & gold for Spain;' and
10   'the consumption of gold & silver in England' and the turning of money into plate.[15]

As we can see, there was certainly no undersupply of presumed causes for the maladies. Merely its number must have bewildered the people at the time. And to increase the confusion, there was no hint of how these factors might operate together to provide the proposed 'want of money'. However, also outside this inner circle an intensive discussion seems to have been going on regarding the causes of the crisis. In his overview of this public discussion Supple emphasises four other explanations highlighted in the discussion besides a generally acknowledged lack of money: the turning out of low-quality manufacture by deceitful manufactures, the emerge of competitive industries in Europe, the outbreak of the Thirty Years' War, and the accusation that trading companies used their monopolistic positions to keep down cloth prices and thus starved off clothiers and workers.[16]

In order to understand the causes behind this dramatic industrial crisis several suggestions have been put forward. In earlier research the failure of the so-called Cockayne's project was often regarded as a major factor. However, in more recent scholarly literature the all-importance of this unsuccessful project has been curtailed.[17]Although the failed attempt to sell only finished dyed cloth to the Dutch might have aggravated the crisis, there were more important structural and short-term causes behind the collapse of the early 1620s. Economic historians such as Hinton, Gould and Supple have argued that this decade experienced a combination of long-term structural changes and sudden shocks. With regard to structural shifts, England had gradually since the end of the sixteenth century experienced a relative decline of the previous almost monopolistic position of its old broadcloth manufacture (the Old Draperies). Thus in the 1620s, increased international competition and the subsequent decline of markets must have been obvious for many observers. After all, many writers during this period, including Misselden, warned for the 'false' supposition 'That the Dutch could not subsist without our English Cloth'.[18] Hence, instead, the late sixteenth century saw the rapid development of such cloth manufacture in continental Europe, not the least in the Low Countries. As a long-run effect of this structural crisis the New Draperies of lighter, colourful and cheaper fabrics aimed at Spain and the Mediterranean market emerged instead. However, this shift did not only necessitate the substitution of techniques and skills. It also implied a drastic re-localisation of industry, which caused distress and underemployment in many of the traditional cloth manufacturing areas.[19]

However, what seems to have worsened this structural crisis were some instant shocks, which upset the normal working of the international economy. As Gould and Supple have emphasised, especially the outbreak of the Thirty Years' War was followed by monetary chaos, which seriously worsened the conditions of the English export trade and manufacture. In order to provide money for warfare, princes and kings in Poland and the Holy German Empire carried through monetary manipulations by enhancing, debasing and clipping their coins. After all, in German scholarship this period has been named the *Kipper- und Wipper-zeit*. Moreover, violent debasement on the continent led to terms of trade turning unfavourable for England as its export wares became increasingly more expensive while simultaneously imports from these parts became cheaper. The latter was mainly an effect of that debasement on the continent and only slowly was followed by a proportional depreciation of local currencies. In an overall sense this all implied a drastic revaluation of the English currency. As Supple shows, inflationary price rises lagged behind 'that of manipulations because of the conventional nature of prices, institutional stickiness, ignorance and confusion'[20] Thus monetary manipulation and debasement was the major short-time factor which made the depression of the early 1620s so severe. As Gould points out this explanation has undoubtedly: 'the weight of inherent theoretical probability overwhelmingly on its side'.[21] In the long run it helped to price English broadcloth out of the market and quickened the pace of a transition from the Old to the New Draperies.

As already noted, an important consequence of the trade depression was the inauguration of several committees. In April 1622 the king's Privy Council appointed a committee (the smaller committee as pointed out by Edward Suprinyak)[22] including members from different trading companies such as the Eastland Company, the East India Company, the Russian Company, and the company of Merchant Adventurers, as well as representatives from the clothier districts and outports to inquire and give advice in the pressing situation. Among them, Mun stands out as the main spokesman of the group. It was at least he who was the author of several memoranda produced by this group during the following months.[23] About the same time another subcommittee was inaugurated with an ambition to 'found out the true groundes and motives, they are then to consider of the aptest and fittest remydie how such exceeding losses and inconveniences to this realme may hereafter be eschewed and avoyded'.[24] Within this body the most important members were Malynes, Ralph Maddison, Robert Cotton and William Sanderson.[25] Very soon the two committees were to part drastically concerning their interpretations of the causes of the trade crisis.

After the Malynes committee had delivered its report in May 1622 it was delivered – according to the king's strict order – to the merchant group for discussion. We can be assured of that it was very critical in its analysis. Moreover in October 1622 a bigger, and this time standing, committee began to work with the difficult issue to find proper remedies to the acute crisis. At least according to the acts of the Privy Council this committee seems to have been very active. A well-known member was the merchant Edward Misselden. He belonged to the Merchant Adventurers, and in 1621 he seems to have been involved with merchants trading with Spain.[26] In the standing committee Malynes was left out, but Maddison was still there, who was regarded to have similar views to Malynes.[27]

It was in this heated atmosphere that the famous pamphlet debate on exchanges and the balance of trade broke out between Malynes, Misselden and Mun. Involved in this *debacle* were also other members sitting in the various committees. It is clear that this discussion highlighted two fundamentally different views regarding the causes behind the crisis as well as its remedies. These disparate opinions are clearly spelled out in the unpublished tracts written by Mun and Malynes as representatives of the different committees, as well as in the well-known published treatises by Malynes, Misselden and Mun.[28]

On one side, we find what we might call the 'monetarists': a group which included Cotton, Maddison, Sanderson and Malynes. It seems clear that they shared the views of Malynes. Not unexpected this is particularly clear with regard to Maddison, who during the next thirty years would repeat that the heart of the problem was the 'exhausting of our money in generall' by the 'Marchant Exchanger'.[29] We will discuss Malynes and his group's ideas more throughly later on so it suffices here to emphasise that for Malynes the situation in the early 1620s seemed to prove what he had been preaching over two decades. Before the committees he referred to his earlier works *A Treatise of the Canker of England's Common Wealth* (1601) and the indeed allegorical *Saint George for England, Allegorically Described* (1601).

Thus in May 1622 he still propounded the view that: 'Therefore it is the Exchange unequally carrieth that is the efficient cause of the Kingdom's loss, and exportation of moneys'.[30] According to his view, exchange dealers and bankers of foreign origin had conspired against the English currency to keep it undervalued – far below his famous *par pro pari*, which we will return to shortly. In effect, this led to an export of money and bullion 'overseas', which explained the 'want of money' in England. Such tricks or 'feats' by bankers had even further disastrous effects as the want of money led to sinking prices at home which forced English merchants to exchange more wares in return for less in order to reap a profit. By both Malynes and Maddison this was described as an 'unequal exchange', which eventuated in a worsened balance of trade. Hence in order to make up for the falling exchange rate the English merchant had to dump his wares abroad. The merchant must, as he wrote in 1622, 'make rash sales of their commodities beyond the sea to pay their bills of exchange whereby they spoil the markette of others, and make them to sell too cheape'. On the contrary the transfer of 'moneys beyond the seas ... causeth the price of forraine commodities to increase'.[31]

As Malynes and his group saw it, the only remedy was to force the exchange rate up to the old par of 1586. Only by such forceful regulative measures to keep up the *par pro pari* could money flow back to England and the terms of trade improve. The only remedy was to see to it 'that not exchange be from hereforth made but acording to the true intrinsique value of our money'[32]. In this sense Malynes can certainly be characterised as a kind of monetarist. His viewpoint that English money was overvalued during this period and therefore exported has also been accepted by most later scholars. This thesis was restated by for example W A Shaw in his work on the history of the British currency as well as by modern scholars such as Supple.[33] That Malynes believed that 'the canker of England' was caused by money exporting bankers and exchange dealers does not immediately make him a bullionist of course – as so often presupposed in literature by Jones and others.[34] Instead, Malynes, as well as Maddison, should Richard rather be regarded as representatives of a line of thought going back to the Schoolmen. Thus his foreign exhange dealers was put on par with usurers. It was his deeply rooted conviction that the malicious feats of bankers and money exchangers in general had caused the crisis. As noted by Misselden this interpretation was of course old hat by the 1620s. For Malynes '... it hath taken more than twenty yeares to bring it to perfection'.[35] As can be seen from the writings of Maddison and Sanderson it was supported by many partakers in the discussion, perhaps a majority.

However, another idea had come up as a consequence of the discussion that challenged the monetarist explanation. In 1623 Malynes reports that some oppositional viewpoints had been raised by the merchant committee (which included Mun: 'some men are of the opinion that the sale of our Natyve Commodities in forraine parte surmount ... the balance of the commodities imported'.[36] Already in April 1622 he made the following observation: 'The adventurers seem to make a difference affirming the Exchange to rise and fall accordingly to the scarcity & plenty of money to be taken'. In their view, Malynes says disapprovingly, it is the 'unequal ballancing' of trade which is 'the sole cause of exportation of coyne, and that the raisening of the wares outwards to oppose the mart inwards will remedy the skill'.[37] The leader of the merchant committe, Mun, developed this idea in his tracts. First he stated that: 'It is not the enhauncing of the Pounds or debasing our own Standards beyond the sea which causeth our undervalued monys to be carried out of the Realm, neither does it hinder the bringing in of the said forrayne Punds'. Mun's simple idea was instead that it was the unfavourable, 'overballance' of trade which lead to falling exchange rates and the export of money. Or as expressed by him: 'this Overballance of our commodities ... must ... be carried away in ready mony'. In principle the level of exchange rates cannot be explained as a consequence of mere speculation, he stressed. 'So it plainelie apppcauseth, that it is not just gain [which] is the effecient cause to carrie away our money, for this underballance must out in money'.[38]

What Mun here says and later on would repeat more comprehensively in his book *Englands Treasure by Forraigne Trade* is that if the balance of trade is unfavourable – a situation that appears whenever a country imports more than it exports – the exchange rate must fall as there is a greater demand for foreign money or bills of exchange. Money and bills of exchange are commodities of which the prices are regulated in the same manner as other commodities: through the mechanism of supply and demand. Thus the value of bills of exchange, for example, is regulated by the 'plenty and scarcity of money'. From this follows, of course, that any attempt to regulate the exchange rate at a certain level is futile. Thus the only effect of forcing the exchange rate of English money to rise to the rate of 1586 – something which Malynes and his group agitated for – would only lead to that 'the English merchant should thereby loose about 15 in one hundred in Germany, the Low countries, and all this arrives to the gain of the strangers ... if the English Merchant cannot raise the price of the cloth in those parts proportionate to this raise of Exchange'. However, such an undertaking would be – as stated in the report by Mun, R Bell, G Kendricke, H Wood, T Jennings and J Skynner in May 1622 – 'difficult if not impossible to be done'.[39]

It is clear that Mun by this had presented a novel and different conception of the economy which challenged earlier interpretations. The

main innovation was to conceive the economy as a system of impersonal laws of supply and demand. He regarded the principal agents in
the marketplace – merchants as well as bankers – as structured by this
system. If an economic crisis occurred this was not caused by evil
feats but by that something was wrong with the complicated economic
machinery. What was wrong in this particular instance was that the
balance of trade had turned unfavourably against England.

Surely, in the long run this vision of an interlinked market system
would win out. However, we must point out that Mun's emphasis on
the balance of trade came out of the heated debate with Malynes'
group and that the general implications of this new view concerning
the economy was not very well understood at the time.[40] Moreover,
whether Mun's explanation of the 1620s' crisis was any better than
Malynes's is of course also a different matter. As we noted, more
recent scholars have tended to choose Malynes's perhaps more short-
term monetary explanation than Mun's rather general and abstract
interpretation. However, as a means to understand the economic problems of the day, the view that 'overbalance' of trade was the crucial
factor became increasingly popular. A sign of such popularity is that
Cotton, who, as we saw, had been a member of Malynes's committee,
most probably shared his viewpoints at that time. However, in 1626 he
was ready to concede that:

> it is not raising of the value that doth it, but the balasing [*sic*] of
> trade: for buy we in more than we sell of other Commodities, be
> the money never so high prized, we must part with it to make the
> disproportion even; If we sell more than we buy, the contrary will
> follow.[41]

A market process

Hence, in the course of this discussion, a new approach emerged
which gave rise to a focus on the balances of trade and payments.
However, it is in these debates that we also can see the birth of a new
vision of the economic realm, which would be further elaborated by a
later generation of mercantilists and classical political economists. For
it is clear that we feel much more at home with the analysis brought
forward by Mun and Misselden than with authors such as Malynes,
Milles and Maddison. This is not because Mun and Misselden focus
on the 'real' economic forces of the marketplace instead of monetary
issues like debasement, clipping, conspiracies against the English currency by 'Lombard' bankers and so on, mentioned in sixteenth- and
early seventeenth-century economic literature. No doubt such practices
were widespread at the time. Instead it is because their vision of the

economic process is quite distinct. Thus they present a stylised picture of the economy as a system which after all is not so far from ours some three hundred years later.

Unfortunately, we do not know very much about *Edward Misselden* (1608–54).[42] What we do know, however, is that he was an influential member of the Merchant Adventurers. And as such he was probably deeply involved in the controversy around Cockayne's project, which stirred up controversy during these years. In the first decade of the seventeenth century the Merchant Adventurers Company had come under severe attack for selling unwrought and undyed cloth to the Low Countries, where it was then worked up for the profit of its manufacturers and workers. The view that it would be better if England would dye and dress up its cloth itself and only export finished wares was commonplace at least since the sixteenth century.[43] Thus already in 1602 John Wheeler had to defend the company exactly on these grounds. Through this company, he pointed out:

> there is shipped out yearly … at least sixtie thousande white clothes, besides coloured of all sorts, kerseys short and long, bays, Cottons.… There goeth also out of England, besides these Wolle Clothes, into the Low Countries, wool, fel, lead, Tinne, Saffron … Leather, Tallow.… By all which commodities a number of labouring men are set on work & gaign much monie, besides that which the Merchant gaineth, which is no small matter.[44]

Paying his dues to the standard policy doctrine, he found it even necessary to argue that:

> I have heard it credible reported, that all the commodities, that come out of all other Countries, besides England, were not wonte to sett so manie people on woorke in the low Countries, as the commodities, which came out of England onley did.[45]

In any case, for right or wrong, in the beginning of the seventeenth century this formula was used for seeking to abolish the privileges of the Merchant Adventurers. Thus the famous Cockaynes project was launched in 1615 by inaugurating exclusive privileges to a new cloth exporting company, The King's Merchant Adventurers. Its aim was explicitly to overthrow the original Merchant Adventurers. Many of its members refused to join the new company at first but had to concede. It seems clear that Misselden was one of the fiercest opponents of the Cockayne scheme. And as it was, Malynes had been a partner of William Cockayne in an earlier project to strike copper tokens in 1613. However, as this project had failed, also the new one did. In 1617 the

King's Merchant Adventurers was dissolved and the privileges of the old Merchant Adventurers were restored.[46]

According to Astrid Friis, Misselden was a spokesman of the Adventurers in 1616 when the Cockayne project was launched. Some years thereafter (as we saw) he sat in the Standing Committee on the trade crisis. And it was during this period that he published two treatises – in 1622 and 1623. As we will see, their content and political message were paradoxically different. While still holding office as a Deputy General with the Adventurers, Misselden joined the East India Company in 1623. As a person he seems not to have been approved of much. In 1649 a group of Adventurers branded him as 'a scandalous man in his life and conversations'.[47]

It is really nothing in his *Free Trade or the Meanes to Make Trade Flourish* (1622) that distinguished Misselden from the standard interpretation of the crisis at this time which mixed monetary and trade issues as we saw. The title of his very first chapter is very illustrative: 'The causes of the want of money in England'. When explaining the 'want' he made a distinction between 'immediate' and 'mediate' reasons. As the principal 'immediate' reason he regarded 'the undervaluation of his Maiesties Coyne, to that of Neighbouring Countries'.[48] Exactly like Malynes, he believed that 'undervaluation' had caused money to have 'turned out of the Kingdome'.[49] In line with what many others said at the time, his main remedy was 'the raising of the King's coine'.[50] That a rise of price was an inevitable consequence of such a devaluation he was aware of. However, he said, 'it is much better to the kingdome to have things deare with plenty of money ... than to have things cheape with want of money, which now makes every man complain'.[51]

When deciding the cause behind the outflow of silver money from England he however held a different view to Malynes. It was really his critical remarks against Malynes's *par* which agitated the latter to write a tract in response and thus triggered the famous controversy. It is not, says Misselden, 'the rate of Exchanges but the value of monies, here lowe, elsewhere high, which cause their Exportation, nor do the Exchanges, but the plenty and scarcity of monies cause their values'.[52] Thus the main problem was the exportation of money, and Misselden could see no other remedy than a more strict enforcement of the Statute of Employment. This Statute from the fifteenth and sixteenth centuries ordained foreign merchants when trading with England to 'employ' their money in order to purchase English wares instead of bringing them back to their native country.

Furthermore, he found the active reason for this drain of silver money when discussing the 'mediate' or 'remote' reasons of the crisis. Here he especially pointed to the 'great Excesse of this Kingdome in

consuming the Commodities of Foreine Countries'.[53] A Commonwealth which continues this policy will sooner or later 'begger itself',
he said. In this context he particularly stressed the 'trade out of Christendome' carried out by the East India Company that led to that the
money 'never returneth againe'.[54] Another important 'mediate' cause
was the 'warres of Christendome', which caused a raising of money in
Germany.[55] Thus the outflow of money played a given independent
role in the explanation of the decay of trade. Misselden could not
avoid the popular explanation that usurious activities by Italian
exchange-dealers had conspired to keep the English money at a low
rate 'for their own advantage'.[56] However, how these 'immediate' and
'mediate' causes were linked together he gave no hint of.

This task was however addressed in Misselden's second published
tract, *The Circle of Commerce or the Balance of Trade* (1623). It is
perhaps best known for its sharp polemic tone directed against Malynes.
Misselden did not hesitate from making insulting remarks concerning
Malynes. 'Is this man madde?', he asked. Malynes was described as a
malicious Dutchman with a 'rude and unmannerly manner of writing'.
Further, he was depicted as a 'poore man with no Genius at all' who had
stolen most of his 'stuff' from authors like Milles and Gresham.[57]
However, for this reason Misselden's little book should not be regarded
as a mere oddity.[58] Thus, for the first time in print, here is presented an
interpretation of the crisis close to what Mun and the merchant committee had arrived at. For example, there were no longer any critical
remarks spurned against the East India Company or foreign money
dealers. One the whole, he was turning his previous analysis upside
down.[59] He started out with a principal remark:

> For it is not the rate of Exchange, whether it be higher or lower,
> that maketh the price of Commodities deare or cheape, as Malynes
> would here inferre; but it is the plenty or scarcities of Commod-
> ities, their use or Non-use that maketh them rise and fall in price.[60]

As previously, he pointed out that it is: 'The plentie or scarcitie of
money which perpetually doth cause the Exchanges to rise and fall'.[61]
However, such an ebb and flow of money was in its turn connected
with demand and supply of commodities on the import and export
market:

> If the Native Commodities exported doe waight downe and exceed
> in value the forraine Commodities imported; it is a rule that never
> faile's, that then the Kingdome growe's rich and prosper in estate
> and stocke: because the overplus therof must needs come in, in
> treasure.

If the opposite happens 'the overplus must needs goe out in treasure'.[62] This was really the first printed presentation, in the English language,[63] of the famous balance of trade doctrine. Misselden hailed this doctrine as an 'excellent and politique invention to show the difference of waight in Commerce of one Kingdome with another'.[64] By using this 'invention' he reformulated what he regarded as the main cause of the economic crisis of the 1620s: 'We are fallen into a great Under-ballance of Trade with other Nations'.[65] There was no longer any place for the 'mysteries' of the money exchange.

We can only speculate about what happened between 1622 and 1623 to set Misselden off in such a different direction. Certainly, as we saw, he had become involved with the East India Company. This perhaps made him less critical of its export of bullion and closer to Mun and his group. It is nevertheless clear that he by this time had come in contact with Mun's work before the merchant's subcommittee. In 1623 he talked very approvingly of Mun: 'his judgement in all trade, his diligence at home, his experience abroad, have adorn'd him with such endownements, as are rather to bee wisht in all, then easie to be found in many Merchants of these times'.[66] Most probably he was aware of what Mun had written on the crisis. Moreover, he accepted the formula and used it for his onslaught on Malynes. This of course did not make Misselden a modern 'free trader'. As is well known, 'free trade' in this age meant something very different than it does in modern times. To be in favour of 'free trade' was to be critical towards the monopoly of old chartered companies and exclusive privileges. However, trade and commerce should still be orderly and serve a public purpose.[67]

It is clear that Thomas Mun (1571–1641) was a central figure in formulating an alternative to the monetarist interpretations of the crisis. Unfortunately, we seem to know just as little about him as we do about Misselden. According to his son, he 'was in his time famous amongst Merchants, and well known to most men of business, for his general Experience in affairs and notable into Trade'.[68] Further, from his own pen we learn that Mun had gained experience as a merchant in Italy. During his stay in this country he had served under Duke Ferdinand of Tuscany and lived in Leghorn for some time.[69] Thereafter, in 1615 he became an official of the East India Company, and it is later on that we find him appointed to several committees and commissions.[70] And it was in such a position that he produced a number of reports and memorandums.

However, only one short treatise was published in Mun's own name during his lifetime. It was a short tract on the East India trade, *A Discourse of Trade From England Unto the East Indies* (1621). It included no reference to the current crisis and might as well have been written some years earlier. Rather, it must be regarded as a partisan defence of the East India Company against 'diverse Objections which are Usually Made against the Same'.[71] And as such, it was not radically different from Wheeler's intervention in 1601 in order to defend the Merchant Adventurers.[72] Mun opened up his little tract by acknowledging the role of foreign trade: 'The trade of Merchandize, is not onely that laudable practize whereby the entercourse of Nations is so worthily performed, but also ... the verie Touchstone of a Kingdome's prosperitie'.[73] Thereafter, he described what in effect is an early formulation of the balance theory:

> So doth it come to passe in those Kingdomes, which with great care and warinesse doe ever vent out more of their home commodities, then they import and use of forren wares; for so undoubtedly the remainder must returne to them in treasure. But where a contrarie course is taken, through wantonnesse and riot; to over waste both forren and domestike wares; there must the money of necessitie be exported.[74]

His defence of the East India Company for the charge that it exported 'gold, silver and coyne ... out of Christendome' is well known. By presenting export and import figures he sought to convince his readers that the Company instead 'bring more treasure into this Realme than of the other trades of this Kingdome ... being put together'.[75] Hence, it brings back wares with a much higher value than the bullion sent out. Moreover, many of these goods will later on be re-exported to other countries, he points out. Hence they will provide England with an 'overplus to the increase of this Kingdomes treasure'.[76]

While Mun seemed satisfied in this small tract to have 'done my task to cleare the East India Trade from imputation',[77] the tone of the posthumous *England's Treasure by Forraign Trade* (1664) is utterly different. Most important, it is a complete misnomer to describe this 'mercantilist manifesto', probably written in the late 1620s, as a spontaneous reflection of reality by a man who was unable to argue in principle. Instead it stands out for its clarity of style and argument as well as for its author's ability to discuss in principle. It is not easily defined as another partisan document defending some company's interests. Certainly, Mun is a partisan of the merchants. But in his defence of this group he points out that it is in the interest of the whole Commonwealth to bring about more trade and manufactures. He does not defend any particular interest. He seeks to develop a general analysis on the factors which can make a nation flourish in wealth and power. In his endeavour to serve the public good he becomes almost 'moralistic', A Finkelstein comments.[78] However, this does not contradict his new views on the balance of trade or even of an economic order of balance between supply and demand. On the contrary, he believed that such a 'natural' order was intrinsically moral as well. This is a view which he shared also with the Scots in the eighteenth century as well as with later political economists.[79]

Hence Mun's ambition in this book is to provide: 'the general meanes whereby a Kingdome may be enriched'.[80] The rule by which this shall be achieved is simple: 'to sell more to strangers yearly than wee consume of theirs in value'.[81] For a country without its own mines the only possibility to achieve more treasure is by foreign trade. Although money is not 'the life of trade', as barter is a possible alternative, a net inflow of treasure undoubtedly has beneficial effects, he thinks.[82] Such an inflow of money quickens trade and makes land values rise. It also provides the prince with more treasure 'in his coffers'. He recognises that an 'overplus' of money may imply rising prices, which in turn might cause sinking exports, 'less consumption'. However, this will only be the effect if we hoard and stop 'trading with our money', he says.[83] We will return to how this undoubtedly central passage shall be understood.

However, besides presenting this new principle, another important aim of this treatise was to counter Malynes's interpretation of the 1620s' crisis. Hence, like Misselden, he argues that exchange rates are regulated by the inflow and outflow of money and exchange bills. Such an inflow and outflow is in turn caused by the 'real' balance of trade. Hence, he argues: 'that which causeth an under or overvaluing of moneys by Exchange, is the plenty or scarcity thereof in those places where the Exchanges are made'. And he presents an example:

> [W]hen here is plenty of money to be delivered for Amsterdam, then shall our money be undervalued in Exchange, because they who take up the money, seeing it so plentifully thrust upon them, do thereby make advantage to themselves in taking the same at an undervalue'.[84]

Further in a passage which almost word for word repeats the manuscript texts from 1622 and 1623, he says: 'it is not the undervaluing of our money in exchange, but the overballancing of our trade that carrieth away our treasure'.[85]

Certainly, as so many have pointed out, Mun's 'balance of trade' should rather be interpreted as a 'balance of payments'. It is clear that he, as well as Misselden, included 'hidden' incomes such as rents, charges and so on, in his famous balance.[86] Thus what we have here, in fact, is more than an embryo of a modern theory of foreign exchange relations. George Goschen has for example pointed out that at bottom 'the exchanges in question are exchanges of claims and debts'.[87] As we have seen, this is in principle what also Mun and Misselden said. However, our task here is not to discuss the advantages or disadvantages of Mun's presentation of exchange relations from the point of view of modern theory. It is more important for us to note that he largely uses this 'classical' theory to argue against Malynes and his followers:

> So by this we plainly see, that it is not the **power of Exchange** that doth enforce treasure where the rich prince will have it, but it is the money proceeding of wares in Foraigne trade that doth enforce the echange, and rules the price thereof high or low, according to the plenty or scarcity of the said money.[88]

It is in *England's Treasure* that Mun presents what later Smith would title the 'mercantile system'. He claims that, in order to prosper, a country must export more than it imports. This gives rise to an inflow of money, which – if we trade with it – increases the stock of the Commonwealth. Further, a country must direct its trade so that it exports manufactured goods and imports raw materials to work up. Indeed, he says, 'our wealth might be a rare discourse for all Christendome to admire and fear, if we would but add **Art and Nature**, our **labour** to our **natural means**'.[89] Explicitly aimed for an English public, this message had an aggressive tone especially directed towards the Dutch. The control over important trades such as the 'fishing of herrings, Ling and Cod … would be sooner decided by swords, than with words', he anticipates.[90]

The message that a country in order to thrive should export more than it imports, as well as export as much worked-up goods as possible, was most certainly a perfect match from the point of view of contemporary orthodoxy. As we saw, such a policy was regarded as the highest wisdom already during the sixteenth century. Misselden for example had been very explicit on this point: 'this Ballance of the Kingdomes trade is no conceit or Novelty, but hath been the wisdom and policy even of elder times'.[91] In accordance with this view, only raw materials of strategic importance for the country (log timber for war ships, etc.), or such which could be worked up by domestic industry, should be imported. Further, an export of raw material should be discouraged. However, old as this policy was, after Mun and Misselden it would increasingly be vindicated by the doctrine of a 'favourable balance of trade'. The balance became a measuring rod for whether a certain state was successful in its foreign trade or not. As emphasised by Mun, it became the 'true rule of our Exchange', and its success was manifested in an increase of the country's 'stock'.

We have already discussed how the balance theory might be interpreted as well as what Mun and other mercantilists understood regarding concepts such as 'wealth', 'stock' and so on. However, it would be wrong only to regard Mun's and Misselden's role in making popular the 'doctrine' of a favourable balance of trade. As we noted, it was largely overlooked in the heated discussion of the 1660s that their main aim had been to explain the 1620s' crisis in more general terms. Even more acutely in this respect their efforts brought forward something new.

For Supple, Mun was 'the economist of a competetive era'.[92] As such, both he and Misselden clearly recognised the all-importance of the market mechanism. Hence according to Misselden: 'Merchants of experience know, that commonly one commidty riseth, when another falleth; and they fall and rise, as they are mor or lesse in request and use'.[93] Certainly, the market was a place where 'every man is nearest to himself'.[94] However, both Mun and Misselden were eager to point out that such egotism was domesticated by the forces of the market. Therefore, bankers or exchange dealers could not randomly make their feats in order to hurt the public. Although characterised by uncertainty, the market was a place of order. The impersonal forces of the market structured the behavioural regimes of different agents. To function properly, this order had to be recognised as a 'natural thing' and therefore freely 'have [its] course'.[95]

Both Mun and Misselden applied this market mechanism to price formation in general. The forces of supply and demand created cheapness or dearness of goods. By conditioning the actual price of 'food and rayment', they at the same time proportioned the wages of the poor.[96] According to Mun and Misselden, as we he have seen, demand and supply also ruled the exchange of bills and money with other countries. Thus the idea that 'exchange by merchant's Bill's' was determined 'according to the plenty or scarcitie of money' had already appeared in the 'humble report' written by Mun in May 1622.[97] Further, they both supposed that demand and supply conditions decided when it was profitable to export money instead of remitting exchange bills, that is, the actual level of the so-called export points. In this context Misselden wrote:

> Now if the gain of the carying out of our money be 10 or 15 per Cent to the stranger, then the Exchange by his owne rule must bee set so much higher to answer the sayd gaine & prevent the exportation.[98]

Particularly Mun was full of scorn against those who thought that the laws of the market could be easily manipulated by merchants, monopolists, bankers or kings. Thus his 'moral' conclusion in *England's Treasure by Forraign Trade* is thunderous:

But let the Merchants exchange be at a high rate, or at a low rate, or at the **Par pro pari**, or put down altogether; let Forraign Princes enhance their Coins, or debase their Standards, and let His Majesty do the like, or keep them constant as they now stand; Let forraign Coind pass current here in all payments at higher rates than they are worth at the Mint; Let the Statute for employments by Strangers do his worst; let Princes oppress, Lawyers extort, Usurers bite, prodigals wast, and lastly let merchants carry out what money they shall have occasion to use in traffique. Yet all these actions can work no other effects in the course of trade than is described in this discourse. For so much Treasure only will be bought in or carried out of a Commonwealth, as the Forraign trade doth over or under ballance in value.[99]

A further important consequence of their stress on the role of the market process must also be acknowledged. Both authors were well aware of higher prices implying lower demand. Moreover, they knew that this rule was applicable also to foreign trade. Demand for export goods was thus in principle elastic. For example, Mun stated that a country must of course try to sell its produce as dear as possible 'so far forth as the high price cause not a less vent in quantity'.[100]

With this in mind, it has been much debated why they did not draw the seemingly logical conclusion that after Barbon, Gervais and Hume would become recognised as the specie–flow mechanism. Especially as they, as Viner pointed out, recognised that foreign demand was elastic as well as acknowledged the principle of a quantity theory of money. Why not then take a third step and recognise that from this followed that an inflow of money would lead to rising prices and lower exports? According to Viner, Mun and Misselden had been unable to combine those two propositions 'into a coherent theory of a self-regulating international distribution of the money metal'. If not so, this would undoubtedly have destroyed the basis for the favourable balance of trade theory, he was convinced.[101] However, as Gould has proposed, it is very doubtful whether Mun not in fact was very well aware of the principle of the quantitative theory of money although he disregarded it for some reason.[102] Thus according to Mun:

[A]ll men do consent that plenty of mony in a Kingdom doth make the native commodities dearer, which as it is to the profit of some private men in their revenues, so is it directly against the benefit of the Publique in the quantity of the trade; for as plenty of mony makes wares dearer, so dear wares decline their use and consumption.... And although this is a very hard lesson for some great landed men to learn, yet I am sure it is a true lesson for all the land to observe, lest when wee have gained some store of mony by trade, wee lose it again by not trading with our mony.[103]

Hence, by applying the supply-demand mechanism to price formation *in general*, Mun and Misselden without doubt provided a new principle with lasting influence. It might of course be stated that this was an insight that they had gained as practising merchants taking part in the daily haggle of the marketplace.[104] Certainly, they explicitly referred to the role of empirical observation for economic inquiry. Thus their 'method' seems quite closely connected to a kind of empiricism which developed during these years and which is connected to Bacon.[105] Already in the 1620s Bacon had presented his general viewpoints to a wide audience in the first editions of his famous *Essays*.

It is certainly difficult to detect a direct influence by Bacon on Mun and Misselden.[106] When Misselden cites and makes reference to philosophical works, it is mostly Aristotle and other classical thinkers he mentions. He quotes from Aristotle in order to emphasise how trade was a natural phenomenon and for that reason pleasing to the 'Creator'. Moreover, his discussion on causality as well as matter, form and essence in *The Circle of Commerce* is unmistakenly Aristotelian.[107] However, references to Aristotle was customary at the time and does not tell us much about what an author's real position was.[108] Simultaneously, Misselden's reference to the controversial 'famous logician of France' Ramus shows that he was well acquainted also with the radical opposition against Aristotelianism. Moreover, at an early stage Bacon had been influenced by Ramus and saw his own work in line with this older master.[109] Hence, what Misselden had to say about Ramus is of even greater interest: 'we must not be so curious in our *Distributions* that in striving for the *Method* we lose the *Matter*'.[110] This citation is picked from a context where Misselden defended his use of making *Dichotomies* against the slanders of Malynes. Surely, it can be read as a critique of the formalism and empty definition making of the Aristotelian school and as such in the spirit of Bacon. Hence in his work *Novum Organum* Bacon pointed out that Aristotle 'imposed innumerable arbitrary distinctions upon the nature of things; being everywhere more anxious as to definitions in teaching and the accuracy of the wording of his propositions, than in the eternal truth of things'.[111]

Hence, most probably from this basis Mun and Misselden argued for more induction and less deduction. They wanted to establish their vision of the economic process upon a sound empirical basis. Thus they argued that they were neither learned nor big thinkers. 'This matter is much too high for me', Mun says at one point.[112] Moreover, when dedicating his 1622 treatise to his royal superiors, Misselden described his subject as a very humble one indeed. It is, he says, perhaps too low for a king to devote his time to.[113] In his first tract defending the East India Company, Mun asks to be forgiven for performing his task: 'for want of learning … without varietie of words or eloquence: yet it is done with all integritie of truth, in every particular, as I shall be readie to make proofe upon all occassions, which may be offered'.[114]

Rather than as instances of mere humbleness, such examples must clearly be envisaged as statements propounding an empiricist methodology. At the same time, we shall not be conceived. Hence, it is too simple to say that they based their conceptualisation of the economic world on simple discrete empirical facts. It is especially misleading to interpret Mun's *England's Treasure by Forraign Trade* in such a fashion. Instead it also presents an abstract economic world of balancing forces ruled by market relations. For example, the extent to which short-run factors such as monetary disturbances might disrupt the self-regulating order of supply and demand he does not take any account of. It is perhaps not the world of modern neo-classical economics. But, to the extent that Mun's vision of the market process also involves moral propositions, this is not original for his time and can also be said of modern economics.

However, there are also other clear linkages between Mun, Misselden and the Baconians.[115] First, especially with Mun, the so-called *panoptery* stemming from Bacon, which implied that everything should be measured in figures, is clearly visible. Thus his *A Discourse of Trade* displays a host of figures in order to show the beneficial effects of the East India trade. Further, in a general way, this new attitude to the study of economy and society is connected with the increasing use of the word 'balance'. This word first appears in an economic text with Malynes in 1601 – in the specific form of 'overbalancing'.[116] But as Beer has shown, 'balance of trade' was explicitly used as a conception in an unpublished report by Sir Lionel Cranfield and Sir John Wostenholme in 1615.[117] The year thereafter it was used by Bacon in a paper 'Advice to Sir George Villiers'.[118] And as we noted, the first time it came into print was with Misselden in 1623.[119] In 1625, lastly, it appeared in an essay in the third edition of Bacon's *Essays*, titled 'Of Seditions and Troubles'.

In a general sense, the increasing use of the concept of 'balance' was connected with increased borrowings of metaphors from the natural world in order to picture processes in society.[120] Such borrowings which became notorious especially in the mid-seventeenth century have often been connected with the breakthrough of a Baconian programme for universal science. For Bacon the noble course of scientific progress was to connect nature, man and society in a huge project of learning.

'Balance' was in this sense a term originally developed by physicists to describe a state of equilibrium in the natural world.[121] Thus both the natural and the social world were regarded as made up by inter-reacting 'mechanical forces'.[122] This idea that the economic world in principle could be studied in the same manner as the natural world undoubtedly had far-reaching consequences.[123] Most profoundly it established the view that also society and the economy were structured by laws and general principles detectable by Man. From there, the further idea that these 'natural' mechanical forces would work better if they were left to themselves was not late to emerge.

Thus, it cannot only be practical experience gained from trade that stimulated Mun and Misselden to perceive of the economy in terms of a mechanical system of 'real' economic forces. The most-simple objection is of course that other observers living at the same time drew totally different conclusions from the very same experience. Furthermore, as de Roover has showed, it is wrong to believe that not also 'monetarists' such as Gresham, Malynes, Robinson and Maddison lived in a world which was just as competitive as Mun's and Misselden's.[124] Or how should one from such a perspective take account of the – one must admit – for us rather strange views of Thomas Milles? It might even be held, as we have seen, that such observers painted an even more accurate picture of the economic situation during this period than Mun and Misselden did. Thus Malynes was perhaps more realistic when he pointed out the role of monetary disturbances and foreign debasement as important causes behind the worsening of English exchange relations in the 1620s. However, Mun and Misselden painted an abstract picture, which was probably more accurate in a long-run perspective.

Moreover, it would be utterly misleading to suppose that especially Mun in *England's Treasure by Forraign Trade* had the ambition to present a precise analysis of what *actually* occurred. Instead his aim – as well as Misselden's – was to provide a framework relying on a set of new principles, the most important being the interplay of the market forces. To this extent it was the working operations of those forces that they were trying to describe – not their actual historical manifestations.[125]

In *Circe of Commerce* Misselden described the economy as a 'natural' system, an independent property almost with laws of its own. When discussing the taking and delivering of exchange bills, he presented the following vision of the micro foundations of this system:

> Which Taking and Delivering, as it is A voluntary Contract, made by the mutuall consent of both parties; so are both alike free to Take and deliver at their own pleasure, as in all other contracts and bargains of buying and selling. And trade hath in it such a

kinde of naturall liberty in the course and use thereof, as it will not indure ro be fors't by any. If you attempt it, it is a thousand to one, that you leave it not worse then you found it.

Further, in this passage he made a clear distinction between 'the naturall liberty in the use of things indifferent' and 'the exercise of government'. And lastly he approvingly cited the proverb *Quod natura dedit, tollere nemo potest* ('That which nature give, no man can take away').[126] More of the same can be found in Mun. His belief in the market economy as regulated by mechanical forces is quite clear from various passages in his texts. He for example stressed: 'for whatsoever is forced in one way must out again another way'.[127] Nor is it possible, Mun believed, for men to interfer with these forces. He pointed out: 'Although a rich Prince hath great power, yet is there not power in every rich Prince to make the staple of Money run where he pleaseth'.[128]

Without doubt, these were radical views during this time. We must remember that we are dealing with a period when royal absolutism was on the march almost everywhere in Europe. And as a consequence of this, must we not rethink the standard conception of the 'mercantile system' as brought forward by Smith? Obviously there are some good reasons for such a revaluation. One important point to press is that, contrary to the popular view, Mun and Misselden believed in the existence of an independent economc sphere outside polity and state. Further, their moral philosophy implied that man was egotistical and full of private vices. They interpreted man in a materialistic fashion. In fact, in their hands, he turned into the stylised 'economic man', which has haunted us ever since. We shall not complain over such things as usury, Mun tells us. It is always so 'that one man's necessity becomes another man's opportunity'.[129] It is a rule that high rates of interest always appear where there is a want of money. Thus usury is merely a reflection of what is natural: the balance of forces in a market economy. Moreover, as we saw, Misselden was clear that 'every man … is nearest to himself'.[130]

However, this basic 'hedonism' did not interfere with the public good as an ultimate end of economic activity. Although we cannot put our full trust in the Christian man conscious of his moral duties and obligations, good order can nevertheless be obtained. Thus, according to Mun, 'The love and services of our Country consisteth not so much in the knowledge of those duties which are to be performed by others, as in the skilful practice of that which is done by our selves'. Therefore, he continued, 'the private gain may ever accompany the publique good'.[131] Certainly, Mun here used the words 'may accompany' quite consciously. Although he emphasised the positive role of economic freedom and the interplay of market forces, the identity between 'private vices and public benefits' presupposed that the Commonwealth adhered to the rule of natural order, that is, to kept up a favourable balance of trade. As we know, eighteenth-century thinkers would draw other conclusions. But it is quite clear that the groundwork for a more radical doctrine was laid by Mun and Misselden.[132]

The bite of usury

Misselden's adversary in the pamphlet war of the early 1620s, Gerard Malynes (1583–1641), was most probably of Dutch origin. Born in Antwerp he named himself *de* Malynes in his first published works, but dropped the particle thereafter – probably to appear more English.[133] A good reputation in this sense could undoubtedly be of importance, as Malynes better than most economic writers of this era fitted to the description of a 'rent-seeker'. He had sought monopoly rights to issue copper coins together with Cockayne, he had been involved in silver and lead mining as well as taking part in a number of economic schemes which presupposed Royal support. Early on he was appointed to different state commissions. The Privy Council asked for his advice on trade matters, and already in 1600 he was commissioned by the Privy Council to establish 'a true Par of Exchange'.[134] Later on he also served as an assay Master of the Mint. First and foremost he was a merchant, of course. As such he 'did not enjoy an untarnished reputation inasmuch as he involved himself in some shady business deals and highly speculative ventures'.[135] Many of these business ventures did not turn out well. Moreover, in 1598 he was imprisoned in Fleet prison for a debt, and in 1619 he was back there for his part in the copper issue project. However, all this must have given him great insight in monetary, financial and trade issues. Hence, without doubt he was able to talk with some authority in the trade crisis discussion of the early 1620s.

As Misselden has informed us, by the early 1620s the idea of a *par pro pari* was an old scheme of Malynes. Already *A Treatise of the Canker of England's Common Wealth* (1601) provided an outline of his general approach. The main problem for England, 'the unknowne disease of the Politicke body of our Weale publique', was 'overbalance'. Moreover,

> This overballancing consisteth properly in the price of commodities, and not in the quantitie or qualities; and to countervaile the same, our treasure must of necessitie be exhausted and spent, to the great impoverishing of the Realme, and the transportation of our monies.[136]

As the reason why 'forrein commodities to be more risen in price then our home commodities', he especially mentioned the transport of money out of the country.[137] According to Malynes, one important factor behind the terms of trade developing unfavourably for England was that the silver flow 'from the West Indies to Christendom' had less benefited England than other European states.[138] This idea was then repeated in his discussion on Bodin and the quantity theory of money in the small pamphlet *England's View in the Unmasking of Two Paradoxes* (1603) as well as in later works.[139] However, his main explanation here, as always, was that such a transport depended upon a low exchange rate for English money, which had made it profitable to export in specie. Already in 1601 he especially stressed that the low exchange rate mainly depended upon manipulations performed by monopolistic foreign bankers and exchange dealers. At bottom, he concluded, it was 'the abuse of the exchange for money to be the very efficient cause of this disease'.[140] And the remedies he proposed are familiar to us by now: the transportation of money should be prevented and money raised to its 'true value'.

Although he further elaborated these ideas in in his subsequent works, they remained fundamentally the same. In his encyclopedical *Consuetudo vel Lex Mercatoria* (1622), Malynes described the foreign exchange alternatively as the 'spirit' ('directing and controlling by just proportions the prices and values of Commodities and Moneys') or the 'Rudder of a ship'.[141] In his view, foreign 'exchange for moneys' played a main role in England's 'overballancing of commodities'. Hence, the undervaluation of English money lead to its merchants having to offer increasingly more wares in order to keep up the old import counted *in value*. As we saw, they must make 'rash sales' and 'sell cheap' in order to pay for their bills of exchange as terms of trade was growing worse due to this spiral process of deteriorating terms of trade.[142] One important consequence, which he used as an argument against Misselden, was that an increasingly less-priced export would make 'unequal exchange' even worse. To increase 'our manufactures … is not like to moderate the overbalancing', he said. This was the case, as 'all men of judgement will say, that the proceed or returne of the said manufactures will come unto us in forraine Commodities, because moneys and Bullion cannot be brought in but to losee, as the case standeth'.[143]

It was especially in *Consuetudo* that he scorned the evil practices of bankers and foreign exchange dealers. His long list of the diabolic 'feats of bankers' was in fact, however, borrowed from a memorandum probably written by Gresham around 1560.[144] Regardless, among the things he accused bankers and exchange dealers of was their exporting of money without consent to 'grow rich and live without adventure of the Seas or travaille' and especially for manipulating the exchange.[145] Lastly, in all his later works, the *par pro pari* appears as the only true remedy to the undervaluation of money and overballance of trade. In *The Centre of the Circle of Commerce* he defined the *par* as:

> The Rule therefore … is infallible that when the exchange doth answer the true values of our moneys, according to their inward weight and finesse, and their outward valuation; they are never exported, because the gaine is answerable by exchange, which is the cause of exportation.[146]

As we have discussed, Malynes's attempt to find the true causes behind the acute crisis of the early 1620s, in the monetary turmoil of the same period, did not really deserve the sarcasms of Misselden. Especially as the accusations Malynes directed against exchange-dealing bankers for cornering the market and being monopolists 'were not altogether without foundation'.[147] Without doubt Raymond de Roover's, Richard Ehrenberg's and R H Tawney's studies of commercial practices and foreign exchange at the end of the sixteenth century have clearly shown the relevance of many of Malynes's observations and arguments.[148] At the same time, as a description of more long-term processes, his insistence upon the role of speculation and monopoly does not seem very convincing. Even further from reality seems his view that it was rather the low prices of English export which were the problem rather than too-high prices. Hence, in contrast to Mun and Misselden, he seems not to have recognised the role of demand elasticity. Instead, his main concern was that English cloth was sold to cheaply in export. He pointed out: 'when they were sold deerer by the one halfe in price then be now sold did never complaine that the Clothes were sold too dere'.[149] Thus to try to cure a diminished trade of cloth 'by abating the price of our Cloth … to undersellour Nations' was not possible 'for Satan cannot cast out Satan'.[150] Instead of 'vilifying the price of Wares [which] can never establish a Trade, nor make Commodities more vendible', he suggested revaluation of the money. However, for Mun and Misselden it was then easy to show that the only effect of this would be to worsen the situation even further.

As Tawney made clear, Malynes's dicussion reflected the emergence of an early international credit system. Hence the exchange of bills and monies had grown considerably after the mid-sixteenth century. It was a consequence of the growth of an international money market and increasing international trade, especially in cloth.[151] For contemporary observers, an exchange trade with bills instead of a 'natural' exchange of commodities for commodities was looked upon with suspicion. Could not a practice by earning a profit by exchanging money be viewed as a good example of the sinister practice 'barren breed of Money metal' condemned by Shakespeare in 'The Merchant of Venice'? In fact, as international credit increased to flow from the mid-sixteenth century, 'the foreign exchanges had become a public question of the first importance'.[152] In London, the Italian colony of exchange dealers were regarded as instigators of the lowered exchange rates that England experienced. Also the bankers and rich merchants of Antwerp were regarded as deliberately conspiring to keep the English money down.[153] From this point of view, Malynes was only one in a long line which condemned 'the great exchangers or *Bankers*' who rule the course of money 'at their pleasure'.[154]

In order to understand Malynes's obsession with the exchange and the *par*, we must, however, look a bit closer at his conception of society. Hence, there is no doubt that he in his views regarding such issues as monopoly and usury was highly influenced by the School-men and canonist of older origin.[155] Still, at this time, 'the usury question' was fought over with bitterness, as we soon will see. The fact that he so fiercely fought these 'evil' practices should not allow us to draw the false conclusion that Malynes was exceptionally conservative for his time. According to Malynes, there existed several forms of foreign exhange with money. In its most pernicious form it was carried out by exchange bills (*cambio sicco*) or through the means of credit (*cambio fictio*).[156] It was such activities that he condemned most furiously and located to small groups of foreign bankers in London as well as Antwerp. The main reason for his wrath was that monopolistic speculation and usury was involved in such 'dry' and 'fictious' exchange.[157] Over again he repeated the existence of such 'illegitimacies'. As a monopoly, he defined

> a kind of Commerce in buying and selling, changing, or bartering, ursurped by a law, and sometimes, but by a person, and forestalled from all others to his or their private gaine, and to the hurt and detriment of all other men.[158]

In *The Maintenance of Free Trade* he violently accused the Merchant Adventurers for being monopolists. About them he said:

> 'For a Society may become to be A Monopoly in effect, when some few Merchants have the whole managing of a Trade to the hurt of a Common-wealth, when many others might also Traffique and negotiate for the Common good'.[159]

Among the forms of monopolistic behaviour he included the practices of a small group of exchange dealers who speculated to keep the value of the currency down. As 'some merchants are so farre wide from the knowledge of the value of Coynes', they lured the merchants to change their money at an unfavourable rate. All this was detrimental to the merchants and the Commonwealth as such, he thought. However, although this might not be totally inaccurate from what actually did occur, it is still difficult to understand why, by some evil force, only the *English* merchants and public were hurt. Mun's and Misselden's solution was of course that unfavourable exchange had to do with an unfavourable balance of trade. However, that 'real' economic forces could work behind monetary flows was never admitted by Malynes. Stubbornly, he defended his view against his opponents.

For Malynes 'the abuse of Monopoly' was a form of usury.[160] It was 'biting usury' according to his vocabulary. Thus in reality 'dry' and 'fictious' exchange was a concealed form of usury. In *Saint George for England* (1601) he described in an allegorical form usury as the dragon which would destroy all that was precious in England: 'charitie', 'equality' and 'concord'. The dragon was 'the chiefest head and cause of rebellion and variance in countries'. He:

> overtroweth the harmonie of the strings of the good government of a common-wealth, by too much enriching some, and by oppressing and impoverishing some others … when as every member of the same should live contented in his vocation and execute his charge according to his profession.[161]

He condemned all forms of usury and brought forward the wrath of God over the dragon,[162] 'Others he maketh voide of all charity, which will lend no money but for gaine'.[163] However, his main target were the exchange dealers: 'they do not consider, that money was ordained as a pledge or right bewixt man and man, and in contracts and bargaining a just measure and proportion.[164] Hence, these men 'maketh money to be the creede of the world'. Further, they have 'Within our land altered the nature and valuation of money, making one hundred pounds, to be one hundred and ten pounds, and having overthrowne charities and free lending'.[165]

It is not difficult to see that 'the biting usurie', which Malynes condemned, was the interest which a foreign exchange dealer charged when buying and selling bills of exchange. Certainly, as a provider of a bill he would always grant a credit for the taker during a certain period of time.[166] However, it was worse when bills of exchange were used mainly to lend and borrow money. According to orthodox moral thinking during this period, such procedures were illegitimate, as they implied gain from changing money for money. Such activities were of course condemned in sixteenth-century literature all over Europe.

However, especially the English literature seems to have been particularly harsh on this point. Thus, the Dean of Durham, Secretary of State and Ambassador to the Netherlands (among other things), Thomas Wilson, in his, *A Discourse Upon Usury* (1572) was more uncompromising towards exchange dealing than for example the catholic Schoolmen of Paris had been two centuries earlier. Most of the latter had accepted an interest taken if profit was doubtful. Now, in his influential work, Wilson dismisses this argument, as the gain of bankers was almost certain.[167] Besides stigmatising usury as morally illegitimate Wilson clearly demonstrated that foreign exchange often involved the taking of interest.[168] He for example stated that 'Thus drye kynde of exchange is utterlye to be abhorred, for that it is none other then a manifest cankered usurye'. This activity 'is altogether against Nature', he pointed out. It was the case as 'For the occupiers thereof doe geeve and sell moneye for moneye, which was not invented and ordeyned to that ende'.

However, that these views were hard to outroot is evidenced by tracts against usury continuing to be printed well into the seventeenth century. As late as 1637, Bolton wrote that 'All usury biteth. Money so lent commeth not empty home; but biteth off, knaweth away, and bringeth with it some part of the borrower's wealth and substance'.[169] Another example was Sir Thomas Culpepper's famous *A Tract against Usury* (1621), which triggered a discussion that continued unto the 1660s with partakers like Culpepper the younger and Child.[170]

Notwithstanding, it is not totally unfair to say that Malynes as a source of inspiration particularly looked back to the sixteenth century. It is not only the negative attitude towards usury that he seems to have shared with this century. In general, his conception of society seemed more old fashioned than his opponents'. For his views of a well-ordained Commonwealth he found ample support from Aristotle and scholastic thinkers. Like them he felt that economic relations ought to be governed by distributive justice. Further, his conception of money as something passive and in principle non-vendible was without doubt an inheritance from the Parisian Schoolmen of the thirteenth and fourteenth centuries.[171] With them he shared the view that commerce, by principle, was hazardous. The greed and profit-seeking of a small group threatened the Commonwealth perceived as a moral order. Men who practised 'biting usury & intolerable extortion' violated the moral code and were 'uncharitable'.[172] In their neglect of the 'need and occassions of the poore & mechanicke people', their 'hearts are overfrozen with the Ice of uncharitableness', he stated.[173] Still in his *Consuetudo vel Lex Mercatora* he repeated the argument that the 'dragon' of usury 'bringeth inequalities in a Common-wealth'.[174] By the tail of this dragon 'the concord is broken, charity is growne cold, inequality is crept in, by falsyfying our measure: the general rule, Do as thou wouldest be done unto, is broken'.[175] Without doubt, the Schoolmen's moral vision of a Christian economy was not very far away.

However, this outlook Malynes most certainly shared with others during this period. As we saw, Maddison was a member of the same committee as Malynes in 1622, which had been inaugurated in order to propose remedies for the depression. In 1640 he was still in principle holding on to the old formula. Thus in his *England's Looking in and out* (1640) Maddison complained of a 'decay of our Kingdomes commodities, and especially the wools of this Kingdom of late yeares much decayed in price'.[176] The main reason for the decay was 'the running out or leaking of our monies into other lands'.[177] According to Maddison, the want of money was achieved either through an unfavourable balance of trade *or* by 'Merchandize exchange'. Thus while holding on to Malynes's original interpretation, he also recognised the conflicting one proposed by Mun and Misselden. The want of money, he wrote, can be achieved 'by two speciall or principall wayes or meanes … namely the overballancing of Trade in commerce with Strangers, And the marchandizing Exchange by bills used betweene us and strangers'.[178] A little later he seemed to have forgotten the first of these causes, however. Now he only stated that the 'Marchant Exchange' is 'the efficient cause of exhausting our moneys in general'.[179] The ideal was a 'just' exchange 'value for value'. But this *par* was obstructed by pernicious bankers 'making monies to ebbe and flow at their pleasure when they please'. They saw to it that a low exchange rate was kept so that they may 'exporteth our money in specie for gain'.[180]

As late as 1652, Henry Robinson put forward a proposal for the improvement of 'Trade and navigation', which stands close to this position. One important remedy that he proposed was to establish a new 'Banck' with the purpose of preventing the 'exportation of our money'. This bank would thus be able to 'overrule the Merchandizing Exchange, whereby the Merchants of this Nation have been meerely cheated in all parts of the world, when exchanging by Bills of Exchange is practiced'.[181] Hence, it was necessary to 'establish the Exchange betweene us, and other Nations according to the Par'.[182] However, also Robinson conceded to some of the new ideas. He, for example, believed that rising prices in England, or decreasing prices elsewhere, might imply an impetus for exporting money out of the realm and thus cause an 'overballancing of trade'.[183]

However, with our last example, Milles, we certainly find ourselves in the sixteenth century. Fiercely attacking the Merchant Adventurers for their export of bullion, this custom officer published several tracts written in a pompous and flowery style, which must have been hard to digest even for a contemporary public.[184] However, it is too easy to dismiss him as a mere crank. As de Roover maintains, he might have been a poor theorist but this does not make him less interesting. His views on the foreign exchange were in fact quite commonplace at the time.[185] For one thing he was of the opinion that the 'confused Trafficke now in London by Bils of Exchange' in reality were maintained by 'Bils of interest'.[186] As the 'Exchange ... holds the whole Bodies of Kingdomes in health', the 'mystery of Exchange' was the key to our want of money and all of our problems, he thought. In his typical jargon, he pointed out

> That Exchange in Marchandize, and Marchandizing Exchange, is that Labyrinth of Errors and private practice, whereby though Kings weare Crowns and seeme powerfuly to raigne, yet particular Bankers, private Socities of Marchants and Covetous Persons, whose Ends are Private-gaine; are able to suspend their Counsels, and Comptroll their Pollicies; offering Bounty to their Sovereign, Kings and Queenes ... and lending for Interest to Emperor and Kinges.... That such was the strength of that staine and stay at Piety, that comtempt of Justice, that Seede of Dissention, that World of warre, that Art of Witch-craft, Usury.[187]

A new turn?

In this chapter we have focussed on the debates of the 1620s in which different views clashed on such matters as the consequences of the outflow of monies, trade balances and the very nature of trade crises like the one that developed in England at the beginning of the 1620s. We have drawn a clear line of demarcation between two different ways to look at these matters: on the one had, a series of arguments of which Malynes was a leading representative and, on the other hand, viewpoints which were developed by men like Mun and Misselden. As we saw this clash became distinct during 1622 and 1623 and ended up in a famous pamphlet debate. While writers such as Malynes, Maddision and Robinson were ready to write off the economic crisis of the 1620s as caused by monetary factors, namely, debasement of coins and a low exchange rate caused by speculators, the group led by Mun and Misselden believed that the evil lay in a negative English trade balance with Europe as well as East India. The latter also conceived that the flow of money between countries was determined by 'real' economic forces, namely, the balance of trade. It was the 'over' or 'underweight' of trade that determined the rate of exchange, not *vice versa*. In line with this as we have argued they recognised the overall importance of the market mechanism, the balance between supply and demand.

Sometimes these differences are regarded mainly as a manifestation of different special interests. Hence Mun and Misselden spoke with the tongue of two of the leading companies at the time carrying out trade with Europe and Asia, the Merchant Adventurers and the East India Company. To this effect they were only defending the right to export bullion out of England. The Malynes group, however, stood for a more conservative outlook on the export of monies. Although it also included merchants, they were not at all so strongly represented as in the other group.

How true this may be, it does not have to rule out the fact that the two parties developed views which were different in *principle* based upon different conceptualisations of what later generations have tended to call 'the economy'. This problem is also acute with regard to Parakunnel Joseph Thomas's without seminal *Mercantilism and the East India Trade* (1926). He strongly emphasised the vital role of the political controversies concerning the French, Irish and, in particular, the East India trade for the lively economic discussion that emerged in Britain during the seventeenth century – to which we will return in the next chapter. According to Thomas Mercantilism was mainly a system of economic policy: 'the strengthening of the State in material terms, it is the economic side of nationalism'.[188] The author was certainly cautious to separate the development of economic policies from economic discourse. However, at the same time, it was easy to infer from him that partisan standpoints regarding such policies played a determinate role also for the development of theory and thinking. Thus Thomas at least implied that the favourable balance of trade idea had mainly been developed in order to counterpose an alleged aggressive trade policy of the French. Particularly during the period from 1680 to 1730, many economic pamphleteers felt that Britain experienced an 'overballance' in its trade with France. Hence, through a 'free' import of French luxeries and wines to Britain, she suffered a damagable loss of bullion.

However, as Thomas continued to argue, the pro and con discussion on the East India trade, which stirred up controversy again in the 1690s, was primarily carried out with other arguments. Instead the question of protectionism and to what extent a cheap import of Indian calicoes might harm manufacture and employment in Britain stood in the forefront. In this new context a 'foreign paid income' version of the balance doctrine seemed more relevant than a formula that emphasised the role of trade surpluses.[189] Thus implicitly, at least, Thomas suggested that it was the rising controversy around the East India trade that caused the gradual replacement of the favourable balance of trade theory for a foreign paid income doctrine during these years. Quite clearly the first of these doctrines stressed the importance for a country to receive a surplus in bullion or money for whatever reason, while the other underpinned the role of domestic production, employment and manufactures for national wealth.[190]

To some extent the picture that Thomas paints is certainly accurate. However, it does not tell the whole story. Thus it would be totally misleading to argue that the existence of stark partisan views by economists on actual political issues exclude their use of analytical categories or a vocabulary of economics which, partly at least, can be regarded as independent from the *parole* context. As we have previously argued, it is crucial that we do not play so much attention to contextual factors that we forget the role played by discursive practices and language. Thus it is important to understand intellectual development also as a development of discourse. The economic texts we refer to cannot be regarded as *tabula rasa* – immediately reflecting some 'outer' reality. Writers used words, concepts, lines of arguments and even certain topics that they had inherited from the past. Hence to some point they were bound to a certain vocabulary, a specific *langue*. However, as we have argued, over time they had to use this *langue* in different discursive contexts. Thus the *paroles* they uttered had to shift over time as the *langue* was used in order to answer different questions. Consequently, such shifting contexts were major factors, which in the long run led to changes in how the *langue* itself was construed.

At last we must then return to Malynes and the pamphlet debate in the early 1620s and emphasise that, although strong material and partisan interest were at stake, the controversies also touched upon different views of what constituted the very basis of commerce and economic relations. Hence, according to Malynes, international trading with money and goods was carried out by actors who often did evil and selfish things. They speculated, filed coins and committed the sin of 'biting usury'. In the other corner, Mun and Misselden most certainly agreed that such practices existed. But they could not explain why some countries had a 'want' of money while others seemed to be more satisfied. Instead their argument was that it was the balance of trade between countries that had such dire consequences. It was less so evil people than the impersonal forces of demand and supply, which sometimes led to a country having an 'overbalance' and at other times an 'underbalance' of trade. As emphasised, we must not from this draw the conclusion that one group was more 'moralistic' in its views than the other. Less prone to believe that markets could be tamed by ethical or church rules, perhaps the Mun group seemed to be more interested in how the market actually worked. Identifying empirical identification as their methodology, they began to think about 'the economy' as constituting a system of forces that worked as a set of balances or a clockwork. These mechanical forces were held together by actors who sold and bought on the market. At the same time they most certainly shared the view with most others at the time that man was a sinful creature and needed to be tamed by Christian values and the force of law. Hence there was no guarantee that selfish behaviour would lead to public purposes. Regulation was needed in order to regulate the forces of the market place – which otherwise would drive its play.

Notes

1 J D Gould, 'The Trade Crisis of the Early 1620s and English Economic Thought'. *The Journal of Economic History*, vol. XV: 2 (1955), p. 133. For a convincing discussion on why it is likely that the book was written 'during the period mid 1626 to late 1630, with a distinct presumption in favor of the earlier half of this period', see the same author 'The Date of England's Treasure by Forraign Trade'. *The Journal of Economic History*, vol. XV (1955), pp. 160f. The answer to why it was not published in the 1620s is discussed in M Beer, *Early British Economics from the XIIIth to the Middle of the XVIIIth Century*. London: George Allen & Unwin 1938, p. 182. Beer speculates that the answer was that it raised sensitive issues concerning the export of money. Was it a total coincidence that the ban of the export of gold was lifted in 1663? However, why would Mun's first pamphlet (*A Discourse of Trade*), which was actually published in 1621 and also argued for the right of the East India Company to export bullion, not have been sensitive to the same degree?
2 T Mun, *England's Treasure by Forraign Trade* [1623] New York: Augustus M Kelley 1986, p. 81.
3 For an overview, see P J Thomas, *Mercantilism and the East India Trade*. London: P S King & Son 1926.
4 Thomas, pp. 8ff., 24, 37ff., 51ff.
5 Mun, pp. 40f.
6 'Advice of His Majesty's Council of Trade Concerning the Exportation of Gold and Silver in Foreign Coind and Bullion'. In: J R McCulloch (ed.), *A Select Collection of Scarce and Valuable Tracts on Money*. London: Political Economy Club 1856, pp. 148f.
7 This quite distinct difference is underrated both in C Wennerlind's interpretation of the pamphlet debate in the early 1620s in his *Casualties of Credits: The English Financial Revolution 1620–1720*. Cambridge, MA: Harvard University Press 2011, p. 32, and by M Poovey, *A History of the Modern Fact*. Chicago, IL: University of Chicago Press 1998, p. 66.
8 B Supple, *Crisis and Change in England 1600–1642*. Cambridge, MA: Cambridge University Press 1959, p. 198.
9 E Lipson, *The Economic History of England*, vol. III, London: A & C Black 1934, p. 305.
10 Lipson, p. 306.
11 Acts of Privy Council of England (A.P.C.) 1619–21, 26.5. 1620. British Library (BL).
12 A.P.C. 1621–3, 17.5.1622. BL.
13 For a full presentation of the work of these committees and their discussions, see C E Suprinyak, 'Trade, Money and the grievances of the commonwealth'. (unpublished, forthcoming paper). He also points out that even before the crisis

conditions within the broadcloth trade had been depressed and the failed so-called Cockayne project for exporting cloth abroad. See also A Friis, *The Alderman Cockayne's Project and the Cloth Trade. The Commercial Policy of England in its Main Aspects, 1603–25.* London: Humphrey Milford 1927 as well as the overview in R Brenner, *Merchants and Revolution. Commercial Change, Political Conflict, and London's Overseas Traders 1560–1653.* London: Verso 2003, ch.V.

14 T Mun, *A Discourse of Trade.* [1621], New York: Augustus M Kelley 1971, pp. 50f.

15 Add. MSS 34324 fol.181 (BL).

16 Supple, *Commercial Crisis and Change in England 1600–1642,* p. 59ff. See also Lipson, III, pp. 307f.

17 See W R Scott, *The Constitution and Finance of English, Scottish and Irish* Joint Stock *Companies to 1720,* vol. I–III, Cambridge, UK: Cambridge University Press 1912; A Friis, *Alderman Cockayne's Project and the Cloth Trade.* See also E Lipson, III, p. 381. For an overview of the discussion see Supple, *Commercial Crisis and Change in England,* chs 2, 3, and R W K Hinton, *The Eastland Trade and the Common Weal,* Cambridge, UK: Cambridge University Press 1959, pp. 12ff. See note 12 above.

18 E Misselden, *The Circle of Commerce or the Balance of Trade* [1623]. New York: Augustus M Kelley 1971, p. 51.

19 On the emergence of the New Draperies, see Supple, pp. 136f.; F J Fisher, 'London's Export Trade in the Early Seventeenth Century', *The Economic History Review,* 2nd ser., vol. III: 2 (1950).

20 Supple, p. 74. See also J D Gould, 'The Trade Depression of the Early 1620s'. *The Economic History Review,* 2nd ser., vol. VII: 1 (1954); and B Supple, 'Currency and Commerce in the Early Seventeenth Century'. *The Economic History Review,* 2nd ser., vol. X: 2 (1957).

21 J D Gould, 'The Trade Depression of the 1620s', p. 90.

22 Suprinyak.

23 Add Mss 34324 fol. 155, 169, 171. British Library.

24 A.P.C. 1621–3. 10.4. 1622. For this see Supple, pp. 66ff., 198ff., 268ff.

25 See Supple, pp. 204f. See also Add Mss 34324 fols 153–4. BL.

26 A.P.C. 1621–3, p. 27. BL.

27 Suprinyak.

28 For these unpublished tracts by Mun and his group and Malynes and his group see Add Mss 34324 fols 153–78. BL. Other important unpublished material is the memorandum by Sanderson, 'A Treatise on the Exchange', Lans. Mss, 768. BL. For a fuller account see Supple, pp. 202ff., 268ff. as well as Suprinyak.

29 R Maddison, *England's Looking in and out.* London: T Badger for H Mosley 1640, pp. 5f., 11.

30 Add MSS fol. 165. BL.

31 Add MSS fol. 165. BL.

32 Add MSS fol. 154. BL.

33 W A Shaw, *The History of Currency 1252–1894.* London: Wilson and Milne 1895, p. 145; Supple, *Commercial Crisis and Change in England.*

34 See above p. 5.

35 See E Misselden, *Free Trade or the Meanes to Make Trade Flourish,* p. 104.

36 Add MSS fol. 167. Suprinyak emphasises the influence of L Cranfield, Earl of Middlesex and Treasurer to the Crown in the beginning of the 1620s for the view of Mun's group.

37 Add MSS fol. 165. BL.

38 Add MSS fol. 169. BL.

39 Add MSS fol. 155. BL.
40 This point is emphasised by Suprinyak.
41 R Cotton, 'A Speech made by Sir Robert Cotton, knight and baronet, Before the Lords of his Majesties most Honourable Privy Council at the Council Table' (first published in 1651). In: W A Shaw (ed.), *Select Tracts and Documents. Illustrative of English Monetary History*. London: Clement Wilson 1896.
42 For some information, see A Finkelstein, *Harmony and the Balance. An Intellectual History of Seventeenth-Century English Economic Thought*. Ann Arbor: University of Michigan Press 2000, ch. 3.
43 E A Johnson, *Predecessors of Adam Smith. The Growth of British Economic Thought*. New York: Prentice-Hall Inc. 1937, pp. 58f.
44 J Wheeler, *A Treatise of Commerce, wherein are Shewed the Comodities Arising by a Well Ordered and Ruled Trade*. Middelburgh, UK: n.p. 1601, pp. 25f.
45 Wheeler, p. 28.
46 For this see Lipson, III; Johnson, pp. 43f., 58f.; Supple, *Commercial Crisis and Change in England*; Friis.
47 See Johnson, pp. 61f.; *Palgrave's Dictionary of Political Economy*. London & New York: Macmillan 1894.
48 E Misselden, *Free Trade or the Meanes to Make Trade Flourish*. London 1622, p. 8.
49 Misselden, pp. 10f.
50 Misselden, p. 104.
51 Misselden, p. 107.
52 Misselden, p. 104.
53 Misselden, p. 12.
54 Misselden, p. 20.
55 Misselden, p. 17.
56 Misselden, p. 89.
57 E Misselden, *The Circle of Commerce or the Balance of Trade*, pp. 4, 14, 26, 23, 29. To be accurate he mentions 'an old manuscript' on 'monies and Exchanges', which Malynes is supposed to have copied material from. As de Roover has pointed out, this manuscript was probably written by Gresham (See Raymond de Roover, *Gresham on Foreign Exchange*. Cambridge, MA: Harvard University Press 1949, pp. 12ff.). Milles is, however, mentioned by name in Misselden's text.
58 E Seligman comes close to this in his *Curiosities of Early Economic Literature*. San Fransisco 1920, pp. viii ff.
59 For a different opinion, see A Finkelstein, *Harmony and the Balance*, p. 54. But her argument that Misselden remained a partisan for a special interest (the Merchant Adventurers) does not substantiate her claims. This might be accurate but does not rile out that what he said was of principal interest, nor does her argument concerning Misselden's view on bullion export. See especially Misselden, *The Circle of Commerce*, pp. 36f., where he talks in great favour of Mun's analysis of the East India trade as well as of T Digges's defence of the same trade.
60 Misselden, *The Circle of Commerce*, p. 21.
61 Misselden, p. 69.
62 Misselden, p. 117.
63 For A Serra, the 'Cambrese', see p. 64.
64 Misselden, p. 116.
65 Misselden, p. 130.
66 Misselden, p. 36.
67 Finkelstein, pp. 62f. Note that her argument for turning down the argument that Misselden came up with something new is mainly taken from his first pamphlet,

The Maintenance of Free Trade, and not from his second, where he expresses his new thoughts. On the concept 'free trade' in the seventeenth century, see L Magnusson, 'Freedom and Trade: From Corporate Freedand and Jealousy of Trade to a Natural Liberty'. *Keio Economic Studies*, vol. XLIX (2013).

68 J Mun's introduction to T Mun, *England's Treasure by Forraign Trade*. See also Finkelstein, pp. 75f.

69 T Mun, pp. 17f. On this see R de Roover, 'Thomas Mun in Italy'. *Bulletin of the Institute of Historical Research*, vol. XXX (1957), pp. 81f. If de Roover is right to place Mun's time in Italy in 1596–8 he certainly could not have been influenced by A Serra. However, that there were earlier Italians who had formulated similar views we saw earlier.

70 More information of Mun is given in *Dictionary of National Biographies*.

71 T Mun, *A Discourse of Trade From England Unto the East Indies.* See title page.

72 Wheeler, *A Treatise of Commerce.*

73 Mun, *A Discourse of Trade*, p. 1.

74 Mun, p. 2.

75 Mun, p. 27.

76 Mun, p. 22.

77 Mun, p. 49.

78 Finkelstein, pp. 74f.

79 On this see, for example, D K Foley, *Adam's Fallacy. A Guide to Economic Theology.* Cambridge, MA: The Belknap Press of Harvard University Press 2006.

80 Mun, *England's Treasure by Forraign Trade*, p. viii.

81 Mun, p. 5.

82 Mun, p. 16.

83 Mun, p. 17.

84 Mun, p. 39.

85 Mun, p. 41.

86 See Johnson, pp. 12ff., etc.

87 G J Goschen, *The Theory of Foreign Exchanges.* London 1866, p. 11.

88 Mun, *England's Treasure by Forraign Trade*, p. 55.

89 Mun, p. 73.

90 Mun, p. 75.

91 Misselden, *The Circle of Commerce*, p. 118.

92 Supple, *Commercial Crisis and Change*, p. 215. For other statements of the same kind see Johnson, *Predecessors of Adam Smith*, and J O Appleby, *Economic Thought and Ideology in Seventeenth Century England.* Princeton: Princeton University Press 1978.

93 Misselden, p. 21.

94 Misselden, p. 62.

95 Misselden, p. 105.

96 Mun, p. 62.

97 Add MSS fol. 155.

98 Misselden, p. 29.

99 Mun, p. 87.

100 Mun, *A Discourse of Trade*, p. 8. See also Misselden, *The Circle of Commerce*, p. 51.

101 J Viner 'English Theories of Foreign Trade before Adam Smith'. *The Journal of Political Economy*, vol. XXXVIII (1930), p. 420.

102 See J D Gould, 'The Trade Crisis of the Early 1620's and English Economic Thought'. *The Journal of Economic History*, vol. XV (1955), pp. 127ff.

103 Mun, p. 17.

104 This is the explicit standpoint formulated in J O Appleby, *Economic Thought and Ideology*.
105 For more recent contributions on Bacon and its eventual influence on economic discourse, see Finkelstein, *Harmony and the Balance*, pp. 89f. and T Leng, 'Epistemology. Expertise and Knowledge in the World of Commerce'. In: P J Stern and C Wennerlid (eds), *Mercantilism Reimagined. Political Economy in Early Modern Britain and its Empire*. Oxford: Oxford University Press 2014.
106 C Wennerlind insists upon such a connection between the Hartlib circle and later seventeenth-century economist writers, such as Petty. However, the Hartlib circle could not have come into existence before the Prussian emigrant Samuel Hartlib came to London in 1626. However, even before that, Bacon's ideas might have spread to such persons as the obviously well-read Misselden and perhaps also to Mun. See C Wennerlind, 'Hartlibian Political Economy and the new Culture of Credit'. In: Stern and Wennerlid, *Mercantilism Reimagined*, p. 77.
107 Misselden, *The Circle of Commerce*, pp. 8ff., 11, 41.
108 Finkelstein, chs 2–3.
109 For an overview, see R W Church, *Bacon*. London 1884 and P M Urbach, *Francis Bacon's Philosophy of Science*. Peru, IL: Open Court 1987. Also consult S Shapin, *A Social History of Truth: Civility and Science in Seventeenth-Century England*. Chicago, IL: University of Chicago Press 1994, and M Poovey, *A History of the Modern Fact*.
110 Misselden, p. 72.
111 J M Robertson (ed.), *The Philosophical Works of Francis Bacon*. London: Routledge 1905, p. 271.
112 Mun, *A Discourse of Trade*, p. 49.
113 Misselden, *Free Trade*, introduction.
114 Mun, p. 49.
115 On this see M Beer, *Early British Economics*. London: Allen & Unwin 1938, pp. 136ff.
116 G Malynes, *Canker of England's Common Wealth*, p. 2.
117 Beer, p. 138. On Cranfield, see above pp. 107, 152.
118 Spedding, Ellis, Heath (eds), *Works of Francis Bacon*, vol. XIII, London: Longmans 1872, p. 22.
119 For a discussion on the origin of the balance of trade concept see for example W H Price, 'The origin of the phrase "Balance of trade". *Quarterly Journal of Economics*, vol. XX (1905); *Palgrave's Dictionary of Political Economy*, vol I, London 1894.
120 On this especially Finkelstein, ch. 7 and the following.
121 G N Clark, *Science in the Age of Newton*, Oxford: Oxford University Press 1947, p. 119. L Sommer, *Die Österreichischen Kameralisten*, vol. I, Vienna 1920, pp. 89ff. See also E F Heckscher, *Mercantilism*, vol. II, London: George Allen & Unwin 1955, pp. 308ff.
122 Especially according to the pioneering work on such issues, L Sommer, *Die Österreichischen Kameralisten*, I, this 'Vorstellung eines mechanischen Kräftespiel' was connected to the princip of dynamics, which orginated from Galileo and ended up with Newton (p. 75).
123 For this see especially Sommer.
124 See de Roover, *Gresham on Foreign Exchange*, pp. 275ff.
125 It is a general mistake made by many who quite correctly emphasise the importance of the depression of the 1620s to regard Mun's and Misselden's work merely as a reflection of actual occurences. However, that these occurances were interpreted by writers in various ways does not at all exclude that this really was the acual framework for their interpretations. As we saw, language is not merely

self-reflective. It is always involved in a dialogue with 'reality', however percieved. To some point Supple seems to be aware of this. But in the end he nevertheless draws the conclusion that Mun and Misselden's writings merely reflected some self-evident 'competetive situaton' from which it was possible only to draw one kind of conclusion. This is not very helpful, thinking of a Malynes or Milles. See Supple, pp. 72, 197ff., 215, 220f.

126 Misselden, *Free Trade*, p. 112.
127 Mun, *England's Treasure by Forraign Trade*, p. 37.
128 Mun, p. 54.
129 Mun, p. 59.
130 Misselden, p. 64.
131 Mun, p. 1.
132 This was to some point admitted by Heckscher, who had great difficulties combining the 'modernism' of mercantilists such as Mun and Misselden in philosophical and methodological sense with their balance of trade theory and their adherence to at least some forms of protectionism. See his *Mercantilism*, II, pp. 273ff., 316ff.
133 On Malynes, see R de Roover, 'Gerard de Malynes as an Economic Writer'. In: J Kirshner (ed.), *Business, Banking and Economic Thought in late Medieval and Early Modern Europe*. Chicago, IL: Chicago University Press 1974; L R Muchmore, 'Gerrard de Malynes and Mercantile Economics'. *History of Political Economy*, vol. I (1969) and E A Johnson, *Predecessors to Adam Smith*, ch. 3. See also *Dictionary of National Biographies* and Finkelstein, ch. 2.
134 Mentioned in his *The Maintenance of Free Trade*, p. 65.
135 de Roover, p. 348.
136 Malynes, *A Treatise of the Canker of Englands Common Wealth*. London 1601, p. 12.
137 For example Malynes, p. 10.
138 Malynes, pp. 9f.
139 Malynes, *The Maintenance of Free Trade*, p. 30.
140 Malynes, *The Maintenance of Free Trade*, p. 18.
141 G Malynes, *Consuetudo vel Lex Mercatoria*. London: Adam Islip 1629, pp. 59, 61.
142 Malynes, *Consuetudo*, pp. 64ff.
143 Malynes, *The Center of the Circle of Commerce*, p. 57.
144 For this see R de Roover, *Gresham on Foreign Exchange*, pp. 14ff. M Dewar has, however, questioned Gresham's authorship of this memorandum. See the discussion between her and de Roover in *Economic History Review*, 2nd ser., vol. XVII (1965), pp. 476ff. and vol. XX (1967), pp. 145ff.
145 Malynes, *Consuetudo*, pp. 408ff.
146 Malynes, *The Center of the Circle of Commerce*, pp. 41f.
147 R de Roover, 'Gerard de Malynes as an Economic Writer', p. 357.
148 See de Roover, *Gresham on Foreign Exchange*; R Ehrenberg, *Zeitalter der Fugger*. Jena, Germany: Verlag Gustav Fischer 1896, translated into English: *Capital and Finance in the Age of Reinaissance* [1928]. New York: Augustus M Kelley 1985, pp. 21ff., 42ff.; R H Tawney, 'Introduction' to T Wilson, *A Discourse Upon Usury*. London: G Bell & Sons 1926, esp. pp. 60ff., 73.
149 Malynes, *The Center of the Circle of Commerce*, p. 79.
150 Malynes, *The Maintenance of Free Trade*, p. 46.
151 R H Tawney, 'Introduction' to T Wilson, *A Discourse Upon Usury*, pp. 60ff.
152 R H Tawney, p. 60.
153 Tawney, pp. 79f. See also R Ehrenberg, pp. 239ff.
154 Malynes, p. 37.

155 See also E A Johnson, *Predecessors to Adam Smith*, ch. 3, and de Roover, 'Gerard Malynes as an Economic Writer', pp. 350ff.; Finkelstein, ch. 2, insists on Malynes's Aristotelian roots.

156 For these terms see R H Tawney, pp. 60ff. For a contemporary definition of 'dry exchange', see T Wilson, *A Discourse Upon Usury*, p. 395. It is practised, he says, 'when one doth borrowe money by exchangue for a strange Region, at longer or shorter distaunce of time, to serve his turne the rather therby, not myndynge to make anye reall payment abroad, but compundeth with the exchanger to have it returned backe agayne accordyng as the exchangue shall passe from thence to London'.

157 De Roover makes an important point when he says that Malynes did not object to exchange dealings 'at rates set by market conditions'. Rather his objection was that exhange in such form concealed usury activities on parts of monopolist bankers. See de Roover, 'Gerard de Malynes as an Economic Writer', p. 356.

158 Malynes, *Consuetudo*, p. 214.

159 Malynes, *The Maintenance of Free Trade*, p. 69.

160 See Malynes, *The maintenance of Free Trade*, p. 69.

161 G de Malynes, *Saint George for England, Allegorically Described*. London: Floure de luce and Crowne 1601.

162 Gerrard de Malynes, pp. 65f.

163 G de Malynes, p. 19.

164 G de Malynes, p. 62.

165 G de Malynes, p. 62.

166 See R H Tawney, 'Introduction' and de Roover, *Gresham and Foreign Exchange*.

167 T Wilson, p. 306. For this see de Roover, *Gresham on Foreign Exchange*, pp. 101f.

168 See T Wilson.

169 *A Short and Private Discussion between Mr Bolton and One M.S. Concerning Usury*. London 1637.

170 See below p. 183.

171 See O Langholm, *Economics in the Medieval School*. Leiden: E J Brill 1992. See also his *Wealth and Money in the Aristotelian Tradition*. Oslo, Norway: Scandinavian University Press 1983.

172 Malynes, *The Maintenance of Free Trade*, p. 41.

173 Malynes, *The Maintenance of Free Trade*, p. 40.

174 Malynes, *Consuetudo*, p. 327.

175 Malynes, *Saint George for England*, p. 15.

176 R Maddison, *England's Looking in and out. Presented to the High Court of Parliament Now Assembled*, introduction.

177 Maddison, p. 1.

178 Maddison, introduction.

179 Maddison, introduction.

180 Maddison, pp. 16, 18.

181 H Robinson, *Certain Proposals in Order to the Peoples Freedom and Accomodation in Some Particulars, with the Advancement of Trade and Navigation of this Commonwealth in Generall*. London: M Simmons 1652, p. 18.

182 Robinson, pp. 14f.

183 Robinson, p. 14.

184 T Milles, *An Outport-Customers Accompt*. n.d.; *The Customers Apoligie*. n.d.; *An Abstract Almost Verbatim of the Customers Apologie Written 18 Years Ago*. n.d. The first of these treatises provoked J Wheeler to write a tract to defend the Merchant Adventurers (J Wheeler, *A Treatise on Commerce*. Middelburgh, UK: n.p. 1601.

185 de Roover, *Gresham on Foreign Exchange*, pp. 104ff.

186 T Milles, *The Customers Apolgiee*, n.p.

187 Milles, *An Outport-Customers Accompt*, n.p. This tract and the one mentioned in n. 186 are included in L Magnusson (ed.), *Mercantilist Theory and Practice. The History of British Mercantilism*, vol. I, London: Pickering & Chatto 2008.

188 P J Thomas, *Mercantilism and the East India Trade* [1926]. London: Frank Cass 1963, p. 3.

189 See below p. 7.

190 Thomas, pp. 22f., 24.

6 A new science of trade

In the previous chapter we sensed the rise of a new discourse dealing with commerce during the turbulent 1620s. As Joyce Oldham Appleby has pointed out, the lively economic discussion taking place in England during most of the seventeenth century must above all have been related to the vigorous 'conflict among the contending parties during England's century of revolution'.[1] However, the great outflow of economic, political and religious books, pamphlets and tracts that resulted from these conflicts had some decisive institutional preconditions. Most importantly, it relied on an unusually high degree of freedom of press as well as the existence of a big reading public, mainly in London. Also a more open and vibrant political system mattered. Hence a sometimes very fierce political struggle in England until the Glorious Revolution in 1688 was carried out between Crown, parliament and different interest groups who competed for power. Moreover, such discussions were increasingly becoming public.[2]

After the 1620s this new way of understanding commercial and market relations increasingly came into use by pamphleteers and economic debaters in order to discuss short- and long-run economic issues. The notion that the economic realm was a system regulated by the forces of supply and demand was increasingly applied. It was used to emphasise that such forces were so strong that trade could not be regulated in detail. Moreover, it was emphasised that a well-regulated or ordered trade would bring wealth and plenty, but a less well-organised trade would produce the opposite result. Hence to clever out the rules for a 'Political Commerce' (as formulated by Postlethwayt in 1757)[3] was the task of a good government. Thus it should, above all, introduce certain protective measures, or urge for more freedom of trade. It was also used in order to discuss monetary issues such as the need for new and better coins or whether the interest rate ought to be kept down by law. As a consequence, a specific type of economic analysis building on the groundwork of Mun and Misselden was further developed.

However, it is really not until the end of the seventeenth century that we can detect the establishment of a more general discourse that aimed to link these bits and pieces together in a more coherent discourse. Something which from especially the 1690s onwards was named a 'science of trade' emerged, which tried to put forward 'maxims' concerning how the market process in general worked and how increased foreign trade in particular might increase the wealth and power of a national economy. During this decade, a number of economic writers sought to establish the principles upon which an independent system based on commerce and trade was built. Against this background we will also present some of the leading English economic writers of this period.

Hence, in this chapter we are tracing a specific English 'science of trade' which also – arguably – contributed to the further development of economic thinking and writing at large. Without falling into the anachronistic trap, we may speak of the development of analysis according to Schumpeter's scheme (see above p. 7). However, this does not imply that analytical developments also were taking place outside England. We have already seen that in a number of major European countries consultant administrators and others developed new tools in order to understand the process of development and underdevelopment or the mysteries of the market place. Nor should we regard English as a measuring rod or blueprint for what occurred elsewhere in terms of intellectual achievements or a development of economic discourse. The different paths taken must be understood in a historical context and against the background of different institutional conditions.[4]

England during the seventeenth century

In 1652 the First Anglo-Dutch War broke out. As it seemed, its immediate cause was hurt national pride. Thus, outside Dover, the Dutch fleet under admiral Tromp had refused to lower its flags out of respect when encountering British naval vessels. But as this war was immediately followed by a second and third war with the Dutch, ending in 1674, there certainly must have been more fundamental factors at work other than this *histoire eventualement.* Moreover, war was by no means over after 1674. Thus, first, a brief war with Spain followed. Thereafter, following the 'Glorious Revolution' of 1688 two long wars with the French were fought: the Nine Years' War (1688–97) and the War of the Spanish Succession (1701–14). Thus, between the establishment of the Navigation Act in 1651 and the Peace of Utrecht in 1713, Britain was almost constantly at war. This situation of permanent warfare most certainly brought forward important economic and political consequences. Most importantly, as generally is the case with wars, it led to the strengthening of state machinery. For example, permanent war necessitated increased control over taxes and revenues. The national interest further demanded increased control over men, industries and trade. Moreover, laws were introduced and new acts were inaugurated to protect national interests. Thus, the kind of authoritarianism that the American historian Philip Buck saw as an inherent part of 'the politics of mercantilism' was really to a large extent a result of permanent warfare.[5]

The economic consequences brought forward by war are more difficult to disentangle. It is clear, however, that with regard to England's trade much happened between 1713 and 1652. In the mid-seventeenth century England to a large extent relied on its export of cloth. Thus for example in the 1640s several economic pamphleteers, including Lewell Roberts and Henry Robinson, had argued that the British economy must become more diversified in order to become less economically vulnerable.[6] Such an increased diversity had largely been achieved half a century later. Through the increase of manufacture production, a rising entrepot trade, the import and re-export of cheap calicoes from India and a colonial trade with 'the plantations', England's trade relations had become much more widespread. Moreover, it had taken its first step to become the world's leading trade nation and to replace the Dutch in this position.[7] In a long-run perspective, this would establish Britain as the workshop of the world during the eighteenth century.[8]

From this it is not far fetched to infer that these wars to a large extent were fought in order to secure or enlarge trade and commercial relations. This was most certainly also how many contemporary observers viewed the situation. Thus in 1698 – a year after peace had been settled with the French –Davenant ridiculed the view that 'Some people have been of opinion that Trade and war could not go together'; but this is plainly a mistake'.[9] Davenant held the contrary view that the state was necessary for the 'care of Traffique'. As he put it: 'For the well governing and protecting trade many things must perhaps be done that may thwart the interest of other nations'.[10]

However, this does not imply that wars were fought merely for private gain in the interest of a conspiracy of merchants, who sought money and privileged positions. On the contrary, as Hinton and Wilson have emphasised, in pushing for increased trade in open and aggressive competition with other states, English governments often pursued policies that directly opposed at least the short-run interest of such private interest groups. Thus it was for example a common theme in government policies, beginning with the Navigation Act in 1651, to replace the private control over trade which regulated companies such as the Merchant Adventurers, the Eastland Company and after 1688 the East India Company[11] previously detained with government control.[12] At the same time, as Robert Brenner points out, there is a justification to talk about 'old' and 'new' groups of merchants that stood close to the revolutionaries in the Commonwealth period pressing for different policies.[13] Hence the new Council of Trade put to work in around 1650 housed 'new' merchants, who were extremely aggressive in their attitude, both to the privileges of the 'old' merchants but even more so towards the Dutch. The work of this Council – including the key moving spirit of Benjamin Worsley, a head figure of the so-called Hartlib circle – pointed forward to the famous Navigation Acts that were inaugurated a little later.

Thus national economic expansion and increased state control was most probably a more persistent motive behind the aggressive and war-like 'politics of mercantilism' (Buck) than the private interest of moneyed merchants. Politicians during this period held the view that power necessitated trade. No country could ever become powerful without a strong economic base. Of special importance in this context were regarded the profits running in from foreign trade. Most certainly, such a scenario helps us to understand why the favourable balance of trade doctrine became such a popular slogan during this period.

During most of the century, the trade of the Dutch Republic was envied by the British. Most certainly it was this covetousness that led to the indictment of the Navigation Act in 1651 and 1662, the Staple Act of 1662 (the act for the encouragement of trade) and the three successive wars with the Dutch from the 1650s. The feeling that the Dutch had captured trades that rightly belonged to England – as we have shown – was a common theme in the economic literature of the period. When one considers the actual situation, this was not particularly strange. As for example described by the economic historian Charles Wilson:

> A Dutch fleet sailed each year from February to September from the Shetlands to the Thames, close in to the coast, fishing up herrings. Salted and barred, these provided food at home and valuable exports abroad. English made cloths were finished, dressed and dyed in Amsterdam, German linens bleached at Haarlem, Norfolk barley distilled or brewed, Carribean sugar, boiled and refined, baltic timber converted into ships, barrels, planks. And a sizeable proportion of these trades, so far as they were driven with England, came and went in Dutch ships, especially in the relatively newly designed flyboats, built for cheap freightage.[14]

However, during the late seventeenth century, another formidable enemy entered the stage: France. In an influential tract from 1673 Samuel Fortrey especially emphasised how much Britain had lost by trading with the French nation. The author pointed out that, because of a great import of luxury wares and wines from France, the result had led to an increasing negative balance of trade for England.[15] This became especially the case as Louis XIV's minister, Colbert, simultaneously had established a system of effective protection against British imports. As many others, Fortrey saw this as the most important cause behind the current economic distress in Britain. This view was also shared by Roger Coke.[16] Although challenged by writers such as Davenant, Barbon, Child, North and Henry Houghton, the view that trade turned unfavourable for Britain since the 1660s, caused by an increasing luxury import from France, became common parlour after Fortrey. Hence, in a dialogue between a fictitious 'Content' and 'Complaint', Houghton let the former win the discussion with the conclusion that 'We have more Wealth now, than ever we had at any time before the Restauration of his Sacred Majestie'.[17] Still, pessimism was a leading theme in the controversy that aroused after the Peace of Utrecht in 1713. In Britain, at this point, a heated debate broke out whether or not the peace treaty with France was unfavourable for Britain. Hence in the serial publication *The British Merchant*, anti-French politicians and writers gathered in order to abolish the treaty. And, as we later on will see, they did succeed.[18]

While trade might have played a key role, the hostility towards France was most certainly also bolstered by political causes. Thus, the restoration of the two Stuarts after 1660, Charles II and Jacob II, clearly aroused anti-French feelings. Furthermore, by the time of the Nine Years' War, France had become militarily and politically powerful enough to challenge the balance of power in Europe. This threat was even more felt at the time of the Spanish Succession, as this occasion had left the possibility open that Spain and its huge empire would fall into the arms of the French king.

Discussions on trade and economy

The political and economic situation just described provided the general framework for the continued economic discussion in England after the crisis of the 1620s. It took use of economic vocabulary to discuss the question of national power, how wealth could be achieved and how the Dutch and French interfered in this general process of wealth making. Furthermore, writers discussed the best means by which the nation could be made rich and powerful. Could this be achieved by lowering the interest rate? Was it necessary to have a favourable balance of trade that would provide the Commonwealth with more money and liquid capital? How could such a favourable balance of trade be achieved? Was the best means to forbid the export of bullion according to the old Statute of Employment? Or should instead an export of bullion be encouraged, provided it brought in an export of wares that *either* could be re-exported *or* worked up in manufactories at home? Furthermore, from the point of view of such questions, different writers took part in the political discussions of the day, which concerned monetary issues, war or peace, the content of treaties with Holland and France, the East India Company, whether or not import from India should be restricted, and so on. Thus, as Wilson pointed out:

> What Adam Smith was to call 'the mercantile system', and later 'mercantilism', emerged from the streams of petitions from private parties directed to these various Committees of State, from the continuous discussions that arose from the frictions between competing private interests and from attempts to reconcile the demands between of the mercantile elements in the State with needs deemed to be those of the Commonwealth as a whole.[19]

However, as we have stated, this does not fully explain what these authors really said and what arguments they used. Surely, the argument here is not to deny that, for example, the discussion focussing on whether the import of cheap calicoes by the East India Company was beneficial was an issue which aroused much controversy and forced writers either to condemn (Cary, Pollexfen and others) or defend it (Child, Davenant and others). In fact, it was most certainly the discussion around the French trade which excited Davenant to put down his views as well as trigger the famous debacle which we briefly mentioned between the journals *The Mercator* (ed. D Defoe) and *The British Merchant* (King, Janssen, Cook, Gee and others) after the Peace Treaty of Utrecht with the French had been made public in 1713. Further, as we said, it was certainly the import of cheap fabrics from the Indies that led defenders of the English manufacture interest, such as Cary and Pollexfen, to publish their tracts. Also, it is noteworthy that both the 1620s and the 1690s were periods of trade depression that especially hit the cloth industry.

To a large extent it was within the context of such political discussions that a discourse of trade developed. Hence it seems to have been specifically during periods of especially heated discussions that most tracts were written and the arguments sharpened. Increasingly, in the economic literature after 1630, we find references to demand and supply explanations of commodity prices, wages, interest rates, money and exchange rates, among others.

Topics of discussion 1640–90

Regulated companies and free trade

Economic writers in England during the seventeenth century talked frequently of 'free trade'. However, when doing so they referred to something quite different to what became common during the eighteenth and especially the nineteenth centuries.[20] During the late medieval period, 'free trade' became a slogan used in order to criticise monopoly privileges granted to so-called chartered companies. Such companies were well established in many European cities from the late medieval period onwards, including London, Antwerp, Bruges, Amsterdam, Florence, Lisbon and Madrid. In the Baltic Sea the famous *Hansa-verband* serves as an international example of a chartered company made up by members from different cities in northern Europe which held a monopoly of the trade of salt, grain and other items. In England the most well-known case was the East India Company, which was inaugurated with a charter, 'The Governor and Company of Merchants of London, Trading into the East Indies' from 31 December 1600, or the much older Merchant Adventurers established already in 1407 with a privilege to export wool to Flemish ports and import draperies and cloth from the same area.[21]

It was the practices of such companies that stirred up political controversies especially in England from the early seventeenth century onwards, which led to a reformulation of the concept of 'freedom of trade', or 'free trade'. Moreover, it was the critique directed against the Merchants Adventurers' export of bullion from Britain to the East Indies – which would make England short of gold and silver – that agitated John Wheeler to publish a small tract, *A Treatise of Commerce*, already in 1601, to defend the company. His argument was that, although England had to export bullion in order to buy the precious goods of the East, its merchants would still be able to re-export these commodities with a profit to other European countries. Through this roundabout trade, England would be a gainer. This argument was even more enforced later on by Mun in his *A Discourse of Trade from England unto the East Indies* (1621). Basically, Mun used the same arguments as Wheeler twenty years earlier. Hence, through its re-exportation, the company would 'bring more treasures into this Realme than of the other trades of this Kingdome ... being put together'.[22]

The attack on the chartered companies undoubtedly originated from merchants or groups of merchants who were jealous of the profits and riches accumulated by the privileged companies. Hence 'freedom of trade' became the political catchword for such who agitated for that merchant companies such as the Merchant Adventurers or the East India Company should be 'open' companies; this distinction was often drawn between 'closed' or regulated companies and open, so-called 'Joint stock' companies. Hence the intense discussion during this century was between two polarised positions; one which defended the position and privileges of the restricted group of merchants to exclusively carry through foreign trade in wools, spices, gold and silver, and the opposite position which wanted trade to be 'free', open to any merchants who had a capital and wanted to partake in the (profitable) trade with Asia or the Baltic states. Hence those who spoke in favour of 'free trade' in England during the seventeenth century were most often criticising regulated companies for upholding a *de facto* monopoly of a certain trade or trade route. However, in 1689 an anonymous writer (Petyt?) blamed the Merchant Adventurers and other trade companies for not allowing 'all English-Men (according to their right) be left at liberty to become Members'.[23] Thus it seems clear that the real controversial point was not that a certain company should have the exclusive privilege to sell or buy at a certain port (or have a privileged position to trade with for example China), but that more merchants should be able to join the company. The privilege of a closed corporation to trade was labelled 'monopoly'. To have no regulations at all was called 'polipoly' – most often referring to a state of anarchy just as detrimental as the monopoly. Hence, until the eighteenth century, most therefore agreed that trade must be regulated and carried out in an orderly fashion.

However, also princes and kings aspiring for absolute rule of their territories in Early Modern Europe talked in favour of 'free trade'. By doing this, their aim was to outroot the exclusive power of special merchant corporations and the privileged position of free cities. At the end of *Mercantilism*, Heckscher draws attention to the perhaps peculiar, but important, element of *laissez-faire* in a *dirigisme* which otherwise characterised the political economy of this period. He points to such statesmen as Colbert in France and Axel Oxenstierna in Sweden during the mid-seventeenth century, who often spoke in favour of 'freedom of trade': 'There are very few slogans of such frequent recurrence in the voluminous correspondence as the phrase "Liberty is the soul of trade"'.[24] What seems to have happened was that kings and statesmen such as Colbert in order to pursue a state interest in fact attacked the ancient privileges of the corporate freedom under the banner of 'free trade'. This is also the reason why, as Heckscher notes, paradoxically enough Mercantilism contributed to the establishment of 'real' free trade in the nineteenth-century meaning of the word.

Hence, it is misleading to speak of 'free trade' in our sense of the word during the seventeenth century. That more freedom of trade was beneficial to a country was for example a position that Mun would have agreed with.[25] However, that did not hinder him to urge for protection in order to achieve a favourable balance of trade. Other authors who argued in a similar way were Fortrey[26] and Houghton.[27] Hence Fortrey in 1673 claimed much the same as Josiah Tucker and Smith would do a century later, namely, that freedom of trade led to a more effective allocation of resources.[28] With a greater freedom of trade we could raise horse, sheep and bullocks on our fields 'to furnish all our neighbours' and instead import corn. He in fact stated:

> And might we freely have the liberty to export them [cattle] ... we should need no laws to hinder the exportation of corn; for we should find thereby a profit so far exceeding that which might be raised out of every acre that we might better afford to give a far greater price to buy it, than we can now sell it for. For the profit of one acre of pasture, in the flesh, hide, and tallow of an Ox ... is so much greater value abroad, than the like yield of the earth would be in corn.[29]

An issue which Fortrey touched upon in this context was whether corn should be allowed to be exported. For decades this had been a controversial political issue. Those who spoke against such exportation argued that corn then would be short in supply if exported. Others, like Fortrey, tended to argue that any export should be allowed if it could be done with a profit. If so it would bring in more income, which could buy whatever was needed from abroad.

Stark criticism directed against regulated companies was already prevalent in the writings of Malynes – but from a specific point of view. He particularly charged the East India Company for its exportation of money 'beyond the seas'. Occasionally he also made use of other arguments. In this context he, for example, propounded the orthodox view that it would be better to work up 'our own stuffes and materials' than to import wares from the East.[30]

However, during the seventeenth century, other critical voices appeared which charged the companies for their alleged monopolistic activities. An example is the pamphlet *A Discourse Consisting of Motives for the Enlargement and Freedome of Trade* from 1645, where an anonymous writer fired his heavy artillery against the Merchant Adventurers.[31] His aim was explicitly to 'demonstrate by clear and unanswerable arguments, the illegality of the incorporation of those who solely ascribe unto themselves the names of Merchant Adventurers'.[32] Whatever might have been the reason for taking up this plight of demonstration – partisan no doubt – the author dressed up his assault in principle terminology. 'Now there is nothing so advantagious and commendable in a Trade, as Community and freedome', he pointed out.[33] He especially charged the Adventurers for their privilege in exporting cloth to Holland. Our author without doubt spoke of the manufacturing interest outside of London – which Lipson called 'provincial jealousy'[34] – when he condemned the Adventurers for their monopolistic activities: buying cheap and selling dear. He went as far as saying that nothing is more 'pernicious and destructive to any Kingdome or Common-wealth than Monopolies'.[35] By using Bacon's money metaphor, he further pointed out that: 'Trade … is like Dung, which being close kept in a heap or two stinks, but being spread abroad, it doth fertilize the earth and make it more fructible'.[36]

In principle, the same argument directed against the regulated companies and their alleged monopolistic behaviour appeared in several tracts during the following decades. We can, for example, find such charges in Coke's treatises from the 1670s, in which he campaigned for 'plenty and cheapness'.[37] Another instance is the remarkable *Britannia Languens or a Discourse of Trade* (1680) most probably written by Petyt.[38] This author was very sceptical indeed towards any 'cloggs upon our trade', especially monopolies. To the extent regulated companies monopolised trade – that is, did not allow 'all *English*-men (according to their right) be left at liberty to *become Members*' – they were damned by Petyt in strong language. He went as far as to criticise the more modern 'Joynt-stock companies' for their monopolistic operations. It is in the nature of such companies that:

> they must be as injurious as may be to all home-manufactures made of our own materialls, and the vent of our other exports, because by trading on a **Joynt-stock** they make but **one buyer**, and therefore have a **Monopoly** for all exportable goods proper.[39]

At times, he explicitly also attacked the East India Company, mainly for their import of wares, which otherwise could have been produced at home.[40]

However, through the seventeenth century, the regulated companies also found support among authors who rather saw an advantage in having a 'well and ordered trade' (Roberts). Already in 1601 Wheeler, serving as a secretary for the Merchant Adventurers, argued that it was to the advantage of the Adventurers that trade and employment increased in England. Especially its traffic with cloth led to that 'a number of labouring men are set to work and gaign much monie, besides that which the Merchant gaineth'.[41] Furthermore, the 'orderlie Gouvernment and rule' does not at all imply fewer buyers and lower selling prices. On the contrary, the market knowledge of the company provides the cloth manufacture with more customers than otherwise would have been the case. Another beneficial effect was that it provided credit to small producers. In fact, he stated, they 'all are provided for, and not some starved for want, whilest others are swollen up to the eyes with Fatt and plentie'.[42] Much of the same arguments in favour of the regulated companies were echoed in the debate during following decades. In 1648 Henry Parker, apparently another official of the Adventurers, disputed against too much 'freedome' in trade. Freedom and regulation were no opposites and could be reconciled to each other, he stressed. On the whole, he repeated Wheeler's argument as well as making explicit references to him in the text.[43]

Further, Roberts, in *The Treasure of Traffike* (1641), recommended that his 'Kingdome' should establish more regulated companies. Thus, according to him, to 'joyn one with another in a corporation and Company, and not to kase their Traffike by themselves asunder, or apart' would lead to increased strength and maximun benefits for a trading nation.[44] And as we have seen, both Mun and Misselden in the 1620s defended the East India Company against attacks, especially from Malynes. However, especially for Mun this defence was mainly directed toward the complaint that this company's export of bullion caused an unfavourable balance of trade.

Interest rates

During most of the seventeenth century, as we have seen, the discussions concerning the importance of commerce and trade for wealth and power were in the foreground. Another topic that triggered a continuous stream of brochure literature involved the issue of interest. The origins of such debates in England lingered at least since the sixteenth century. It was in such a context that for example Thomas Wilson published his famous *Discourse Upon Usury* in 1572. To some degree, echoing the position taken by the medieval Schoolmen, the issue of usury was also a leading theme in most of what Malynes wrote at the beginning of the seventeenth century. In much of this literature, usury was of course condemned as an evil practice. For Malynes, usury in different guises was the very 'Canker' which tormented England. In fact, up until the 1630s, the view that 'all usury biteth' was widespread in economic literature.[45]

Hence, when Culpepper the elder's *A Tract of Ursurie* (1621) appeared in print, it must be seen in the context of a long tradition of denunciations of usury and taking of interest in England. John Culpepper (1578–1662), who had studied in Oxford but left without a degree and later became lord of Leeds castle, has sometimes been dealt with as a scholastic writer. However, this can be doubted. In his tract, which was presented to the parliament in 1623, he was quite casual with regard to the moral or origin of rent. He did not claim that high interest rates were the consequence of malicious speculation, as Malynes did. Rather, he turned the argument around and said that the reason for example why merchants leave their trade and instead take to 'usurie' is because 'the gaine therof being so easie'.[46] Therefore, more than another tract condemning usury in the old way, his text must be seen in the context of the current discussion during the 1620s dealing with the trade crisis. While he argued for a reduction of the interest rate to 6 per cent, Bacon, whose essay titled 'On Usury' was first published in 1625, demanded a reduction to 5 per cent.

Bacon's main interest lay in the general economic consequences of a high rate of interest. Although he starts out to mention that usurers are regarded to have broken 'the first law that was made for mankind after the fall' and thus because they 'Judaize? ... they should have orange-tawny bonnets'. Still he defended at least some practices of 'usury'. It is not totally against nature 'to beget money, and the like'. He ponders, 'I say this only, that usury is a *concessum propter duritiem cordis*: for since there must be borrowing and lending, and men are so hard of heart as they will not lend freely, usury must be permitted'. He opines that few have spoken of usury in a useful way. His analysis of the phenomenon is then the following:

> The discommodities of usury are, first, that it makes fewer merchants; for were it not for this lazy trade of usury, money would not lie still but would in great part be employed upon merchandising, which is the *vena porta* of wealth in a state: the second, that it makes poor merchants; for as a farmer cannot husband his ground so well if he sit at a great rent, so the merchant cannot drive his trade so well if he sit at great usury: the third is incident to the other two; and that is, the decay of customs of kings or states, which ebb or flow with merchandising: the fourth, that it bringeth the treasure of a realm or state into a few hands; for the usurer being at certainties, and others at uncertainties, at the end of the game most of the money will be in the box; and ever a state flourisheth when wealth is more equally spread: the fifth, that it beats down the price of land; for the employment of money is chiefly either merchandising or purchasing, and usury waylays both: the sixth, that it doth dull and damp all industries, improvements, and new inventions, wherein money would be stirring if it were not for this slug: the last, that it is the canker and ruin of many men's estates, which in process of time breeds a public poverty.[47]

Much of the same had been said by Culpepper in his 1621 tract. The central issue here was why Holland had risen to such a wealth while

England had harked behind. As a main answer he stressed the higher level of interest in England than in the Dutch Republic. Thus Culpepper's proposition was that the present 'high rate of usury decayes trade'. The main consequence of a high rate of interest was that 'generally all Merchants when they have gotten any greath wealth, leave trading and fall to usury, the gaine thereof being so easie, certain and great'.[48] And it is against this background that he proposed that the interest rate should be lowered by statute and law. In his tract he takes careful notice of the arguments that might be raised against his scheme. The obvious objection that money may 'be hard to be borrowed' when a maximum interest rate is established, he repudiated in the following fashion: 'I answer that this if it were true, if the high rate of Usurie did increase money within this Land; but the high rate of Usury doth inrich onely the Usurer, and impoverish the Kingdome'.[49]

When disavowing that increased interest rates in fact might increase the fund of loanable money, we certainly seem to stand on familiar ground. On this point he undoubtedly (as well as Bacon) was closer to Malynes than to Mun and Misselden. Thus Culpepper was aware that an increased quantity of money might decrease the rate of interest. At the same time, he does not think that this will make the number of lenders less.[50] However, this was really an exception, and it is interesting to notice that this seemingly illogical position was shared by a number of later authors, including Child.

In the 1660s, Culpepper's arguments were once again rehearsed and his pamphlet republished. In 1668, the author's son John, Thomas Culpepper the younger, and Child published pamphlets which dealt with the rate of interest. By this time, Child was already a representative of the East India Company (on Child see further p. 193). However, Child's *Brief Observations Concerning Trade and Interest of Money* (1668) was clearly a result of his work for the newly established Council of Trade and cannot only be regarded as a partisan intervention in the interest of this company.[51] In fact, his argumentation was cast in principal terms. Thus Child saw the cause for the present trade crisis in England in: 'The prodigious increase of the Netherlanders in their Domestick and foreign Trade'.[52] Furthermore, one of the most important causes for their superiority was 'the lowness of interest of Money with them, which in peaceable times exceeds not three per cent per Annum' – while the English interest rate was at six per cent.[53] This implied, according to Child, that money was more abounding in Holland than in England – and easier to borrow; trade could be carried out in Holland which was unprofitable in Britain due to a high rate of interest. But also trades in Holland that gained relatively lower profit margins than in England would be established. From this point of view, like Culpepper the elder almost fifty years earlier, Child argued that a law should be inaugurated to fix the rate of interest, this time not to rise above 4 per cent.

Closely following his father, Culpepper the younger, agreed with Child on the urgency to put down the interest rate by statute. Thus his tract abounded with vivid illustrations regarding the benefits that would accrue if interest rates were reduced. For example, he assured that 'it will in a short time double, if not treble, the yearly fruits of our Lands ... it will revive our dying Manufacture'.[54] However, he as well as Child had even less to say than Culpepper the elder about the forces which regulated the level of the interest rate. None of them was afraid that a lowered interest rate might induce potential lenders to do other things with their money than to offer it on the loan market. Child opined that they would have to consent to the new conditions. Most certainly, this argument relied upon the qualification that money-capital was not transferable between countries, for example from Holland to England. As hard evidence he sufficed to point out that in Holland lenders seemed to be satisfied with three per cent.[55] Undoubtedly, from the perspective of the 1660s, this supposition is not altogether unrealistic. As we have seen, England and Holland were at war with each other for a long time. This together with war-like conditions in general did not to any greater degree allow a flow of loanable capital between countries.

Child's and Culpepper's tracts – which were followed by several others from Culpepper's pen during the next couple of years – aroused severe criticism. In 1668 a certain Thomas Manley argued that it was 'to force nature' to lower the interest rate by statute. The reason that the rate was so low in Holland stemmed from 'natural' causes, he argued. He referred directly to an argument Mun and Misselden had used against Malynes:

> [I]t is with money in Holland and in all other parts (in point of interest) as in the Exchange with us, the more money there is, and fewer takers, the lower is the Exchange, and when we have more lenders than borrowers interest will be low without a law for it.[56]

Thus while Culpepper the younger and Child seems to have regarded the interest rate as an independent variable, which through its fluctuations determined the level of wealth, Manley turned the argument upside down. He denied outright 'that the lowness of interest is the cause of riches'. On the contrary, he regarded this rate as the dependent variable.[57] Like most contemporaries, he believed that the interest rate was regulated by the amount of money (or loanable capital) in the country.[58] Child, however, was unhappy with this doctrine. Without doubt, Child and Culpepper were quite in opposition to for example Mun and Manley on this whole issue. Whether this is enough for talking about two conflicting 'schools' – as Bowley does – is perhaps to say too much. However, this is an interesting contrast that shows that Mercantilism was not a closed and static doctrine, but a series of discussions which employed a common vocabulary used for different purposes.

Money

Monetary issues were always central in the economic discussions during the seventeenth century.[59] Moreover, during most of this century, it was generally believed that England suffered a constant shortage of bullion. This supposed shortage, in turn, was most often referred to as caused by an almost constant drainage of money from England to foreign nations. As we saw, the cause of the drainage was either seen as a consequence of speculation leading to an overvaluation of the British coin, or as a consequence of a negative balance of trade.[60]

Whatever the reasons for the 'drainage of coynage', three main methods for increasing the money supply in Britain were discussed during the seventeenth century: debasement of silver coins, the introduction of a par of exchange and the establishment of a positive balance of trade (payments).[61]

The first method was generally rejected as detrimental. Certainly, debasement of the silver coin had been a common policy during the sixteenth century in order to increase the stock of money – not the least during the reign of Henry VIII. However, from the middle of the century this method was heavily criticised. Such a critique was in fact the leading theme in the tract *A Discourse of the Common Weal of this Realm of England*. Once believed to have been written by Shakespeare, as we saw, and now commonly attributed to the scholar and statesman Thomas Smith (1513–77), who was Vice Chancellor of Cambridge University and Master of Request at the court of the Duke of Somerset, it propounded the view that: 'is the chiefest greife that all men complaine most on'.[62] The author was certainly aware of the quantity principle: 'it is the wares that be necessarie for mans use that are exchanged indede for the outward name of the coyne, an yt is the raritie and plentie thereof that maketh the price thereof base or higher'.[63] Apart from causing higher prices, the debasement of coin had lead to the result that 'our coine is discredited already amongst strangers which evermore desired to serve us before all other nations, of all our nedes, for the goodness of our coine'.[64]

Moreover, also during the ensuing period, debasement had few supporters – if any. Hence in the 1620s Malynes would speak fiercely against debasement.[65] Also in the mid-1620s when debasement once again was presented as a solution to present urging problems, Cotton spoke fervently against this method before His Majesty the King and the Privy Council. Debasement was no real solution, he argued. A change in the nominal value of the silver coin would only mean that 'a less proportion of such commodities as shall be exchanged for it, must be received'.[66] Moreover, as Cotton pointed out, the king would lose by debasement. He would 'suffer by the Rents of his Lands', by receiving less in customs, by the increase of his soldiers' wages, as well as 'discourage a great proportion of the trade in England'.[67] As noted, such a disapproving attitude was shared by a clear majority of authors and debaters during this century, including Vaughan, Robinson and later Locke.

The second method for increasing the supply of money had of course been especially recommended by Malynes: the notorious par of exchange. The suggestion of a stable *par*, which would determine the relative value of English and foreign money in exchange, most often went together with the advice to enforce the ancient Statute of Employment, which outlawed the export of bullion. However, as we have seen, increasingly during the seventeenth century the view that undervaluation of English coin was caused by exchange manipulations carried out by usurious bankers and exchange dealers was replaced by the ideas of Mun and Misselden. However, the suggestion that a statute which forced the value of the coin to stay at its 'intrinsick value' – that is, a stable relation between the nominal value and the monetary value in silver – was still offered in the middle of the century. For example in 1652 Henry Robinson was entirely against the export of coin and proposed that exchange should be carried out according to a decided *par*.[68] The 'Marchandizing Exchange' must be regulated, he thought. According to his view, it was in fact 'the most mysterious parts of Trade'.[69]

However, a third solution for increasing the money supply was gaining ground during this period. For a country which had no mines of its own, as it was increasingly argued by Mun and others (for example: Serra in Naples, as we saw),[70] the only valid method would be to increase the money supply through a net surplus from its foreign trade. Simultaneously, however, another opinion was also spreading, which really was a logical step once the quantity theory of money was accepted. In the long run it made the whole issue of enlarging the money supply by more or less *dirigiste* means obsolete. It was the view that money was a commodity which price was regulated by supply and demand. Ironically, this view was also to some sense a logical outcome of the kind of supply and demand analysis propounded by Mun and Misselden, but which they did not themselves fully apply with regard to money. The question why they did not recognise this has of course been standard in the controversy around Mercantilism ever since the eighteenth century their awareness of the so-called specie–flow mechanism we have already discussed. For most interpreters, it has, indeed, been difficult to understand why they would have pressed for a net surplus with regard to bullion while at the same time they recognised the overall importance of the supply-and-demand mechanism.[71]

By the end of the seventeenth century, the view that the price of money was regulated by its demand and supply had largely become accepted. A further step had also been reached, namely that the demand for money was related to the amount of trade carried out. This was for example evidenced in the great controversy that arose during the 1690s when a new re-coinage project was launched. As we will see later, especially Locke would argue that money had a stable intrinsic value, determined by 'common consent', in its relation to its denominator, silver and gold. At the same time he surely agreed that this 'intrinsic' value of money (i.e. silver and gold) was regulated by 'the Plenty or Scarcity of Money in proportion to the Plenty and Scarcity of those things [trade-able goods]'.[72]

The most important implication of the view that the price of money, or value as Locke would insist upon, was regulated by supply and demand related to trade was that the issue of an absolute shortage of money in a country became futile. A relatively small circulation of money would only mean deflation, while an opposite situation would induce inflation. With regard to the effects of inflation and/or deflation, different authors most certainly took different standpoints – as for example the discussion around the re-coinage project amply proves. However, it is clear that the agreed upon view that the price of money was regulated by supply and demand was difficult to reconcile with a traditional favourable balance of trade view seems clear. Certainly, also, such an approach ruled out the possibility to establish a par of exchange. It implied, that the relative value of money in exchange was caused by monetary flows between countries and/or by the demand and supply for bills of exchange. This in turn meant that in the sixteenth century suspicion was rejected that the lack of minted coin was caused by foreign speculators who had consciously manipulated it so that English money was worth more abroad than at home.[73] Certainly, if only a small amount of coins were issued by the Royal mint, this implied that silver was worth more as bullion than as money. But the low valuation of the king's money was mainly caused by a negative trade balance that created low demand for them in exchange.

These new viewpoints, which only received mature expression during the 1690s, are clearly visible already in Vaughan's *A Discourse of Coin and Coinage*, published in 1675 but written already in the 1630s.[74] According to Vaughan the value of money was regulated by its 'Raritie'. The 'rarity of money' grows from four causes, he says. First, from the 'Want of means to bring in the materials of money'. Second, 'the facility of exporting them' leads to the same consequence. Third, from 'the wasting of them in the Kingdome' and, fourth, from 'the great encrease of the proportion between Gold and Silver, and the things valued by them'.[75] Furthermore, he stated that the reason why foreign countries 'raise their money', while England was not able to do the same, solely depended upon the 'rarity of money' caused by a net exportation of money.[76]

That such views became increasingly common during the mid-seventeenth century seems quite clear. In 1660 the Council of Trade once again discussed monetary questions and the causes behind the supposed outflow of money. Against the view that the Statute of Employment should be reinforced and no bullion exported, an anonymous writer for example stated 'that Money and Bullion have always forced their way against the several laws; that the trade of the world will not be forced, but will find or make its own way free to all appearances of profit'.[77] Instead, he stated in a quite familiar fashion that: 'The Balance of Trade ... being the sake or principal cause of the exportation or importation of Bullion'.[78]

A new science of trade

Perhaps not surprisingly the debates on trade and commerce as well as its advantages for the nation dominated the economic discussions in England during the seventeenth century. As we have seen, building upon the new groundwork provided by the 1620s discussion this would lead forward to the development of a new language of vocabulary culminating in what Hutchison named 'the economic boom in economic thinking' in England during the 1690s. Moreover, around this time many authors did struggle to join together ideas, theories and concepts that had been used in the previous discussions into a more coherent 'discourse of trade'. The aim, at least by some, was to put forward a number of general principles upon which commerce and trade were instituted.[79]

This interpretation is undoubtedly on the mark. Such an ambition is for example clearly discernible with Child's *A New Discourse of Trade* (1693). Hence this book was much more than a mere extension of his *Discourse of Trade*, published three years earlier. Thus the 1690 text mainly enclosed Child's repeated opinion that the interest rate ought to be lowered by statute. The new edition, however, was enlarged with much new material. In *New Discourse*, Child was trying to present a number of general principles on the overall role of trade and commerce for economic development. As this work was to be published in numerous editions over the next century, it is clear that it was widely read. Other works with the same ambition, which perhaps did not achieve such commercial success, were also published by other authors, some of which we will portrait in this chapter: Davenant, Barbon, Simon Clement, North and others. Another important author of this period – Cary, a merchant from Bristol – would even use the word 'science' when attempting to present some general principles regarding trade:

> In order to discover whether a Nation gets or loses by its trade, 'tis necessary first to enquire into the Principles whereupon it is built; for Trade hath its Principles as other Sciences have, and as difficult to understand.[80]

It is not so difficult to understand why particularly the 1690s implied a boom in economic writing and thinking. The Glorious Revolution had turned the political scenery upside down. With the Stuarts, many old favourites fell in disrepute while the fortune of others rose. For the East India Company, for example, the future definitively looked less bright than before. During the restoration it had been transformed into a joint-stock company. At the time of the Glorious Revolution, as Cunningham showed, it was not only a trade monopoly but also a political and judicial power.[81] However, in the 1690s, the company received sharp opposition from competing merchants, wool manufacturers and Whig politicians who looked with envy at the privileges upheld by the company. As a result, many of those were discarded. It was also a clear sign of the new situation when a rival 'Whig' East India Company was set up in 1700.[82]

Another major issue that stirred up much controversy during this decade was a new re-coinage project. As we saw, since the 1620s, there had been no attempts made by the Crown to debase the currency. However, among the public an almost present fear existed that money would be wanted in circulation. This anxiety became even more pronounced after 1663, when the old prohibition against the export of bullion was dissolved.[83] In reality a more important problem than the alleged export of coin was probably the tendency for old silver coin to get worn out in circulation. Hence, their actual silver content tended to decrease over time. In accordance with Gresham's law, this seems in practice to have led to newly minted silver coin never going into circulation. As new coins contained more silver, they would be melted down and sold as bullion – at least to some extent to foreigners. In response to this, a new re-coinage project was launched. It declared the withdrawal of old and worn coins and the circulation of new ones.

According to the original plan, made by William Lowndes, the introduction of the new coin would imply a debasement of the silver crown from 60 to 75 pence. However, not the least, Locke's intervention meant that this attempt was halted (see below). Instead the old standard was preserved. During the next years this would result in a severe deflation that severely worsened a trade crisis already in existence. Hence, with respect to the controversial political situation, which also included a heated debate around the establishment of the Bank of England in 1694, it is perhaps no wonder that the 1690s must have been a fruitful decade for economic debate and speculation.

However, in order to understand the 'boom of the 1690s', we must also take account of the prevailing intellectual *milieu*. We must further acknowledge that the foregoing discussion during the seventeenth century described in the last chapter had led to a development of concepts and ideas which formed the basis of the synthetic attempts made during this decade.

First, it is necessary to point out that the late seventeenth century saw the continuation of a natural scientific approach to economic phenomena which had emerged earlier during, particularly, the 1620s.[84] The idea that the commercial economy could be regarded as an independent body with its own laws of motion was the most important result of this approach. Within this body of literature it is amazing to notice how often the human body and its functions was used metaphorically in order to depict economic processes.[85] For example, the blood metaphor was very often compared with money and/or trade. Hence, for example, Pollexfen would emphasise that 'Trade is the Body Politick, as Blood to the Body Natural'.[86] Furthermore, in reference to a country growing poor from an ill-regulated trade, Cary would fill in: 'For as in the Body Natural, if you draw out Blood faster than the sangufying parts can supply, it must necessarily wast and decay'.[87] Another author, Erasmus Phillips, would fill in some decades later: 'Trade is to the Body Politick as the Blood is to human Body, it diffuses itself by the minutest Canals into every part of a Nation, and gives Life and Vigour to the whole'.[88] Most certainly, such references can be multiplied almost endlessly.

However, with the application of such a natural scientific approach, a fashion for quantification and empirical investigation spread. The 'laws' of commercial society were to some sense analogous with the laws of the natural world. Thus it was conceived that the laws of commerce could only be manipulated to some limit. Otherwise the sensitive machinery could be destroyed and not function properly. From this point of view, it can be no mere coincidence that some of the most-important economic writers during the 1690s – Barbon, Petty, Locke and others – were trained as physicists and could be regarded as well read in the contemporary natural scientific literature. At the same time the gradual breakthrough for a philosophy of logic, which built on Cartesian principles and the subsequent dismantling of Aristotelian formalism, must have played an important role in this context.[89]

Second, this natural scientific approach was also at times merged with a moral philosophy building on natural law ideas. This influence was especially noticeable with Locke. But such inclinations can also be traced in the writings of, for example, Davenant and Barbon. Especially Pocock has drawn attention to an Atlantic republication tradition with clear neo-Machiavellian influences especially concerning Davenant, but also Defoe and others. Their civic humanism was mainly shown in their discussion on such themes as the 'common good' versus corruption, between wealth and inequality or how long freedom can survive without equality in property. Also, for example, Davenant's discussion on republics versus empires and kingdoms is unmistakably neo-Machiavellian, Pocock insists.[90]

However, also from the broader discussion dealing with natural law, especially during the latter half of the seventeenth century, the economic writers would in a general sense be forced into believing in the existence of a 'natural system' of trade relationships. However, this influence is explicit only with some writers. Thus for example Barbon's insistence on the subjective foundation of exchange relations and price is close in line with Hugo Grotius and, especially, Samuel Pufendorff. As is well known, Pufendorff based his theory of price (or value) on a solid subjective basis. His conception of value stemmed from his general theory of man as a social creature guided by *sociabilitas*.[91]

Of the many economic writers who can be regarded as part of the boom of the 1690s, we will here look a little more in detail at five of the perhaps most important – or at least they can serve as examples – other economic writers: Child, Davenant, Locke, Clement and Petty.

Josiah Child (1630–99)

Child was the well-known director and later on chairman of the East India Company. Over this company he was said to rule 'as absolutely as if it had been his private business'.[92] Thus, by the time of his death, Child was a man of great wealth able to leave a fortune of approximately L 200 000. In political terms he started out as a Whig, but with wealth and fortune his sympathies changed towards the Tories. Especially during the short reign of Charles II he and the East India Company accomplished great success. After 1688, however, things changed for the worse. But Child himself seems not to have been financially affected by the company's increasing problems.

As an economic writer Child was able to reach a great audience. His first published tract, *Brief Observations Concerning Trade and Interest of Money* (1668) was written, as we have seen, in order to advocate an 'abatement' of interest by law to four per cent. According to Child, a low rate of interest was the main 'cause of the prosperity and riches of the nation'.[93] He had written the tract mainly for practical political reasons during his work for the Council of Trade. In 1690 when the issue of a fixed interest rate once again was brought forward, the tract was republished with some slight amendments under the title *A Discourse of Trade*. Furthermore, when *A New Discourse of Trade* appeared in print three years later, it once again included Child's views and arguments on interest. But a number of additional chapters were supplemented which dealt with topics such as the role of merchant companies, the Navigation Act, the employment of the poor, the overseas plantations and 'the Ballance of trade'.

It is true that Child was not a very systematic thinker and writer. However, in *New Discourse of Trade* he made it explicitly clear that his main objective was to explain why the Netherlanders had been able to achieve such a 'prodigious increase' in their 'Domestick and Foreign trade, Riches and multitude of Shipping'.[94] For this purpose he presented a list of in all fifteen reasons: the Dutch had lower interest rates, they were more experienced merchants, they had established a great fishing industry in the Nordic Sea, they encouraged (and enumerated) new inventors, they had established an outstanding shipbuilding industry and so on.[95]

However, beyond these particulars, he was searching for some general principles which could make a commonwealth rich and powerful. Hence, according to Child, national wealth – the material well-being of its population – is mainly a result of production. Of special significance were modern worked-up goods in manufactures. He pointed out that:

> It is multitudes of People and good Laws, such as Cause an encrease of People, which principally Enrich our Country; and if we retrench by Law the Labour of our people, we drive them from us to other countries that gives better Rates.[96]

Thus Child started out with production and the employment of the poor. To this extent he certainly differed from, for example, Mun, Fortrey and Petyt, who emphasised that England's 'great happiness' lay in much foreign trade that could bring in treasure. Moreover, it is noteworthy that the aspect of foreign trade surpluses was almost totally lost with Child. The issue of foreign trade, though, was certainly important also for him. If well organised, it would support production and employment to grow at a fast rate. Basically, however, it was people employed in manufactures and trade who provided for the material wealth of the nation.

Besides employment, as we saw, Child emphasised the need for good laws. With regard to labour, he shared the view of many of his contemporaries that workers were lazy and behaved in accordance with a backward bending supply curve: when times were good they simply retreated from work.[97] Hence, such laws which encouraged productive work, stimulated foreign craft workers to immigrate and stay were necessary to implement. However, also foreign trade must be organised in a beneficial fashion. As such a beneficial regulation, in accordance with Adam almost a hundred years later, he especially pointed out the Navigation Act:

> I am of Opinion that in relation to Trade, Shipping, Profit and Power, it is one of the choicest and most prudent Acts that ever was made in England, and without which we had not now been owners of one half of the Shipping, nor trade, nor Employed one half of the Sea-men which we do at present.[98]

As we can see, Child here particularly spoke in favour of protection for the sake of keeping up employment within the shipping industry. But his arguments extended far outside such a narrow context. In fact, *A New Discourse of Trade* must to a large extent be understood as an argument for the establishment of more manufactures and increased domestic production. For this purpose he sometimes propounded protection from foreign competition. But domestically he rather argued for more freedom of trade and fewer restrictions, a dismantling of trade and craft regulations and so on.[99] In this he was not consistent, however. Hence, in order to encourage growth he always seemed to return to his old proposal that the interest rate should be put down by force to become equal or lower than the rate prevailing in the Dutch Republic. With a lower interest rate Englishmen could compete with the Dutch more easily, he believed. If loanable money became more accessible, they would be able to engage themselves in trades and projects that would have been unprofitable given a higher rate of interest.[100]

It is also in the light of his preference for production and employment that we must discern Child's critique of the orthodox favourable balance of trade theory. Certainly, however, his main argument is that it would be impossible for practical reasons to establish such a balance. He felt that it was impossible to compute an accurate balance because of all the technical complications involved. However, he pointed out, even if such a balance could be found, it would not present any conclusive proof of whether a country won or lost through its foreign trade. Child here pointed at Virginia and Barbados, which both had a favourable balance but still lost by their trade (mainly because they exported raw materials and imported manufactured goods).[101]

Thus, instead of being so concerned with the balance of trade and payments, we should regulate our trade so that manufacture and employment is encouraged, he propounded. And this was best accomplished by keeping to the following formula: 'To encourage those Trades most, that vent most of our Manufactures, or supply us with Materials to be further Manufactured in England'.[102] From this point of view he was prepared to defend the East India Company from its antagonists. England very much benefited from the trade carried out by this company, he emphasised. Particularly, it helped to encourage employment in England through its re-exportation of finished wares and its import of such wares that could be worked up by domestic manufacture.[103]

Hence, Child in *A New Discourse of Trade* as well as in a later work, *A Discourse of the Nature, Use and Advantages of Trade* (1694), presented an explicit critique of the orthodox favourable balance doctrine. Finding it useless he instead suggested another important 'balance' for the authorities to take notice of. This was the so-called 'labour balance' based upon a theory of 'foreign paid incomes' which we discussed earlier.[104] To this 'balance' we will return to shortly as it is best formulated in some later texts. However, our main point here is the extent to which Child emphasised production and employment as the main progenitors of material wealth and national power. For this aim good laws must be inaugurated. Therefore, to some point he was certainly a promulgator of state *dirigisme.* Thus to call him a free trade Tory, as Ashley did, is not very helpful. As we saw, he was certainly ready to defend economic freedom to a certain extent.[105] As he was a Tory and Director of the East India Company, he was very suspicious towards the increased war cries for protection, which mounted up especially during the 1690s. However, the achievement of wealth was to him part and parcel of the efficiency of the machinery of the state and its powers. This certainly made him avert a more radical free trade gospel.

Nicholas Barbon (1640–98)

In this last sense, Barbon was quite differently inclined. He was by principle averted to *dirigisme* – being the speculative building tycoon after London's great fire that he was. Like Child he was sternly critical of the favourable balance of trade thesis. It is in fact with him that we first can see the full implications of the 'foreign paid income' doctrine.

As the son of the famous Praisegood Barbon, or Barebone, who had the notorious Barebone parliament named after him, Nicholas was graduated a MD at Utrecht and became a Fellow of the College of Physicians there in 1664.[106] Taking use of the opportunity that the great fire of London 1666 offered, he became a builder–speculator, a considerable banker and the first to introduce a system of fire insurance in England. He wrote two small, but remarkable tracts, *A Discourse of Trade* (1690) and *A Discourse Concerning Coining the New Money Lighter* (1696). The general tone of the first of the treatises can at least partly be explained by Barbon's experience as a builder and banker. His aim to publish it was most probably triggered by his wish to combat regulations that according to him had hampered a healthy increase of trade and production. The second treatise was in effect quite different. It was mainly a critical response to Locke during the re-coinage discussion in the mid-1690s.

In the second treatise directed against Locke, Barbon started out by firmly stating that Locke's main mistake was the belief that there existed an 'intrinsick' value in silver. He implied that the view that this intrinsic value should be 'the instrument and measure of commerce' was mistaken.[107] Instead, according to Barbon, silver as well as money in general were commodities which price varied depending on use and quantity. Thus, there was neither an 'intrinsick' value in silver nor a necessary relationship between nominal money and silver. 'Value' he defined as 'the price of things' determined mainly by use:'There are two general uses by which all Things have a Value: They are either useful to supply the Wants of the Body, or the Want of the Mind'. Riches, in turn, he defines as 'all such Things as are of great value'.[108] On the basis of such a definition of value he went forward to criticise the favourable balance theory of trade. The opinion, he argued, that silver and gold have an 'intrinsick' value stemmed from the same confusion which had haunted King Midas.[109] This mistake was granted upon the false supposition 'that Gold and Silver are the only Riches'.[110] Hence, the notion of a favourable balance of trade was a simple 'mistake'.[111] He placed his critique upon two different arguments. First, he repeated Child's conviction that it would be almost impracticable to account for such a balance. Not even the fact that foreign exchange 'run high upon a Nation' is a true sign of an unfavourable balance of trade; especially as bills of exchange 'rise and fall every week and of some particular times in the year run high against a Nation'.[112] Second, however, from this he carried on by stressing a more principal point:

> But if there could be an account taken of the **Balance of Trade**, I can't see where the advantage of it could be. For the reason that's given for it, **That the Overplus is paid in Bullion, and the Nation grows so much the richer, because the balance is made**

in Bullion, is altogether a mistake: For Gold and Silver are but commodities; and one sort of commodity is as good as another, so it be of the same value. A hundred pounds of worth of Copper is as good to a merchant, as if he imported a hundred pounds worth of Silver, and he may get as much by it.... For a Nation grows rich, by the Inhabitants growing rich.[113]

Replacing an account of the balance of trade he suggested another method to judge whether a nation grew rich or poor by its trade. First, it might be judged by observing whether the inhabitants were 'growing rich'. Second, to know whether a nation gained or lost in its trade the method would be to consider 'what sort of Goods employ most hands by importing and manufacturing'. Thus, a well-regulated trade should be ordered so that a maximum of people are employed, as 'the more there are employ'd in a nation the richer the Nation grows'.[114]

Moreover, besides presenting an alternative to the balance of trade 'doctrine' in such terms, he developed a critique of the generally accepted view that an 'overballance' of trade must lead to that 'money is carried out' of the realm. In fact, anticipating the specie–flow mechanism, which later on was developed by Gervaise, Hume and others, he stated that a negative trade balance would merely lead to the price of English bills of exchange falling and with them export prices being measured in value: 'That all sorts of Goods of the value of the Bill of Exchange, or the Balance of the accompt, will answer the Bill, and Balance the Accompt as well as Money'.[115] Thus, a net outflow of money would not be feasible, at least not in the long run. However, he did not explicitly mention that such a neat balancing out in the long run necessitated, for example, that demand on foreign markets was elastic and that a lowered export price would mean higher foreign demand. But at the same time he was clearly aware of the principle of elasticity. Therefore, it is highly plausible that he presupposed this precondition without spelling it out very clearly.

Barbon's earlier work, 'A Discourse of Trade', had been more general in character and presented the framework for the later treatise particularly directed against Locke. In this work he, at some length, discussed the concepts of value and riches. 'Things of no use has no value', he pointed out.[116] Moreover, as he continued, 'the market is the best judge of value: for by the Concourse of Buyers and sellers, the quality of wares, and the occassion for them are Best known'.[117] He took the same position with regard to money and pointed out that it would be a grave mistake to believe that money had an 'intrinsick value by itself'. Instead, like any commodity, it varied in its value.[118]

In this treatise he also discussed the general benefits of trade. An abundant foreign trade would raise the value of land, improve the natural stock of the country, increase wages as well as the revenues of the state. Moreover, by its civilising effects, trade would not only bring increased wealth, but also peace.[119] Contrary to Child, Barbon did not so much emphasise the visible hand of governments in order to make trade prosperous. Instead, trade was mainly promoted by the 'industry of the poor' and the 'liberality in the Rich'. Thus the consumption of luxury wares among the rich classes should not be opposed but rather encouraged, he propounded. He even went so far that he defended 'prodigality' with the argument that, although it was vicious from the individual point of view, it brought social benefits by raising demand:

> Prodigality is a vice that is prejudicial to the Man, but not to the Trade; It is living a pace, and spending that in a Year, that should last all his life; Covetousness is a Vice, prejudicial both to Man & Trade; It starves the Man, and breaks the Trade: and by the same way the Covetous Man thinks he grows rich, he grows poor.[120]

As causes behind the prevailing and much debated decay of trade in England he especially pointed out the 'many prohibitions and high rents'.[121] On the whole, in this pamphlet his tone was quite 'liberal'. He of course admitted that the best for England would be 'if our Serges, Stuffs, or Cloth are Exchanged for Unmanufactured Goods ... because of the difference in Number of Hands in the making of the First, and the Later'.[122] However, to draw the conclusion from this that more prohibitions should be introduced was wrong, he pointed out. Rather, as a better solution he stressed that English wares should be made more competitive by low interest rates, low prices on provisions and low wages. For this purpose, not the least, an 'increased industry' among the poor was most necessary.

Thus with Barbon we seem quite far from the stylised version of a mercantilist writer. Instead of the advantage of having a trade surplus, he rather stressed the role of production and demand as dynamic economic forces propelling growth and increased wealth. From this point of view it is very typical indeed that he takes notice of the relationship between interest as a price paid for the loan of money – which was the definition most economic pamphleteers of this age employed – and the *real* rate of interest. Thus Barbon in his *Dicourse of Trade* defined interest as a 'Rent of stock' and compared it with the rent accruing from land.[123] This line of reasoning would in the eighteenth century be further developed by, for example, Joseph Massie, Tucker and Hume.

However, if we take an even broader view of Barbon's accomplishment, it is impossible not to notice the influence from the contemporary natural rights discussion. As Barbon did not explicitly cite any works of this kind, we cannot be exactly sure of the exact influence he gained from this literature. However, most of the discussion on political, moral and judicial matters during this period was carried out within the context of natural rights discourse. And for Barbon we can see this influence directly in his subjective theory of value most often connected with the name of Puffendorf. As such, however, this theory of course had longer roots back to the moral philosophical discussion among the Schoolmen of the Middle Ages.[124]

Quite clearly, Barbon's *A Discourse of Trade* contained several such references to the civilising function of trade, which was a typical feature of this tradition. Moreover, our author presented a historical sequence – almost a stage theory – of a rise from barbarism to modern civilisation almost in the same mode as would become popular during the eighteenth century.[125] Therefore, it must be concluded, in Barbon we find an author who does not fit very well into a stylised 'mercantilist school', as once perceived.

Charles Davenant (1656–1714)

Davenant was the son of the noble, once so famous, poet Sir William D' Avenant. He left Balliol, Oxford, as it seems, without taking a formal degree, for a career as a politician and writer. He sat in parliament for St Ives, Cornwall, and during 1683–9 he was commissioner of the excises. Although he remained loyal to William III, after the *coup détat* of 1688, he did not hold any office. However, after Queen Anne's succession to the throne, he once again gained recognition and was appointed Inspector General of Exports and Imports in 1705.[126]

Davenant was a prolific writer and his collected printed works run to five volumes. As such he was recognised as a militant Tory who opposed the Whigs exuberantly. In stark language in his political tracts he denounced ministerial abuse and corruption. A representative example is the bemusing, *The True Picture of a Modern Whig in Two Parts* (1701–2) in which he charged the Whigs for exploiting the public treasury for own personal gain. His most important works dealing with 'economic' matters were, however, *An Essay on Ways and Means of Supplying the War* (1695), *An Essay of the East-India Trade* (1697) and *Discourses on the Public Revenues and the Trades of England* (1698). He also wrote an important treatise on 'political arithmetic', which was clearly inspired by Petty (but surpassed him in style and method): *An Essay on the Probable Methods of Making the People Gainers in the Ballance of Trade* (1699).

In contrast to, for example, Child and Barbon, Davenant never published a general and principal work on trade. Nor should we expect that he regarded himself as a 'pure' economist (whatever that could have meant at the time). Rather, his more general views on trade, wealth and the balance of trade are scattered around in texts which deal with concrete economic matters, the war with France, political issues and so on. Moreover, as an economic writer he in fact fits in well with the straw man created by Ashley, the 'Tory free trader'. He particularly resisted the strong anti-French feelings bolstered by the Whigs during the 1690s. He seems to have accepted the contemporary war with France as inevitable but argued at the same time against the dogma that France had ruined England through its export of wines and luxuries, while at the same time prohibiting English cloth to enter the French market.[127] Thus to some extent he was a 'liberal'. He opposed the prohibitive act of 1678 that had prevented the free import of French wines, vinegar, linen and so on to England. Furthermore, he argued vigorously against the computations which Fortrey published in 1673, which pertained to show how much England lost in its trade with France. Most of the argumentation from the 1670s onwards that England lost in its trade with France was in fact based upon Fortrey's pamphlet.

Moreover, it is clear that Davenant also was a 'free trader' in a, for that time, radical sense. In order to multiply trade and wealth, he did not exclude the role of 'good laws and government'. However, as a general principle, he stated that:

> Trade is in its nature free, finds its own channels, and best directeth its own course: and all laws to give it rules and directive … may serve the particular ends of private men, but are seldom advantageous for the public.[128]

Thus, according to Davenant, the best way to promote for example the English woollen industry was not by means of protection, but by such good laws that could secure that its products would be 'manufactured cheaply'.[129] Moreover, 'To make England a true gainer by the woollen manufacture, we should be able to work the commodity so cheap, as to undersell all comers to the markets abroad'.[130] In the soundness of this basic principle he seems to have been at least as certain as Barbon. He even went so far as to state that 'Wisdom is most commonly in the wrong when it pretends to direct nature'.[131]

In the literature dealing with Mercantilism, Davenant, most often, is depicted as a representative of a school of 'late' mercantilists who attach to the principle of a great population, low wages and the increase of manufacture as the best way to make a nation wealthy and powerful. This is certainly true to a certain degree. At the same time, however, this does not make him into what is sometimes offered as a true picture of this school: a ruthless brute ready to sacrifice the well-being of the public in order to gratify the interest of the state or some private rent-seekers. Quite on the contrary to the popular view, as outlined most profoundly by Edgar Furniss almost a century ago, for example, Davenant saw no advantage *per sé* in low wages and a poor working class.[132] In fact, such a position is hardly visible anywhere in the economic literature of this period. Thus when Davenant communicated his view that wages ought to be low, he at the same time based it upon the important presupposition that food and other provisions should be kept cheap as well.[133] Besides, Furniss's interpretation is hard to incorporate with Davenant's often stated view that 'We understand that to be wealth, which maintains the prime and the general body of ... people in plenty, ease and safety'.[134]

Nor does this interpretation fit with Davenant's comparison between such developed countries, which had many manufactures, and the under-development that for example haunted Spain. The first category of countries had a prosperous population living in a certain ease and comfort, while Spain abounded in silver and gold but 'whose subjects are poor'.[135] Last, such a view is difficult to concur with Davenant's philosophical outlook. It might be so that much of his bitterness directed against corruption was coloured by his dislike for the Whigs. However, at the same time, he dressed up his discussion of corruption in a vocabulary of civic humanism, which was common parlour in political discourse during the seventeenth century. As we have seen, Pocock has emphasised that civic humanism from Machiavelli and onwards regarded corruption as a deadly threat to civic virtues. Much of the political discussion centred around the question which forms of government – either monarchy, republic or despoty – would best safeguard public virtues against corruption.[136] In his political writings, Davenant often refered to 'this great man' Machiavelli and his discussion of corruption. Hence, in line with this tradition, also Davenant would argue that in order to preserve civic virtues the ruler must pursue 'the common good', 'serve the people' and work in the 'nation's service'.[137]

Using much of the same arguments as Child and Barbon, also Davenant would criticise the idea of a favourable balance of trade. A true balance was impossible to achieve for practical reasons, he stressed. Nor was it certain, if in fact achieved, 'whether a scrutiny so very nice would be of any use'.[138] Rather, the only way to know whether a country lost or gained by its foreign trade was to examine how the development of material wealth fared in general terms. As gold and silver were only the measure of value, 'and not its spring and original', it was of no special significance to hoard these precious metals. Instead, in order to gain enlarged material wealth, the development of industry and manufacture played a leading role. If exported abroad, wrought goods would give rise to 'foreign paid incomes' and a manufacturing sector of a much more considerable size. However, it was in this context he mentioned the peculiar view which several English economic writers without doubt shared: that too much domestic consumption was wasteful as it hindered export to foreign countries. Hence, he said, if manufactured wares are exported abroad and not so much consumed at home, the nation will gain: 'since by what is consumed at home, one loseth only what another gets, and the nation in general is not at all the richer; but all foreign consumption is a clear and certain profit'.[139]

It is difficult to interpret what Davenant and others may have meant by such a statement. For Heckscher it was a direct sign of the mercantilist's 'fear of goods', and for others it has served as an illustration that even the 'late' mercantilists adhered to the principle that only money was riches. However, it is easier to interpret him here against what we already have learnt concerning the so-called foreign paid balance 'theory': to consume such raw materials at home, which could be worked up by labour and then sold to the foreigner, could be considered as a loss to the nation. Hence, through such value adding, more wages, profits and rents would accrue to masters and workers. Therefore, to some extent, it was possible to argue that these extra incomes were paid by foreigners. To modern strategic trade theory, this might not seem so far off the mark. However, for those who always seek 'otherness' in older economic discourse, this interpretation can seem disappointing.

John Locke (1632–1704)

By one authority in the field the great philosopher Locke has been depicted as perhaps 'more liberal' in theory and 'more mercantilist' in practical policy making.[140] However, to the extent that the distinction between 'mercantilism' and 'liberalism' is of any use at all – we have already seen that this is not self evident; it seems more pertinent to argue that Locke most profoundly was a 'mercantilist' in both these respects. It is of course true that Locke did not write very much on economic matters. However, from his professional point of view he seems to have taken quite an interest in economic affairs. He was after all one of the founding fathers of the Bank of England and served as a salaried commissioner in the Council of Trade and Plantations 1696–1700. Moreover, already in the 1670s he was engaged in the affairs of an earlier Council of Trade.[141]

As an economic writer, he published two tracts during the 1690s dealing with agitated political issues. First, in 1691 he published his arguments against Child's and Lord Somer's proposal to 'regulate by law … the price of the hire of money'.[142] Interest, he said, was a 'natural phenomena' regulated by supply and demand of money. Therefore, if all 'the Creditors at once call in their Money there would be a great scarcity of Money'.[143] As we have seen, the idea of economic equilibrium regulated by the forces of the market was by no means unusual at the time. Nor was he especially original in his views regarding the balance of trade. Rather he tended to repeat the most-simple version of the favourable balance theory:

> For we having no Mines, nor any way of getting, or keeping of Riches amongst us but by Trade, so much of our Trade is lost, so much of our Riches must necessarily go with it; and the over-ballancing of Trade between us and our Neighbours, must inevitably carry away our Money, and quickly leave us Poor, and exposed.[144]

In this context, he used Mun's analogy between a nation state and a person who either spent or saved his money in his lockers.[145] In fact, Locke was also indebted to Mun when he pointed out than an increased circulation of money was especially pertinent for a fast-expanding trading nation.[146] We also find with in Locke the often repeated statement that England was a country without mines of its own.

Thus Locke in his tract of 1691 appeared an orthodox 'mercantilist' mainly repeating what Mun had said much earlier. In his next tract, *Further Considerations Concerning Raising the Value of Money* (1696), he seemed even more traditional. His main point here was to argue against William Lowndes's re-coinage project, which he conceived as a form of debasement. Instead, he insisted that the old ratio between nominal money and silver and gold should be retained. Most probably did Locke's disapproval of the recoinage project stem from the general seventeenth-century hostility towards debasement. For, in fact, he never really explained why he so sternly believed that 'the standard once settled by Publick Authority' should never be altered.[147] From the point of view of his natural rights inspired interpretation of property, he might have felt that it would be unlawful to 'raise the value of money', as this would undoubtedly hurt the interest of some people, mainly creditors and landlords. However, he is not very explicit about his reasons. Moreover, his insistence of an unaltered standard between money and precious metals is hard to reconcile with his demand and supply theory of commodity prices. Hence, as he argued repeatedly with regard to the price of money: 'That which regulates the Price, i.e. the quantity given for Money (which is called buying and selling) for an other Commodity (which is called Bartring) is nothing else but their Quantity in Proportion to their vent'.[148] Or with regard to the interest rate: 'Tis in vain therefore to go about effectually to reduce the price of Interest by a Law;

and you may as rationally hope to set a fixt Rate upon the Hire of Houses, or Ships, as of Money'.[149]

From this basis it would most certainly have been more consistent to argue, as for example Barbon did, that silver as well as money were commodities which could be altered in absolute value as well in their relative affiliation. However, the moral gist of his argument why 'debasement' was illegitimate is quite clear:

> And whether this will not be a publick failure of Justice, thus arbitrarily to give one Man's Right and Possession to another, without any fault on the suffereing Man's side, and without any the least advantage to the publick, I shall leave to be considered.[150]

Simon Clement (–1720)

With regard to Clement, 'merchant of London', not much is known. However, in 1696 he was depicted by Lord Bellamont as 'a merchant ... who wrote an ingenious book about trade'. Further, he was said to be 'a good sort of man and has a good understanding for business'. By Bellamont, he was officially recommended to his appointment as 'state secretary to New England'.[151] Furthermore, in 1712–14 we know that Clement resided in Vienna, probably on behalf of some governmental commission concerning trade.

The 'ingenious book' mentioned in this context was Clement's *A Discourse of the General Notions of Money, Trade and Exchange* (1695). We are by now quite familiar with the general ideas expressed in such attempts to synthesise a 'science of trade'. Thus Clement started out with a historical sketch clearly influenced by natural rights discourse, which emphasised the civilising function of trade:

> But when the world became more Popolous, divers persons addicted themselves to more peculiar Managements, either from the Prosperity of their Genius, or the Conveniency and Aptitude of those Habitations that fell to their lot ...[152]

Furthermore, that kind of foreign trade 'bringst most Profit to the Countrey, when he returns with most Money'.[153] It can be advantageous to export money, he said. But only if 'it is so be the Money they draw in by their Trade with other Countries, doth in the whole surmount the Value they shall send out'.[154]

Money, according to Clement was the precious 'Medium of all Commerce'. Silver and gold was used for such a purpose in all international trade. He considered bullion as 'a finer sort of commodities', which are 'capable of Rising and Falling in Price'.[155] Much bullion in the country is a sign of wealth, and 'according to this Rule – the Riches or Poverty of a Countrey is to be Computed even as the Riches of a Private Man is reckon'd from the weight of Bullion he can command'.[156] From this he drew the conclusion that 'abating the Standard of their Coins' was a true sign of shortage of bullion in a country. This statement presented for him an opportunity to attack Lowndes scheme in much the same manner as Locke would do a year later. The abatement of the value of money in relation to silver with 20 per cent was thus both a sign of poverty as well as a cause for further empoverishment. Nor will this act hinder the further exportation of our money, he said, as the root cause of the problem was the unfavourable balance of trade. As long as this 'overbalance' remained, the price of our bullion would still tend to be higher than our money, he concluded. As so many others, Clement believed that England's unfavourable balance had been caused mainly by 'trafick' with France. However, he defended the East India trade, as it returned 'more Money and Moneys worth than that we first set out for India'.[157]

Hence, Clement can hardly be characterised as a very original writer even during his time. Instead, it is rather his style and the context in which he puts his argument which might deserve our recognition. He presented his ideas as general propositions in an almost aphoristical form. Without doubt, his aim was to present his views in the form of axiomatic maxims. Consequently, he left the actual applications of his general maxims to appendices. The 'science' he wanted to establish and contribute to he perhaps would have preferred to call 'Trade in general'. However, in such an attempt to construct a more scientific discourse of trade and exchange based on general 'natural' principles he was of course a quite typical offspring of the 1690s.

William Petty (1623–87)

In contrast to Clement, Petty *was* a highly original thinker who hardly can be described as a typical 'mercantilist'. As with Locke we cannot here present Petty's achievements in full figure.[158] However, at the same time it is impossible even in this context to pass over him in silence. Petty is usually referred to in the doctrinal literature as a political arithmetician. However, the distinction between a mercantilist and a political arithmetician is definitively blurred. Thus while Mercantilism might be described – as we do in this book – as a series of discussions dealing with the role of trade and commerce for economic growth and modernisation, political arithmetic was rather a specific method to solve or illustrate certain problems of economic nature. Thus Davenant, for one, was certainly both a 'mercantilist' and a 'political arithmetician'. Second, however, it is also necessary to pay attention to Petty as he indeed was of great importance as a writer and thinker during the boom of the 1690s. It was in fact during this decade, while written earlier, that most of his works were posthumously published, for example, *Political Arithmetick* (1690), *Political Anatomy of Ireland* (1691), *Verbum Sapienti* (1691) and *Quantulumcunque Concerning Money* (1695). Consequently, it was during the 1690s that Petty reached a wider audience for his ideas and proposals. This does not mean that he played no intellectual role earlier. As is well described by Ted McCormick in his biography on Petty, he was a leading member of the Hartlib group previously discussed. To this extent he certainly contributed to the general revolution in science that took place in England in the middle of the century.[159]

The intricacies of his ideas regarding labour and land as the source of value need not concern us here. Without doubt, his suggested 'theory of value' has had a much greater impact on later economists – such as Marx – than it had on his contemporaries.[160] Thus we will only say something of his general attitude to economic questions and his positions in the general economic discussions of this age. In this context, it is generally acknowledged that Petty can be said to have belonged to neither a 'liberal' nor a 'protectionist' camp. As he himself recognised Thomas Hobbes as a clear influence, it is no wonder that he was of a rather *dirigiste* stance. However, his belief in state interventionism should not be overemphasised. Thus while his first published work, *A Treatise of Taxes and Contributions* (1662), best is described as a collection of small essays on public charges, religion, lotteries, free ports and taxes – in the style of Bacon – his later published works point in another direction. They are much more integrated and bear the stamp of an author who clearly regarded the economy as a systematic whole. Thus, for example, in *Quantulumcunque* he discussed monetary issues from the point of view of a natural scientific methodology. With sharp clarity he illustrated the systematic effects – *ceteris paribus* – which would accrue if for example the value of money were raised. Against this background he regarded the laws aimed to hinder the export of bullion or for lowering the rate of interest as 'impracticable' and 'against the Laws of Nature'.[161] Hence, good government was to rule according to the natural laws of the clockwork economy, and not against them.

Certainly, what made the biggest impact at the time was the method propounded by Petty. In *Political Arithmetic* (printed 1690) he presented an empirical methodology which closely resembles Bacon's: 'The Method I have to do this is not yet very usual; for instead only comparative and superlative words, and intellectual Arguments, I have taken the course ... to express my self in Terms of Numbers, Weight and Measure'.[162] Thus, he said, only by knowing the 'true State of the People, Land, Stock, Trade etc.,' was it possible to put forward true principles and find the correct remedies to current problems.[163]

However, with regard to his actual proposals he was in fact quite conventional. In fact, like most writers during this period, he pointed out that England could only have a great population in proportion to Holland if she developed her trade, fishing and manufactures. Furthermore, Petty especially emphasised the importance of manufactures based on home commodities, but also such which used imported foreign raw materials. Moreover, like many others, he presumed that economic growth and improvement was a consequence of more employment. From this point of view a great population, *a priore*, is of no advantage at all: 'Now if there were spare hands to *Superlucrate* Millions of Millions, they signifie nothing unless there were Employment for them'.[164] Against this background he was highly ambivalent with regard to the favourable balance theory. He still conceded that money was of special importance for a state because silver, gold and jewels were 'not perishable, nor so mutable as other commodities'.[165] At other times, however, he viewed that: 'Money is but the Fat of the Body-politick, whereof too much doth as often hinder its Agility, as too little makes it quick'.[166] Whether his views were inconsistent or not on this point is perhaps not so important to decide. Clearly, like most others, he was influenced by the balance theory and the significance it gave to a net surplus of bullion from foreign trade. However, his second statement fits better with his general approach to economic matters. Clearly, also it fits in much better with his general notion of land and labour as the source of value and wealth.[167]

Continuity and change

We have so far discerned the emergence of an economic literature during the seventeenth century that shared a common terminology and dealt with a common set of problems. It certainly did not constitute a 'school' with a single theoretical creed, as Judges pointed out long ago. Nor did 'mercantilist' writers, as we have seen, necessarily agree on political matters. Some of them defended protectionist legislation, while others emphasised freedom of trade, either partially or more in principle. A third group seems not to have been able to make up their minds on this matter, and Coke stressed the self-evidential that 'all Beneficial Trade ought to be made free'.[168]

Against this background it is more fruitful to perceive the English literature on economic issues as a series of continuous discussions. As we have seen, they dealt with many different issues, and protectionism versus free trade *in general* was not a key focus in any of them. While discussing whether the interest rate should be fixed by law, the East India Company and so on, these writers developed a common language or vocabulary. They elaborated on the role of foreign trade for economic growth and development. They cultivated some common views concerning money, the role of supply and demand and perhaps even the notion of an independent economic realm with laws of its own. Over time such economic discussions created a common language that was developed further during the eighteenth century.

Thus to some extent the eighteenth century only implied a gradual process of development of an economic language inherited from the preceding century. Slowly over time, concepts and theoretical propositions became clearer and more coherent. With regard to value and price theory, there were no definitive disruptions until Ricardo. In monetary theory there was certainly a clear continuity from Vaughan in the 1630s up to the 'classical' Harris in the 1750s.[169] Slowly also the classical notion of interest as dependent on the real rate of profit was gaining ground. We traced it already with Barbon in the 1690s; during the eighteenth century it matured in the hands of, for example, Joseph Massie and Hume.

Also in other respects we must certainly stress continuity rather than rapid transformation and change. The view that 'the economy' was a self-equilibrating 'system' was of course further developed during the eighteenth century – but as we saw it was certainly a part already of the 'mercantilist breakthrough' of the 1620s. Moreover, the view that growth to some extent was linked to a positive net inflow of bullion from abroad would disappear during the eighteenth century. However, already in the 1690s this idea was heavily attacked by authors such as Child, Davenant and Barbon, who rather stressed the role of employment and manufactures for the process of growth. Instead of disappearing, this viewpoint was even further emphasised by eighteenth century writers such as Tucker, Hume and Smith. There might have been some disagreement with regard to how such manufactures might be established and improved, of course. However, free trade positions in principle are possible to discern at least during the early eighteenth century. To what extent Smith was more radical on such issues than some of his 'mercantilist' forerunners is still an open issue.

Notes

1 J O Appleby, *Economic Thought and Ideology in Seventeenth-Century England*. Princeton, NJ: Princeton University Press 1978, p. 4. Also R Brenner, *Merchants and Revolution. Commercial Change, Political Conflict, and London Overseas Traders, 1550–1653*. London: Verso Press 2003.

2 More on the English *Sonderweg* in this context, see P O'Brien and D Winch (eds), *The Political Economy of British Historical Experience 1688–1914.* Oxford: Oxford University Press 2002.

3 See above p. 173.

4 See L Magnusson, *Tradition of Free Trade.* London: Routledge 2004, ch. 1.

5 P S Buck, *The Politics of Mercantilism.* New York: Henry Holt & Company 1942.

6 On the economics of diversification proposed by writers in the 1640s see B Supple, *Commercial Crisis and Change in England 1600–1642.* Cambridge, UK: Cambridge University Press 1959, pp. 221ff.

7 For perhaps the best presentation of this shift, see D Ormrod, *The Rise of Commercial Enterprises: England and the Netherlands in the Age of Mercantilism, 1650–1779.* Cambridge, UK: Cambridge University Press 2003.

8 L Magnusson, *Nation, State and the Industrial Revolution.* Abingdon, UK: Routledge 2009, pp. 80f.

9 C Davenant, 'Discourse on the Public Revenues and on Trade'. In: *The Political and Commercial Works of the Celebrated Writer Charles D'Avenant,* vol. I, London: R Horsfield 1771, p. 399.

10 C Davenant, 'Discourse on the Public Revenues and on Trade', I, p. 424.

11 For this see especially W J Ashley, 'The Tory Origin of Free Trade Policy'. In: W J Ashley (ed.), *Surveys. Historic and Economic.* London: Longmans 1900; and W Letwin, *The Origins of Scientific Economics. English Economic Thought 1660–1776.* London: Methuen 1963.

12 R W K Hinton, *The Eastland Trade and the Common Weal in The Seventeenth Century.* Cambridge, UK: Cambridge University Press 1959, pp. 90ff.; and C Wilson, *England's Apptenticeship.* London & New York: Longman 1984, pp. 61ff., 172ff.

13 Brenner, pp. 598f.

14 C Wilson, *England's Appenticeship*, p. 41.

15 On the Anglo-French wine trade, see J V C Nye, *Wine and Taxes. The Political Economy of the Anglo-French Trade, 1689–1900.* Princeton, NJ: Princeton University Press 2007.

16 See R Coke's strongly anti-French, *A Discourse of Trade, in Two Parts.* London: H Brome 1670, for example, pp. 37ff. See also his *A Treatise Wherein is Demonstrated that the Church and the People of England Are in Equal Danger with the Trade of it.* London 1671, p. 81.

17 H Houghton, *England's Great Happiness or a Dialogue between Content and Complaint.* London: Edward Croft 1677. The restauration referred to here is from 1660 when Charles II was appointed King.

18 Still the best overview of this in E A Johnson, *Predecessors of Adam Smith.* New York: Prentice Hall 1937.

19 C Wilson, p. 58.

20 For the following passages, see L Magnusson, 'Freedom and Trade: From Corporate Freedom and Jealousy of Trade to a Natural Liberty. *Keio Economic Studies,* vol. XLIX, 2013.

21 K N Chaudhuri, *The English East India Company: The Study of an Early Joint-Stock Company.* London: Frank Cass 1965, pp. 11f. See also P Lawson, *The East India Company. A History.* London and New York: Longman 1993.

22 Mun, p. 62.

23 *Britannia Languens*; *A Discourse of Trade.* London 1689, p. 72.

24 Heckscher, II, pp. 273f.

25 See above p. 145.

26 S Fortrey, *England's Interest and Improvement*, p. 16.

27 J Houghton, *England's Great Happiness or a Dialogue between Content and Complaint*. London: Edward Croft 1677, pp. 10f.

28 The term 'resource allocation' to describe this thinking is from M Bowley, *Studies in the History of Economic Thought before 1870*. London & New York: Macmillan 1973, p. 33.

29 Fortrey, p. 17.

30 G Malynes. *The Center of the Circle of Commerce* [1623]. New York: Augustus M Kelley 1973, p. 127. See also pp. 103ff.

31 For a full presentation of the controversies around the Merchant Adventurers from around 1600 onwards, see E Lipson, *The Economic History of England*, vol. II, London: A & C Black Ltd 1934, pp. 243ff.

32 Author unknown, *A Discourse Concisting of Motives for the Enlargement and Freedome of Trade*. London: Richard Rowtell 1645, p. 3.

33 Author unknown, *A Discourse Concisting of Motives for the Enlargement and Freedome of Trade*, p. 3.

34 Lipson, II, p. 244.

35 Lipson, p. 4.

36 Lipson, p. 25.

37 R Coke, *A Discourse of Trade, in Two Parts; England's Improvement, in Two Parts*. London 1675.

38 It was Foxwell who first attributed this book written by the pseudonym 'Philangus' to W Petyt. See Schumpeter, *A History of Economic Analysis*. London: George & Unwin 1972, p. 197. See also Heckscher, II, p. 115.

39 *Britannia Languens*, p. 51.

40 *Britannia Languens*, p. 59.

41 J Wheeler, *A Treatise of Commerce*, p. 25.

42 Wheeler, pp. 78f.

43 H Parker, *Of a Free Trade. A Discourse Seriously Recommending to our Nation the Wonderfull Benefits of Trade, Especially of a Rightly Governed and Ordered Trade*. London: F Neile for Robert Bostock 1648, pp. 7, 9ff.

44 L Roberts, *The Treasure of Traffike*. London: E.P. for Nicholas Bourne 1641, p. 30.

45 *A Short and Private Discussion between Mr Bolton and M.S. Concerning Usury*. London 1637, p. v.

46 T Culpepper, *A Tract against Usurie* (1621). London: Elizabeth Calvert 1668, p. 1.

47 F Bacon, 'On Usury'. *Essays*, ch. XLI. Harmondsworth, UK: Penguin 1986.

48 Bacon, 'On Usury'. *Essays*, ch. XLI.

49 Culpepper, p. 14.

50 For a different interpretation of Culpepper the Elder, see M Bowley, *Studies in the History of Economic Ideas before 1870*. London: Macmillan 1973, p. 41. Bowley's opinion that 'the Culpeppers implicitly denied the traditional view that changes in the supply of money se ipse were the factor of major significance in this connection' is directly opposed to what Culpepper himself had to say on p. 14 in his tract:

> and it is the plenty of money within the Land that maketh money easie to be borrowed, as we see by the examples of other countries, where money is easier to be borrowed than it is with us, and yet the rate tolerated.

51 W Letwin, 'Sir Josiah Child. Merchant Economist'. *Baker Library*. Boston, MA Harvard Graduate School for Business Administration, Publications, Kress Library, no 14 1959, pp. 2f.

52 J Child, *Brief Observations Concerning Trade and Interest of Money*. London: Elizabeth Calwert 1668, p. 3.

53 Child, pp. 6f.
54 T Culpepper the younger, *A Discourse Upon Usury*. London 1668, p. 155.
55 Child, p. 11.
56 T Manley, *Interest of Money Mistaken*. London 1668, p. 14.
57 Manley, p. 13. See also his answer to Culpepper in, *Usury at Six Per Cent Examined and Found Unjustly Charged by Sir Th Culpeppper and J.C.* London 1669.
58 See G S L Tucker, *Progress and Profits in British Economic Thought 1650–1850*. Cambridge, UK: Cambridge University Press 1960, pp. 19ff.
59 For an overview especially concentrating on the Hartlib circle's views on monetary matters, see C Wennerlind, 'Hartlibian political economy and the new culture of credit'. In: P J Stern and C Wennerlid (eds), *Mercantilism Reimagined. Political Economy in Early Modern Britain and its Empire*. Oxford: Oxford University Press 2013.
60 W A Shaw, *The History of Currency 1252–1894*. London: Clement Wilson 1896, p. 144.
61 See for example G de Malynes, *Consuetudo vel Lex Mercatoria*. London: Adam Islip 1629, and R Vaughan, *A Discourse of Coin and Coinage*. London: Th Dawks for Th Basse 1675. For example, pp. 23ff.
62 T Smith, *A Discourse of the Common Weal of this Realm of England*. Cambridge, UK: Cambridge University Press 1893 (ed. Elizabeth Lamond), p. 98.
63 Smith, p. 71.
64 Smith, p. 78.
65 At length for example in G Malynes, *Consuetudo vel Lex Mercatoria*, pp. 254ff.
66 R Cotton, 'A Speech Made by Sir Rob Cotton, Knight and Baronet, before the Lords of his Majesties Most Honourable Privy Council at the Council Table'. In: W M Shaw (ed.), *Selected Tracts and Documents*. London: Clement Wilson 1896, p. 31.
67 Cotton, pp. 31ff.
68 H Robinson, 'Certain proposals in order to the peoples freedome and accomodation'. In: W M Shaw, *Selected Tracts and Documents*.
69 Robinson, p. 75. Although Robinson mentions 'overballance of trade' as a cause behind the exportation of money, there are no signs that he did not accept Malynes's basic view that such an 'overballance' was caused by the exchange and not *vice versa*.
70 See p. 64.
71 This dilemma is perhaps most acutely expressed by J Viner, 'Early English Theories of Trade'. *The Journal of Political Economy*, vol. XXXVIII (1930).
72 J Locke, *Some Considerations of the Consequences of the Lowering Interest and Raising the Value of Money*. London 1691, p. 46.
73 For a discussion of such views during the late sixteenth century see for example de Roover, *Greesham on Foreign Exchange*. Cambridge, MA: Harvard University Press 1949.
74 See McCulloch, *A Select Collection of Scarce and Valuable Tracts on Money*, London: Political Economy Club 1856, p. vi.
75 Vaughan, *A Discourse of Coin and Coinage*, pp. 37f.
76 See Vaughan, ch. 12, esp. p. 73.
77 'Advice of His Majesty's Council of Trade Concerning the Exportation of Gold and Silver in Foreign Coins and Bullion, Concluded 11 December 1660'. In: J R McCulloch, *A Select Collection of Scarce and Valuable Tracts on Money*, pp. 148f.
78 'Advice of His Majesty's Council of Trade Concerning the Exportation of Gold and Silver in Foreign Coins and Bullion, Concluded 11 December 1660'. In: J R McCulloch, *A Select Collection of Scarce and Valuable Tracts on Money*, p. 145.

79　T W Hutchinson, *Before Adam Smith, the Emergence of Political Economy 1662–1776*. Oxford: Basil Blackwell 1988, ch. 5.

80　J Cary, *An Essay Towards Regulating the Trade and Employing the Poor of this Kingdom*. London: Susanna Collins 1717, p. 2.

81　W Cunningham, *The Growth of English Industry and Commerce in Modern Times, Part II: The Mercantile System*. New York: Augustus M Kelley, pp. 262ff.

82　Cunningham, pp. 265ff.

83　This reform is defended in 'Advice of His Majesty's Council of Trade, Concerning the Exportation of Gold and Silver in Foreign Coins & Bullion. Concluded 11 December 1669'. In: J R McCulloch (ed.), *Old and Scarce Tracts on Money*. London 1856.

84　On this L Sommer was a pioneer (see above Chapter 5, footnote 122). For a modern discussion, see A Finkelstein, *Harmony and the Balance. An Intellectual History of Seventeenth-Century English Economic Thought*. Ann Arbor: The University of Michigan Press 2000.

85　For this see also Cunningham, pp. 380f.

86　J Pollexfen, *A Discourse of Trade and Coyn*. London 1697, p. 108.

87　J Cary, *An Essay on the State of England in Relation to its Trade, its Poor, and its Taxes for carrying on the Present War against France*. Bristol 1695, pp. 1f.

88　E Philips, *The State of the Nation*. London: J Woodman and D Lyon 1725, p. 2.

89　D North is most outspoken about his general influences, see the preface to his *Treatises on Trade*. London 1691.

90　J G A Pocock, *The Machiavellian Moment. Florentine Political Thought and the Atlantic Republican Tradition*. Princeton, NJ: Princeton University Press 1975, chs 13 and 14.

91　See for example T W Hutchison, *Before Adam Smith*, pp. 87ff. I Hont has especially dealt with the role of Pufendorf's sociability theory for the Scottish enlightment but they were without influence long before that. See I Hont, 'The language of sociability and commerce: Samuel Pufendorf and the theoretical foundations of the Four-Stages Theory'. In: A Pagden (ed.), *The Languages of Political Theory in Early-Modern Europe*. Cambridge, UK: Cambridge University Press 1987.

92　*Dictionary of National Biographies*. For a presentation of Child see the unfortunately highly biased W Letwin, 'Sir Josiah Child, Merchant Economist'. *Baker Library*. Boston, MA: Harvard Graduate School for Business Administration, Publications, Kress Library, no 14 1959.

93　J Child, *Brief Observations Concerning Trade and Interest of Money*. London: Elizabeth Calwert 1668, p. 10.

94　J Child, *A New Discourse of Trade*, London 1693, p. 1.

95　Child, p. 2.

96　Child, preface.

97　For a discussion, see D C Coleman, 'Labour in the English Economy of the Seventeenth Century', *Economic History Review*, 2nd ser., vol. VIII (1956) and A W Coats, 'Changing Attitudes to Labour in the Mid-Eighteenth Century'. *Economic History Review*, 2nd ser., vol. XII (1958).

98　Child, p. 91.

99　Child, pp. 127ff.

100　See for example J Child, *A Short Addition to the Observations Concerning Trade and Interest of Money*. London 1668, p. 11. Child is thus, implicitly at least, indicating that the level of investment seems to be dependent on the interest rate. No wonder then that for example Vickers regarded Child and the late seventeenth-century economic writers as forerunners to modern macro and growth economics (Vickers, *Studies in the Theory of Money 1690–1776*. Philadelphia, PA: Chilton & Co 1959.

101 Child, pp. 136ff.
102 Child, pp. 156f.
103 See J Child's argumentation in *A Treatise Concerning the East India Trade*. London 1681 and *The Great Honour and Advantage of the East India Trade to the Kingdom Asserted*. London 1697.
104 Child, *New Discourse of Trade*, p. 153.
105 W J Ashley, 'The Tory Origin of Free Trade Policy'. In: W J Ashley (ed.), *Surveys. Historic and Economic*. London: Longmand 1900.
106 *Dictionary of National Biographies*. See also S Bauer, 'Nicholas Barbon. Ein Beitrag zur Vorgeschichte der klassischen Oekonomik'. *Jahrbücher für Nationalökonomie und Statistik*, vol. XXI, vd 6 (1890).
107 N Barbon, *A Discourse Concerning Coining the Money Lighter*. London 1696, introduction, p. 1.
108 Barbon, p. 2.
109 Barbon, p. 4.
110 Barbon, p. 36.
111 Barbon, p. 35.
112 Barbon, p. 39.
113 Barbon, p. 40.
114 Barbon, p. 41.
115 Barbon, p. 265.
116 Barbon, *A Discourse of Trade*. London 1690, p. 13.
117 Barbon, p. 20.
118 Barbon, p. 24.
119 Barbon, pp. 35ff.
120 Barbon, p. 63.
121 Barbon, p. 71.
122 Barbon, pp. 76f.
123 Barbon, pp. 31f.
124 On Pufendorff and this tradition, see A Oncken, *Geschichte der Nationalökonomie*, vol. I, Leipzig: Verlag von C L Hirschfeldt 1922, p. 226; W Roscher, *Geschichte der National-Oekonomik in Deutschland*. Munich: R Oldenbourg 1874, pp. 304 ff.
125 See above note and also I Hont & M Ignatieff, *Wealth and Virtue*. Cambridge, UK: Cambridge University Press 1983.
126 *Dictionary of National Biographies*: C Davenant; *Palgrave's Dictionary of Political Economy*. London & New York: Macmillan 1893.
127 See W J Ashley, pp. 270ff.
128 C Davenant, 'An Essay on the East India Trade'. In: *The Political and Commercial Works of that Celebrated Writer Charles D'Avenant*, vol. I, London 1771, p. 98.
129 Davenant, p. 100.
130 Davenant, p. 100.
131 Davevant, p. 104.
132 The Yale assistant professor in economics Edgar Furniss's furious attack on European nationalism in general – just after the First World War – led him to formulations such as: 'the Mercantilist ... came to believe that the majority must be kept in poverty that the whole might be rich'. This has often been cited but remains a grossly unfair interpretation of what most 'mercantilist' writers said.

See E Furniss, *The Position of Labour in a System of Nationalism* (1920). New York: Augustus M Kelley 1965, for example p. 8.

133 See for example, C Davenant, 'Discourse on the Public Revenues'. In: *Works*, vol. I, p. 358.
134 Davenant, p. 358.
135 Davenant, p. 382.
136 Pocock, *Machiavellian Moments*.
137 Davenant, pp. 336ff., 348ff.
138 C Davenant, 'An Essay Upon the Probable Methods of Making People Gainers in the Balance of Trade'. In: *Works*, vol. II, London 1699, p. 171.
139 Davenant, *An Essay Upon the East India Trade*. In: *Works*, vol. I, p. 102.
140 Hutchinson, p. 72.
141 *Dictionary of National Biographies*: J Locke; *Palgrave's Dictionary of Political Economy*: J Locke & C M Andrews, *British Committees, Commissions and Councils of Trade and Plantations, 1622–1675*. Baltimore, MD: John Hopkins Press 1908.
142 J Locke, *Some Considerations of the Consequences of the Lowering of Interest and Raising the Value of Money*. London 1691, p. 1.
143 Locke, p. 10.
144 Locke, p. 14.
145 Locke, p. 27.
146 See below Chapter 6.
147 J Locke, *Further Considerations Concerning Raising the Value of Money*, London 1696, p. 9.
148 Locke, p. 55.
149 Locke, p. 11.
150 Locke, p. 11.
151 *Calendar of State Papers*. Dom. ser. 1 January–31 December 1696. London 1913, p. 461.
152 S Clement, *A Discourse of the General Notions of Money, Trade and Exchanges*. London: n.p. 1695, p. 3.
153 Clement, p. 5.
154 Clement, pp. 5f.
155 Clement, p. 7.
156 Clement, p. 7.
157 Clement, p. 16.
158 The literature on Petty is vast. For an older biography see E Strauss, *Sir William Petty. Portrait of a Genius*. London: The Bodley Head 1954. He is also portraited in *Aubrey's Brief Lives*. London: Penguin 1987. See also the introduction by C Hull to *The Economic Writings of Sir William Petty. I-II*. [1899] New York: Augustus M Kelley 1986. A new valuable contribution is T McCormick, *William Petty and the Ambitions of Political Arithmetic*. Oxford: Oxford University Press 2009.
159 McCormick, pp. 41f.
160 See McCormick, pp. 306f. On Petty and Marx, see also P Groenewegen, *Essays on 19th and 20th Century Economic Thought*. London: Routledge 2002; T Aspromourgos, *On the Origins of Classical Economics from William Petty to Adam Smith*. Abingdon, UK: Routledge 2011.
161 *The Economic Writings of Sir William Petty*, p. 445.
162 *The Economic Writing of Sir William Petty*, p. 249. See further McCormick, pp. 42–3, 50, 54 and other places.
163 *The Economic Writing of Sir William Petty*, p. 313.
164 *The Economic Writing of Sir William Petty*, p. 309.

165 *The Economic Writing of Sir William Petty*, p. 259.
166 *The Economic Writings of Sir William Petty*, p. 113.
167 See Bowley, *Studies in the History of Economic Thought before 1870.*
168 R Coke, *England's Improvement, in Two Parts*. London 1675, p. 47.
169 J Harris, 'An Essay Upon Money and Coins I-II'. London 1757–8.

7   Then what was Mercantilism?

For historians and economists alike, the concept 'mercantilism' traditionally designates – either or both – a system of economic policy and an epoch in the development of economic thinking during the seventeenth and eighteenth centuries. As we know, the concept 'mercantilism' first appeared in print in de Mirabeau's *Philosophie Rurale* in 1763 as the *systeme mercantile.* By him and many others this concept was utilised in order to describe an economic policy regime characterised by direct state intervention in order to protect domestic merchants and manufacturers in accordance with the regulative policies of Louis XIV's finance minister, Colbert. However, the main creator of 'Mercantilism' proper was in fact Adam Smith. According to his famous definition, its core – 'the commercial system', as he called it – consisted of the popular folly of confusing wealth with money. Although the practical orientation of the mercantilist writers in general, they nevertheless proposed a principle: namely that a country must export more than it imports which would lead to a net inflow of bullion. This was the core of the much-discussed so-called positive balance of trade theory.

As we have shown in this book, this stylised picture of Mercantilism as a coherent system of thought and practice is untenable for a number of reasons. First, 'mercantilism' was never a well-structured doctrine built on a number of well-settled principles by which one could describe economic behaviour and/or prescribe the right policy measures. Moreover, it is not very fruitful to regard Mercantilism as an all-encompassing phenomenon appearing from country to country during most of the Early Modern period. On the contrary, as we have seen, in the early economic political discussion in Spain, Italy, France, but also in the German-speaking countries, several of these ideas came to use. The political, economic and institutional contexts were however quite different.

Second, from Smith to Viner in the 1930s the orthodox view that the mercantilist writers had confused money with wealth has been repeated over and over again. However, more recent research has agreed that this explication is misleading and has little support in actual texts from this period. For example, in 1699 the English economic and political writer Charles Davenant wrote: 'Gold and Silver are indeed the Measure of Trade, but that the Spring and Original of it, in all nations is the Natural or Artificial Product of the Country; that is to say, what this Land or what this Labour and Industry Produces'.[1] It is quite clear that a majority of writers – in England but also elsewhere – by and large shared the same viewpoint. Some of them might have added that to have abundance of money in the country was of great importance for economic progress and the wealth of the nation. But this did not at all imply that money was identical with wealth. Rather, many would argue that a net inflow of money was a barometer that signalled whether a nation won or lost in its trade with other countries. Others would say that abounding money would help to speed up intercourse in the market place and stimulate growth and development. Thus, a net inflow of money could be a means to *procure* wealth (or plenty), but wealth itself was always the result of production and consumption.

Third, thus, the so-called favourable balance of trade 'theory' was never a finished doctrine but instead a number of diverse propositions held together by the balance metaphor, which was 'good to think with' together with a determined view that commerce and trade were especially important for power and plenty. Several suggestions have been put forward in order to disentangle this 'doctrine'. Some have stated that the mercantilists sought to fill the prince coffers with bullion – a view, however, that seemed to gain little empirical support. Or it has been said that they regarded price inflation as something beneficial in itself, understanding very well the specie–flow mechanism later on formulated by Hume and others. Yet others have suggested that the crux of this 'doctrine' was the idea of the need for more money in circulation: 'a struggle for liquid assets'. Hence, a main worry of, for example, the economic writers in England of the seventeenth and eighteenth centuries was that the shortage of money would curtail economic development. Also Serra in Naples was much concerned with how a country without silver and gold mines of its own could have enough bullion to run a commercial economy.

However, whatever interpretation we choose, it is clear that the favourable balance of trade 'theory' had been abandoned in its simple form already at the end of the seventeenth century. Indeed in some countries – like Italy, Spain, France and Germany – we find very small traces of such a 'doctrine' at all criticised by Smith in 1776. Here instead the idea that own manufactures and value-added production should be stimulated and enlarged was dominant from the sixteenth century onwards. In England particularly during the 1690s, writers such as Child, Davenant and Barbon developed an idea that alternatively has been called the theory of 'foreign paid incomes' or the 'labour balance of trade theory'. Instead of holding on to the dogma that a country should receive an inflow of bullion through the balance of trade, these authors stressed that a country should export products with as much value-added content as possible and import as little of such products as they could. The more manufactured goods were exported the more income would accrue to England, they thought. The profit would accrue through the buyer – in Spain, Portugal or other countries – paying England for not only its raw materials but also its labourers. In perhaps a little more sophisticated form, this was very much what Serra in Naples and Ortiz in Spain suggested much earlier on.

Hence, then, what *was* Mercantilism? I have elsewhere suggested that we need not stop using the concept but perhaps be more careful when we apply it.[2] First and foremost, it was literature in the form of books, manuals, tracts, pamphlets and periodicals dealing with everything from political controversial issues to practical issues concerning commerce, trade, shipping, the beneficial role of domestic manufactures and immigration of skilled workers from abroad, how to hold interest rates low in order to stimulate business, how to enrich the state and much more. It was also formulated in political statements by kings, princes, statesmen, other policy-makers, commissions and bureaucrats. Moreover, such a literature as well as ordinances appeared in a number of European countries from the sixteenth century up until the mid-eighteenth century.

To the extent that there is a common thread holding together such texts and proposals – something we might want to name Mercantilism – we must begin with treating them as discourse(s) rather than doctrine(s). This means that what we are trying to trace is a common set of questions, concepts, vocabulary and interpretative frameworks that emerge over time. Hence the existence of a common set of conceptual tools and a shared vocabulary further suggests that the economic pamphleteers and writers to some extent at least shared certain notions of how the economy operated. Moreover, in order to unfold such discourse(s), we must adopt a historically based reading of texts. Instead of construing a history backwards, we must instead seek to understand ideas and concepts within their proper historical context. Hence here we are not mainly interested in tracing the doctrinal development of modern economics but instead understanding what these old writers of tracts wanted to say at the time and in their own contexts. As we saw, the great historian of economic analysis, Joseph Schumpeter, preferred to call such authors 'consultant administrators'.

Certainly some of them were exactly that but others were merchants, bankers, swindlers, politicians or learned men from the academies.

Moreover, what held them together was their preoccupation – not all, but most of them – with the question of how plenty could be achieved and how it was connected with increased power. Very often in discussions concerning what Mercantilism 'really was', the goals of power and plenty have been looked upon as opposites – either one or the other. But this is hardly a fertile point of departure. At least for the mercantilist writers, it seemed clear that power presupposed economic affluence. Power in this context does not always have to refer to the state. The German historical economist Schmoller used 'birth-hour of modern states and national economies' in order to depict the current situation. Hence 'state' was not the coherent machinery of power that we might adhere to today.[3] Instead it was still a contested arena and consisted of competing interests, corporations and constituencies. Nevertheless, such powers together with kings and princes perceived that power and plenty were clearly linked phenomena. Theirs was also a world where commerce and trade were identified as providers – or destroyers – of plenty. In Naples the Calabrese Serra pondered over how his homeland was so poor while Venice was so rich. In England the merchant writer Mun accused the Dutch for snatching the fish in the North Sea from the nets of his countrymen. During the seventeenth century many wondered why Holland had grown so rich and wanted to emulate and learn. In England during the last decades of the same century a fear arose that the French with their wines and manufactured goods would out-compete the English. In the following century, something that the Scotsman Hume called 'jealousy of trade' came to dominate international policies, and different strategies of protection and establishing plantations overseas were set in place. This 'birth-hour of modern states' was, once again according to Schmoller, 'characterised by a selfish national commercial policy of a harsh and rude kind'.[4]

Moreover, should we go along with the economic historian Barry Supple and draw the conclusion that 'mercantilist' discourse, particularly in England from the 1620s, was an 'ideology of a competitive era'?[5] To some extent this is undoubtedly true. But as we have argued such an interpretation, perhaps too much, downplays the independent role played by language and discourse, which cannot merely be reduced to a simple reflection of economic and historical events. Hence over time something that I have chosen to call a new 'language' of economics developed. Within this process, a certain set of concepts and a vocabulary were evolving and set to use in order to make sense of a this brave, new and bewildering world of commercial relationships emerging in Early Modern Europe. Thus to an extent language is self-reflective. But this does not imply that language is disclosed from an outer world of praxis. Instead the relation between language and *praxis* as well as *langue* and *parole* is interactive. This means that language is changed through acts of communication. By using language in praxis it is gradually transformed.

Such a case is the new language, which emerged in order to cope with the English trade crisis around 1620. Dissatisfied with old ways, to grasp what was going on it emphasised that rulers of the realm should look to the *real* balance of trade in order to find effective means to the current crisis. By doing so, as we have argued, they at the same time started to explore new ways to analyse and understand the market economy. Gradually, a view of the economy as a system or process with 'laws' on its own was developed – very much stimulated by new and novel ways to look at the natural world using a new methodology for us today connected with the name of Francis Bacon. In England at the end of the seventeenth century, this new way to grasp the market economy was even hailed as a 'science of trade' and could be summarised in a number of 'maxims'. Thus the market was a place of interchangeable forces. It constituted a balance upheld by the twin forces of supply and demand. Hence, as proposed by Munn and Misselden in the famous pamphlet war with Malynes in the early 1620s: if the balance of trade is unfavourable, the exchange rate must fall, as there is a greater demand for foreign money or bills of exchange. The value of money and bills of exchange in foreign exchange situations is regulated in the same manner as other commodities, through the mechanism of supply and demand. Such 'natural' forces could be tamed and regulated – but only to a certain extent. Thus, against the popular view of this literature, the bulk of its writers were ready to argue for fewer restrictions on trade rather than for more.[6]

Still, good governance consisted of guaranteeing that a country or realm profited especially from foreign trade, the 'Political Commerce', which for example the often-described 'arch-type mercantilist' Postlethwayt asked for. Such a commerce meant an urge to export more and import less. However, more pertinently, it implied that statesmen should introduce beneficial regulations in order for more value-added production to be sent abroad creating more employment and incomes. It is, however, a mistake to believe that such suggestions always went with the view that a poor population was the greatest wealth of a nation. In fact, this view was quite unusual during the seventeenth century. Instead the rationale behind the quest for low wages seems more frequently to have been that low wages certainly implied low costs – but also more employment and low prices of provisions.

At last some words of continuity and change. As we saw, Smith's description of Mercantilism depicted its 'otherness', something alien

222 Then what was Mercantilism?

to which his own viewpoints could be contrasted. However, perhaps more pertinent is continuity: how the literature and texts we have analysed in this book rather look forward to later periods. We might even dare to say that many of the issues that the mercantilists dealt with are still with us today – certainly those which are tied to and effected by modern forms of economic globalisation. But we can perhaps also see continuity in terms of theory and our modern conceptualisation concerning the workings of a market economy, which was complex enough to grapple in the seventeenth century, but perhaps even more so today.

First, it is clearly the case that the view that wealth and power are linked is nothing that distinguishes writers from the seventeenth century from later 'schools' of economic thinking and writing. Hence in the 19th century we can refer to the so-called American system with names such as Alexander Hamilton or Matthew and Henry Carey, as well to Friedrich List who developed ideas which were based on the quest for national industrial protection.[7] Although quite distinct in temper, style and ideas, they shared the view that an agricultural economy was always inferior to an industrial economy. For example, in 1791 Hamilton presented before the American Congress a 'Report on Manufactures'. In this report Hamilton presents a number of arguments for the protection of infant industry, which has been commonplace ever since. The resemblance to earlier adherents of the 'labour balance theory' is striking.

Moreover, List in his famous *Das Nationale System der politischen Ökonomie* (1846) constructed a stage theory of economic development in which a nation started out from free trade in its agricultural stage, turned protectionist during its early days of industrialisation and then in its mature stage returned to free trade. He fiercely attacked the false or 'chimerical cosmopolitanism' of the British, which he regarded as a cloak for self-interest – that nations peculiar version of 'individualism'. Instead each nation must concentrate on the building-up of their own 'productive forces' and not forget the future for the immediate present. Moreover, it was only through such a national build-up of productive powers that true cosmopolitanism can be achieved in the future, he argued.[8]

We can also look to the twentieth century for similar views – in quite different contexts no doubt. From the end of the 1970s, strategic trade theorists such as Lester Thurow, James Brander, Barbara Spencer and Paul Krugman sought to replace Torrens and Ricardo's theory of comparative advantages with something which Porter prefers to call 'competitive advantage'.[9] Their argument has been that the pattern of international trade cannot be explained on the basis of comparative advantage or with the help of the simple Heckscher-Ohlin theorem. Instead, the flow of international trade is a consequence of scale and scope, economic muscles and increasing returns to scale. Thus the basis of the Brander-Spencer model and pleas for 'strategic trade policy' was that countries which through early investments had reached a strong position in a certain export market for a particular good would tend to keep such a leading position. In the case where competition is not perfect (and who cannot find such instances?), sunk investments will lead to barriers of entries – at least in industries with a high value added or high-tech content – which in its turn will serve as a competitive advantage. The political implications of this were pretty straightforward: governmental support could bring forward a competitive advantage for a certain industry which would be of long-run gain for a specific nation. Certainly, this was another way to defend the infant-industry argument with clear implications for trade policy. Also in twentieth-century import substitution we can hear a remote echo of earlier viewpoints. According to this theory with stark policy implications, the establishment of industry will give rise to value-adding production and more employment. Hence, economists critical of free trade, such as Raul Prebisch and Gunnar Myrdal, stressed in the 1960s and 1970s that international trade is characterised by an unequal advantage for the parties involved, which is dependent on the value in use of the commodities exchanged, or to put it differently, on the different productive potentials of their value in use.[10] Also some of those we call mercantilists were aware several hundred years ago that a higher productive potential in the form of value-added industry provided the more developed country with a technological advantage that could be used in order to create plenty.

Second, in the new views emerging from, for example, the English discussion in the early seventeenth century, it was stressed that on both consumer and factor markets the forces of supply and demand create cheapness or dearness. Without doubt, the increased application of the supply-demand mechanism to price formation in general was an extremely important step in its own right. Moreover, the view that the economy must be perceived as a system made up by interreacting 'mechanical forces' implied that also economic society was structured in a law-like manner and relied on a number of principles which might be detected. This emphasis on system-like regularities implied that society operated in a predictable fashion. The market processes linked together variables such as prices, wages, interest rates, monetary value and exchange rates. When, for example, Misselden insisted upon that 'Which Taking and Delivering, as it is A voluntary Contract, made by the mutuall consent of both parties; so are both alike free to Take and deliver at their own pleasure, as in all other contracts and bargains of buying and selling', this was clearly a viewpoints that has stayed with us since then. The same goes for what he followed up by stating, and which has been hotly debated since 1622:

> And trade hath in it such a kinde of naturall liberty in the course and use thereof, as it will not indure to be fors't by any. If you attempt it, it is a thousand to one, that you leave it not worse then you found it.[11]

Notes

1 C Davenant cited from p. 101 above.
2 L Magnusson, 'Is Mercantilism a Useful Concept Still?'. In: M Isenmann (ed.), *Merkantilismus. Wiederaufnahme einer Debatte*. Stuttgart, Germany: Franz Steiner Verlag 2014.
3 G Schmoller, *The Mercantile System and its Historical Significance*. New York: The Macmillan Company 1897, p. 77.
4 G Schmoller, *The Mercantile System and its Historical Significance*. New York: The MacMillan Company 1897, p. 77.
5 B Supple, *Commercial Crises and Change in England 1600–1642*. Cambridge, UK: Cambridge University Press 1969. See also for a similar view J O Appleby, *Economic Thought and Ideology in Seventeenth Century England*. Princeton, NJ: Princeton University Press 1978.
6 This does not make them 'free traders' in a modern sense of course. See L Magnusson, 'Freedom and Trade: From Corporate Freedom and Jealousy of Trade to a Natural Liberty'. *Keio Economic Studies*, vol. XLIX (2013).
7 On this see L Magnusson, 'Introduction'. In: L Magnusson (ed.), *Free Trade and Protectionism in America 1822–1890*, vol. I, London: Routledge 2000.
8 On F List see K Tribe, *Strategies of Economic Order: German Economic Discourse, 1750–1950*. Cambridge, UK: Cambridge University Press 2007.
9 Consult J Spencer and B Spencer, 'Tariffs and the Extraction of Foreign Monopoly Rents under Potential Entry'. *Canadian Journal of Economics*, vol. XIV (1981); R Kuttner, *The End of Laissez-Faire. National Purpose and the Global Economy after the Cold War*. Philadelphia, PA: University of Pennsylvania Press 1991; M Porter, *On Competition*. Boston, MA: Harvard Business School 1998; and P Krugman, *Pop Internationalism*. Cambridge, MA: The MIT Press 1999.
10 On Prebisch see the biography by E J Dosman, *The Life and Times of Raúl Prebisch, 1901–1986*, Montreal Kingston, Canada: McGill-Queen's University Press 2008. For Myrdal's views on trade and development consult, for example, G Myrdal, *An International Economy: Problems and Prospects*, New York: Harper, 1956.
11 E Misselden, *Free Trade or the Meanes to Make Trade Flourish*, p. 112. It was of course passages like this that made W D Grampp draw his conclusion of the liberal element in many of the mercantilist texts. See his 'The liberal elements in English mercantilism'. *The Quarterly Journal of Economics*, 4, 1952.

Index

administrative economics 79–80
agricultural economy 222
Ailesbury, Richard 107
Anglo–Dutch War (1652–74) 174
Appleby, J O 17, 173
arch-type mercantilist 221
Aristotle 47, 75, 151, 160
artificial wealth 115–16
Ashley, W J 7, 16, 21, 22, 32, 63, 74, 196, 201

balance of payments 147
balance of power 177
balance of trade 135, 141, 147; and creation of wealth 101–7; decline in 123–6; definition of 117; doctrine of 17, 20, 27, 29, 38, 41, 45, 63, 77, 93, 108, 112, 145, 195–6; favourable *see* favourable balance of trade; foreign paid incomes and 117–22; labour 117; in retrospect 126–7; specie-flow mechanism for 110, 115, 125, 218
Bank of England 192, 203
bankruptcy 135
Barbon, Nicholas 9, 11, 56, 61, 102, 104, 123–6, 150, 177, 191–3, 196–200, 202, 205, 209, 219
barter system 204
Beccaria, Cesare 82–3
Becher, Johann Joachim 86–9, 91; on system of reciprocal relationships 87
Beer, M 111–12, 152
Bellamont, Lord 205
bills of exchange 115, 139, 147, 161–2, 189, 198, 221
Blaug, M 7, 18
Bodin, Jean 71–2, 74–5, 111, 156
Borniss, Jacob 83, 85

Botero, Giovanni 55, 65, 83, 118
Brenner, Robert 47, 176
Breve Trattato (1613) 46, 64, 67, 117
Brief Observations Concerning Trade and Interest of Money (1668) 185, 193
Britain's Commercial Interest (1757) 62
Britannia Languens (1680) 12, 57, 60, 103, 109, 111, 113, 182
British Corn Laws (1846) 3
Buck, Philip 175–6
bullion 112, 146, 189, 206; import of 114, 117; restrictions against export of 134, 191; surplus from foreign trade 124, 208
Burke, P 10
buying and selling, mechanism of 223

Cambridge School of Intellectual History 8
Cantillon, Richard 77–8
Carey, Henry 222
Cary, John 66, 104, 118–19, 178, 191–2
ceteris paribus 207
Chamberlain, J 21–2
Chamberlen, Peter 102
chartered companies 145, 179
Child, Josiah 9, 11, 56, 58, 61, 104, 118, 122–4, 126, 160, 177, 185–6, 190, 193–7, 199–203, 209, 219
Circle of Commerce or the Balance of Trade, The (1623) 144
civic humanism 193, 202
Clark, G N 34
Clement, Simon 191, 193, 205–6
Coats, A W 33–4, 37
Cockayne, W 142, 155
Cockaynes project 136, 142–3
coin, debasement of 187

Colbert, J B 3, 62, 70, 76–7, 83–5, 89, 91, 177, 180, 217
Coleman, D C 1, 9, 17, 32–4, 36
commodity prices, demand and supply theory of 178, 204
Consuetudo vel Lex Mercatoria (1622) 156, 160
consultant administrators 33, 54, 63, 69, 72, 74, 78, 92, 174, 219
corruption 193, 200, 202
Council of Trade 134, 176, 185, 190, 194
Council of Trade and Plantations (1696–1700) 203
Cranfield, Lionel 107, 152
Culpepper, Thomas 160, 183–6
Cunningham, W 16, 21–7, 31–2, 191

Davanzati, Bernardo 82
Davenant, Charles 6, 9, 11, 58–9, 61–3, 77, 101, 104, 106, 110, 118, 123, 124, 126, 175, 177–8, 191, 193, 200–3, 218–19
de Azpilcueta, Martin 67
de Boisguilbert, Pierre Le Peasant 77
de Mercado, Tomas 67
de Mirabeau, M 3, 217
de Montchrétien, A 70–1, 74–6, 83, 89–90; economic policies proposed by 76
de Santis, Marc Antonio 65
de Soto, D 67
de Uztáritz, G 68
de Vauban, Sebastian le Prestre 77
de Vitoria, F 67
Decker, Matthew 56, 104, 110, 112, 121–3
Defoe, D 119, 178, 193
Della ragion di stato (1589) 65
Der Teutsche Furstenstaat (1655) 84
Discourse Concerning Coining the New Money Lighter, A (1696) 197
Discourse of Coin and Coinage, A (1675) 189–90
Discourse of the Common Weal (1581) 107, 187
Discourse of the General Notions of Money, Trade and Exchange, A (1695) 205
Discourse of the Nature, Use and Advantages of Trade, A (1694) 196
Discourses on the Public Revenues and the Trades of England (1698) 200
Discourse of Trade, A (1621) 105, 134, 145, 179, 194

Discourse of Trade, A (1690) 197
Discourse Upon Coins (1588) 82
Discourses Upon Trade (1691) 124
Discourse Upon Usury, A (1572) 160, 183
drainage of coynage, reasons for 187
Dutch Republic 176; balance of trade 61; methods in order to snatch the trade of others 59–63; monopoly of the trade 60; National Freedoms to Foreigners 57; political power and military strength 55; rise of trade and industry 58; war of liberation against the Habsburgs 55
Dutot, C 77

East India Company 12, 118, 134, 137, 143–6, 152, 176, 178–81, 183, 185, 191, 193, 196
Eastland Company 137, 175
economic doctrines: history of 7–8, 25, 121
economic globalisation 222
economic language 7–9, 12, 209
economistes 67, 76–8
economy: Aristotelian concept of 76, 81
Edward Misselden (1608–54) 142
Ekelund, R E 17, 42–4, 55
England: balance of trade for 177; cloth industry in 118, 134; during the seventeenth century 174–7; Navigation Acts (1651) 58, 133, 174–5, 194–5; peace treaty with France 177
England's Looking in and out (1640) 161
England's Treasure by Forraign Trade (1664) 5, 102, 108, 133–4, 146, 149, 152–3
England's View in the Unmasking of Two Paradoxes (1603) 156
English currency: revaluation of 137, 139, 141
English Royal Society 91
English textile industries 118, 134; 1620s discussion on 135–41; cloth manufacture, development of 137; market process 141–55
Essay of the East-India Trade, An (1697) 200
Essay on the Probable Methods of Making the People Gainers in the Ballance of Trade, An (1699) 200
Essay on Ways and Means of Supplying the War, An (1695) 200

Essays (1625) 107, 112, 151–2
exchange for moneys 156

factory income 117
factory trade 118
Factum de la France (1705) 77
favourable balance of trade 148, 150, 196, 208; concept of 107–8; decline in 123–6; foreign paid incomes and 117–22; foreign surplus 116; increase of the kingdom's stock and 115–17; inflation and 110–11; money as liquid assets 111–15; and money in the king's coffers 108–9; objective of 109; profit from 108
Ferguson, Adam 82
Filip V, King 68
fishing trade: in England 60–1; competition from Dutch over 60
foreign exchange relations, theory of 147, 160
foreign money, demand for 221
foreign paid incomes 163, 202; balance of trade and 117–22; doctrine of 100, 125, 196, 219
Fortrey, S 62, 102, 111, 176–7, 181, 194, 201
France, kingdom of 69–78; agricultural and other natural resources 75; balance of trade 77; ban of bullion export 70; Colbert's rise to power 70; commerce and foreign trade, role of 70, 77; consultant administrators 69; domestic production 72; economic nationalism and self-sufficiency 71; *economistes* 76–8; inflation and rise of prices 71; metal craft industry 75; policy of provision 70, 72; religious and political turbulence 69; trade regulations 76–7; wealth creation 77
Frederick the Great 19
Free Trade or the Meanes to Make Trade Flourish (1622) 143
'free trade' system 3, 12, 45, 122, 125, 145, 180, 208, 223; concept of 179; during eighteenth and nineteenth centuries 179; imperialism in 63, 126; international system of 24; protectionism *versus* 24, 208–9; regulated companies and 179–83
freedom of press 173
Fürstliche Schatz- und Rentkammer (1686) 91

Further Considerations Concerning Raising the Value of Money (1696) 204

Galiani, Ferdanando 66–7, 82
Gee, Josiah 59–60, 106–7, 119–20, 122, 178
Gemeinschaft industrial order 22
General Wealth of the Nation 58
Genovesi, Antonio 66
German countries 78–84; Cameralism 79–80, 84; commercial rivalry and power struggles 83; consultant administrators 78; Habsburg dynasty 78; history of economic thought and doctrines in 79; importation of luxury wares 79; international trade and commerce 78; nexus between science and economic development 80; tax burden of citizens 78; Thirty Years' War (1618–48) 79, 84; *Verfassung* of 85
German *Sonderweg*, idea of 16, 79–80
Gervaise, Isaac 125, 198
Gesellschaft industrial order 22
Glorious Revolution (1688) 173–4, 191
Goschen, G 147
Gould, J D 35–6, 113–14, 133–4, 136–7, 150
Gournay circle 3
Grampp, W D 41
Gresham, T 35–6, 144, 153, 156
Gresham's law 191
Grotius, Hugo 193
Guicciardini, Francesco 65

Habsburg dynasty 55, 68, 78
Hamilton, Alexander 222
Hansa-verband 179
Harris, Joseph 6, 124, 209
Hartlib circle 48, 169n106, 176
Hartlib, Samuel 47
Heckscher, E F 1; *magnum opus* 25; *Merkantilismen* (1931) 23; work on mercantalism 23–8
Heckscher-Ohlin theorem 24, 222
Henry IV, King 69, 72–3
Hewins, W A S 21–2
historical economics in Britain, school of 21–2
History of Italy (1537–40) 65
Hobbes, Thomas 91, 207
Holy Roman Empire 78, 80, 86

industrial competition 121
industrial protection, national 222
inflation: issue of 110–11; and principle
    of price elasticity 110
interest rates 2, 40, 117, 124, 173, 177–8,
    183–7, 194–5, 199, 204, 209, 219, 223
international trade 61, 164; patterns of
    222
Isenmann, M 76

'jealousy of trade' 2, 46, 55, 61, 118, 220
Jevons, S 67
Johnson, E A J 2, 33, 45, 117
'joint stock' companies 47, 180, 191

Keynes, Lord 8, 16, 31, 37–41
king's coffers, money in 108–9

labour balance, theory of 45, 100, 121,
    196, 219
Laffemas, Barthélemy 72–4; economic
    policies proposed by 76
laissez-faire 16, 22, 24, 28–9, 38, 87,
    180; *versus* protectionist tendencies
    126
Law, John 9, 77
Le Détail de la France (1695) 77
liquid capital 114, 116, 126, 177
loan market 186
Locke, John 67, 110–13, 117, 122,
    188–9, 192, 197–8, 203–6
'Lombard' bankers 141
Lous XIV, King 70, 89, 177, 217
Lowndes, William 192, 204, 206;
    re-coinage project 204

Machiavelli, Niccolo 55, 60, 64–5, 202
Malynes, Gerard 17, 36–7, 66, 101, 107,
    110, 114, 134, 138–48, 151–64,
    155–6, 158–9, 164, 181, 183–8, 221
Manley, Thomas 186–7
marchandizing exchange, regulation of
    161–2, 188
Marchant Exchanger 138
Marx, Karl 8, 43–4, 78, 207
Melon, Jean-Francois 77
Menger, C 21
mercantile system 16, 148; Brander-
    Spencer model of 223; concept of 1,
    2–7, 19, 217; definition of 19–21;
    development and underdevelopment
    44–6; economic aspects of 24;
    economic history of 31–7; German

Sonderweg of 79; Heckscher's work
    on 23–8; historical development of
    19–23; Keynes views on 37–41;
    politics of 175–6; in Prussia 20–1; as
    rent-seeking society 42–3; social order
    of 42; strategic trade policy 223
*Mercantile System and its Historical
    Significance, The* (1884) 79
Mercantilism and the East India Trade
    (1926) 163
mercantilist manifesto 133, 146
Merchant Adventurers 137–8, 142–3, 163,
    175, 179–80, 182; export of bullion
    from Britain to the East Indies 179
Mill, J S 4, 121
money: beneficial influence of steady
    inflow of 117; in circulation 112;
    demand of 204; drainage of 187;
    foreign exchange 221; foreign money,
    demand for 221; impact on demand
    113; in the king's coffers 108–9; as
    liquid assets 111–15; methods for
    increasing supply of 187; negative
    balance of trade, impact of 123; net
    inflow of 116, 218; net surplus of 116;
    overplus of 147; price paid for the loan
    of 199; quantity theory of 67, 71, 114,
    150, 188; rarity of 190; in seventeenth
    century 187–90; stock of 105, 111;
    supply of 111, 188, 204; value of
    189–90
Money Answers to All Things (1734) 123
money-capital 186
monopoly 42–3, 45, 60, 89, 121, 145,
    155, 157–9, 179–80, 182, 191
Monroe, A 67
Montanari, Geminiano 82
Mun, Thomas 113–14, 133–4, 137–8,
    145, 148, 152–3, 161, 187, 220;
    emphasis on balance of trade 141;
    humble report (1622) 149; mercantilist
    manifesto 133–4; presentation of
    exchange relations 148
Myrdal, Gunnar 45, 223

Naples, Kingdom of 64–7; currency
    exchange rates 65; 'favourable balance
    of trade' in goods 65; public debt 64;
    share-cropping practices 64; shortage
    of money 65; social and economic
    crisis 64
national gain: concept of 106; by foreign
    trade 103

national income 106–7, 109
National Product (GDP) 106
national stock, of treasure 104
natural rights, doctrines of 28
Navarra, kingdom of 68
Navigation Act (1651) 58, 70, 133,
    174–5, 194–5
Neapolitan Enlightenment 66
New Discourse of Trade, A (1693) 190,
    194–6
Nicole, Pierre 78
Nine Years' War (1688–97) 174, 177
North, Dudley 104–5, 123–4, 126, 177,
    191

*Observations Upon the United Provinces
    of the Netherlands* (1673) 57
offshoring 62
Ortiz, L 68, 219
overbalance: of commodities 155–6; of
    trade 141, 147, 161, 164

Parker, H 183
Peace of Utrecht (1713) *see* Utrecht,
    Peace of (1713)
Perrotta, C 45–6, 68
Petty, William 104, 113, 192–3, 200,
    206–8
Phillips, Erasmus 68, 192
physical capital stocks 115
polipoly 180
Political Anatomy of Ireland (1691) 207
Political Arithmetick (1690) 207
political commerce: administration of
    120; rules for 173
political economies, creation of 2, 19–20,
    141, 147
political power, through economic means
    54–5
Politische Discurs 88
Polizei-wissenschaften 82
Poor Man's Advocate, The (1649) 102
Postlethwayt, M 59, 62, 104–5, 108–9,
    112, 116–17, 120, 173, 221
poverty 46, 61, 68–9, 74, 103, 184, 206
Prebisch, Raul 45, 223
price: competition 62; inflation 110, 218;
    principle of elasticity 110; revolution
    68; theory of 193
Projet d'une Dime Royale (1707) 77
protection and money, system of 25
public debt 64, 68
Pufendorff, Samuel 78, 84, 193, 200

Quantulumcunque Concerning Money
    (1695) 207

'rarity of money', causes for growth of
    114, 190
ready money 41, 105, 116
regulated companies 175, 179–83
Reinert, Erik 46, 66
Renaissance 55
rent-seeking society, mercantilism as
    42–3
'Report on Manufactures' (1791) 222
Roberts, L 59, 103–4, 175, 182–3
Robinson, H 56, 60–1, 153, 161–2, 175,
    188
Royal mint 189
Russian Company 137

*Saint George for England, Allegorically
    Described* (1601) 138, 159
Schaeffer, R 18
Schmoller, G 2, 11, 15–16, 19–28, 30,
    46–7, 54, 220; definition of
    mercantilism 20
Schumpeter, Joseph 3, 7, 10, 17–19, 33,
    54, 64–5, 69, 72, 82, 101, 103, 105,
    174, 219
'science of trade' 174, 190–6, 221;
    discussions on trade and economy
    177–8; England during the seventeenth
    century 174–7
Sen, A K 41
Senior, N W 4
Serra, A 46, 63–8, 117, 218–20
Shaw, W A 139
Smith, Adam 2–4, 8, 11, 18, 29, 100,
    217
Smith, Thomas 187
social imperialism 21–2
Spain, kingdom of 67–9; bullion trade
    67–9; consultant administrators 69;
    domestic industry 69; foreign
    competition in agriculture products 68;
    price revolution 68; tax system 69
specie-flow mechanism 110, 115, 125,
    150, 189, 198, 218
Staatswirtschaft (175) 81
Staple Act of 1662, 176
statute of employment 136, 143, 178,
    188, 190
stock of money 104–5, 109, 113, 187
Supple, Barry 17, 36, 136–7, 139, 149,
    220

supply and demand 149; economic order of balance between 146–7; mechanism of 78, 141, 151, 173, 189, 221, 223
Surviranta, Bruno 100

tabula rasa 164
tariff barriers 20
Tautscher, A 81
Temple, W 57–8, 64, 102, 104
Thirty Years' War (1618–48) 36, 79, 84, 136–7
Thomas, Joseph 163
Tollison, R 17, 42–4, 55
Tory free traders 63, 77, 105, 201
Tract of Ursurie, A (1621) 160, 183
trade and economy, discussions on 124, 177–8
Trade and Navigation of Great Britain, The (1729) 120
trade depression 17, 35, 137, 178
trade leading, 'overplus' of 117
trade relationships 32, 175, 193
trade surplus, impact of 110, 163, 194, 199
trade unions 22
Trattato della Moneta (1751) 67
Treasure of Traffike, The (1641) 103, 183
Treatise of the Canker of England's Common Wealth, A (1601) 138, 155
Treatise of Commerce, A (1601) 179
Treatise of Taxes and Contributions, A (1662) 207
True Picture of a Modern Whig in Two Parts, The (1701–2) 200

'underbalance' of trade 164
unemployment 39, 134–5
Universal Dictionary of Trade and Commerce (1751–5) 59

Utrecht, Peace of (1713) 119, 174, 177

value of money 189–90, 204, 206–7, 221
value-added goods, export of 118
value-added industry 223
Vanderlint, J 110, 115, 123, 125
Vaughan, R 114, 189–90, 209
Verbum Sapienti (1691) 207
Verri, Pietro 82
Vickers, Douglas 40
Villiers, George 107, 152
Viner, J 2, 16–18, 24–5, 29–31, 38, 101, 105, 108–10, 150, 217
von Hörnigk, Philipp Wilhelm 89–90
von Justi, Johan Heinrich Gottlieb 81
von Schröder, Wilhelm 90–2
von Seckendorff, Ludvig 84–6, 91
von Sonnenfels, Joseph 82

wages, issue of 62–3
Wakefield, A 80
War of the Spanish Succession (1701–14) 174
wealth: artificial wealth 115; creation of 101–7; national stock of treasure and 104; physical capital stock and 115; ready money 105; stock of money 105
Wealth of Nations (Smith) 3, 29, 37
Wheeler, J 142, 146, 179, 182–3
Wichman, Christian August 66
Wilson, Clement 17, 34–5, 38–9, 115, 175–6, 178, 183
Wilson, Thomas 160
Worsley, B 176
Wostenholme, John 152

Zeitschrift 23